Introduction
to
Contemporary
Microeconomics

Introduction
to
Contemporary
Microeconomics

VIVIAN CHARLES WALSH

Visiting Professor of Economics
University of Washington

McGRAW-HILL BOOK COMPANY

New York   San Francisco   St. Louis   Toronto   London   Sydney   Mexico   Panama

for Winifred Ann Macaulay Walsh

**INTRODUCTION TO
CONTEMPORARY MICROECONOMICS**

Printed in the United States of America.

Library of Congress catalog card number: 77-85170

34567890   PEPE   787654321

FOREWORD

The science of choice is the core of the theory of rational behavior, and therefore it lies at the heart of economic science. It has great relevance in the applied fields of economic, social, and political policy, both as a basis for disciplined discussion and as a rationing principle for discarding empirically untenable propositions.

There is no royal road to practical economic theory or to the deep philosophical mysteries that lie beneath the axioms on which it is based. But Professor Walsh has opened the door to an approach of elegance and generality. He has, for the first time, started the serious student off at the axiomatic foundations of the science and has communicated to him the key to his own original contributions and advanced work in the theory of choice. What emerges is an apparatus of thought and an algebra of reasoning of great vitality and promise.

R. A. Mundell

v

PREFACE

Any scientist realises that his subject is moving in time—
that he knows incomparably more today than better, cleverer,
and deeper men did twenty years ago. He knows that his
pupils, in twenty years, will know incomparably more than he
does. Scientists have it within them to know what a
future-directed society feels like, for science itself, in its human
aspect, is just that.

Lord Snow of Leicester
Science and Government

All, all, of a piece throughout;
Thy Chase had a Beast in View;
Thy Wars brought nothing about;
Thy Lovers were all untrue.
'Tis well an Old Age is out;
And Time to begin a New.

John Dryden
The Secular Masque

If one leaves a happy, spirited discussion with friends about currently debated topics in microeconomics to get down to the job of arranging introductory lectures on the subject for a large audience, one may be struck by a certain oddity. The two worlds seem to have no intersection. Granted immediately, scientists, in the absence of laymen, tend to discuss the newest and most problematical of their interests. Nevertheless, it is still surely odd that there should be *no* resemblance between what passes for microtheory[1] in the introductory texts currently being used, and the set of topics, their manner of statement in the current grown-up talk, and the literature around which this talk revolves.

[1]By "microtheory" I mean simply the theory of individual decision units, as distinct from aggregates of choosing agents.

This assertion sounds extreme, but a simple test will show it to be vastly more reasonable than would at first appear. Look through the standard introductory texts for any recognition, any treatment—however cursory—of choice theory written since the first edition of Sir John Hicks' *Value and Capital*. (Hicks' great work made popular, in 1939, the technique—of indifference curves—that has been standard in texts ever since.)

If one depended on the extent to which anything has filtered through into the introductory texts, one might get the impression that no radical changes had taken place in microtheory for an embarrassingly long time. Of course, nothing could be further from the case. Yet if all scientific writings in the field except these texts were to be destroyed in some disaster, a future Martian historian of human economic ideas might go in ignorance that the work, for example, of Arrow, Debreu, Koopmans, or of any of the younger men had ever seen the light of day.

Can it be that the authors of the texts have honestly felt, on surveying all this literature, that none of the work done since the early Hicks was usable in an introductory book?

It may be said that all the newer work is "highly mathematical." Let us look into this. In discussions at meetings where the content and manner of large introductory lectures is being mooted, one picks up a recurrent suggestion. It is not that anyone would precisely want to come out and say in so many words that the old economic theory is easy to teach whereas the new is difficult. It is, as it were, that the older ideas are held up confidently for approval, are handled as one would a familiar object one had grown used to, like a slipper; whereas the new concepts are approached with circumspection and hesitance, as one would a hard, spiky, gently ticking object in a briefcase.

However, with the greatest respect, it must be pointed out that the old ideas are familiar simply to those who grew up with them, whereas, notion for notion, the new concepts may in point of fact be *simpler* to a new generation. The internal combustion engine is not, merely because of its venerable age as a piece of engineering, simpler to explain to a child of today than the jet engine.

As for being "mathematical": The neoclassical utility theory of Jevons, Edgeworth, and Marshall was not without its dependence on concepts that most people would regard as "mathematical," nor was the so-called Hicksian revolution accomplished wholly without the use of weapons of this kind. Yet generations of undergraduates have been introduced to the concepts of diminishing marginal utility, and later of marginal rates of substitution and the indifference curve, without such concepts being considered, or proving to be, beyond their strength or fatal to their peace of mind.

This book shows that the few concepts really logically necessary to introduce contemporary theory come more easily to the fresh mind than those needed to set up either neoclassical utility theory or indifference-curve analysis. One may yet go further; I have found, as a matter of experience, that undergraduate audiences find it easier to grasp the properties and limitations of the two older mechanisms of analysis when these are introduced as particular models—distinguished by their limiting characteristics—among the set of possible models for a simple contemporary choice theory. I have, therefore, plunged in and written this whole book, from the beginning, in terms of the set-theoretic approach of contemporary mathematical economics, and I have consistently developed the theory in the axiomatic manner characteristic of current advanced writing.

Perhaps it is time to offer a word or two about in what sense this is or is not a mathematically oriented book. It is assuredly concerned with certain formal, abstract structures—although these are introduced and spoken of quite informally and often in terms of very humanly concrete examples. It has a point of view—if you like, it is in a tradition—of which the full-dress version comes with axioms elaborately justified, proofs formally derived, and the resulting theory logically distinguished from possible interpretations.[2] However, it is *not* a mathematical book in the sense of presupposing any prior aquaintance with a notation or with any techniques whatever.

May I suggest, nevertheless, that one cannot start learning up-to-date techniques too early? Even now, it is quite usual for a scientist in our subject to be trained throughout his undergraduate years (and even in first-year graduate school) in nothing but traditional economic theory and classical mathematical techniques. Then all at once he finds that the young men who are making contributions at the

---

[2]See the forthcoming *Axiomatic Choice Theory* by the present author, to be published by McGraw-Hill Book Company, New York.

frontier are using techniques that depend on properties of point sets and not on calculus, and which do not require many of the restrictive assumptions that he had been brought up to regard as absolutely part and parcel of any economic theory. Is it any wonder he feels hopelessly lost and betrayed by his mentors?

Now, it may be asked, if you use this book as an introduction to the new scene, where are its readers to go afterwards—short of the extremely advanced literature, which is clearly too great a jump?

Even a few years ago, this would have been a problem. Now, however, there is a clear road that one can point out. The reader of this book should (with a little work!) go on to read James Quirk and Rubin Saposnik's *Introduction to General Equilibrium Theory and Welfare Economics.*[3] Then, in first-year graduate school, he should read Kelvin Lancaster's *Mathematical Economics.*[4] There is now a clearly marked channel out to the advanced literature.

As I go to press, I have just received a book called *An Introduction to Modern Microeconomics*, also by Kelvin Lancaster,[5] which could certainly be read by sophomores and juniors. Lancaster says that "traditional elementary price theory texts are at least a generation behind advanced theory in content and approach"[6] Olé!

Lancaster says that "there is no attempt in this book to give an elementary account of the methods of modern advanced theory"[7] and it is true that he has not joined me in the use of an explicitly set-theoretic approach, or of the axiomatic method.

But I think we can see now how the tide is beginning to run: There is no longer the excuse of lack of books at intermediate levels to justify keeping students away from the new literature.

But what about undergraduates who take only one or two courses in economics: Is this new tradition an esoteric specialism with which they need not, indeed should not, bother?

[3]McGraw-Hill Book Company, New York, 1968.

[4]The Macmillan Company, New York, 1968.

[5]Rand McNally & Company, Chicago, 1969.

[6]*Op. cit.*, p. v.

[7]*Ibid.*

I am deadly serious in believing that the answer is absolutely *no*. Everyone, to be literate and aware of the dangers facing our society, needs to have some grasp of what the mathematical science of optimization is becoming. It can become a sinister science of our control and manipulation by hidden power—it will, if we do not watch our precious liberties vigilantly. It could also become a science of the search for the truly best, if we control, and are not controlled by, the ever more subtle and sophisticated systems that are coming to determine the very structure of our lives.

Everyone needs to know that at the core of today's mathematical economics lies a theory, not just of market decisions, but of all decisions subject to constraints. A theory not just of prices, or commodities, or conventional industry, but of all choices, all human and cybernetic optimizing activity, of all systems. A theory, moreover, for which it is claimed that behavior in conformity to its axiom set is behavior that merits the name "rational." Let everyone who is concerned with the structure of human society scrutinize carefully, and ponder long, any set of axioms supposed to guarantee the beneficence of control and the rationality of the systems with which we are forced to live. Let us try to root out illusion and pretension and hidden prejudice from these structures, as far as possible while they are still in the writings of scientists, and before they have penetrated too deeply, and become lost to sight in the corridors of power.

It is precisely for this reason that I have stressed again and again the general theory of choice, of optimization, that lies at the core of contemporary mathematical economics, even here in a book that is only an introduction.

The word might bear some consideration: What counts as an "introduction"; what ought we to be "introducing," and—no less important—to whom? The nineteenth-century Whig historian, Macaulay, once expressed the ambition of writing a history that would be read by young girls. Since we know him to have been a sober man, we cannot suppose that he intended to falsify the history of England. On the other hand, he was making vivid that he expected that some minimum, over which as a professional he was prepared to stand, would *get over* even to the youngest and greenest. One gathers what he was after. This text should achieve these goals.

We have all felt over the past few years in America the fresh strong wind of unmistakable change in the tone and direction of undergraduate attitudes and commitments. Our youth are disposed to give a deadly serious hearing to serious things, of which the new science is assuredly one, but equally strongly disposed to reject intellectually and morally any offerings that may be suspected to have survived through their momentum[8] rather than by virtue of their internal logical rigor or their truth to life, or to bear less than the utter seriousness of science.

VIVIAN CHARLES WALSH

[8]Survived, if you like, through the resistance of a science to changing its paradigm. On all this, compare Thomas Kuhn, *The Structure of Scientific Revolutions;* (University of Chicago Press, Chicago, 1962), with Louis Althusser's *Pour Marx* and *Lire Le Capital* (Hadamard, Paris 1965). The striking similarity between the concepts of Kuhn and Althusser is clearly shown in an unpublished paper "The Problem of Knowledge: Philosophy of Science" by David Loud. I owe this reference to Hilary Putnam.

ACKNOWLEDGMENTS

The main influence in my early years in economic science will become only too clear from Chapter 3 to those who do not already know it. If anyone should be surprised, it would be only at the extent of this influence and its persistence. On this I have only two concerns: First, to acknowledge everything I owe in that quarter, and second, to absolve the noble Lord concerned from any responsibility for the present result of that influence.

As for any contemporaries in America, many of them will see in these pages informal renderings (I hope not too vulgarly popularized) of their ideas, and of some of our mutual friends' ideas. Happily, these know one another too well for me to need to list them here.

There are, however, a few notions about the idea of incomparability in choice theory appearing in these pages, together with some of the structure of Chapter 9, that may possibly be new. Since they are taken from the results of a most pleasant collaboration and are about to appear elsewhere, it seems fitting that I mention that my collaborator on that work was my old friend Professor Hilary Putnam of Harvard University.

The book would contain many more mistakes but for Professor William Baumol, and it would have been much slower in appearing but for Professor Robert Mundell. Professor Kevin Sontheimer, who was one of a little group who used it in a preliminary edition, suggested several improvements. Responsibility for any remaining mistakes is mine.

VIVIAN CHARLES WALSH

CONTENTS

Part 1 General Choice Theory

1
ECONOMISTS
AND
THE SCIENTIFIC
REVOLUTIONARIES

2
THE
CHOICE
SET

Part 2 Welfare Theory

12
AXIOMATIC WELFARE ECONOMICS

Part 3   Consumption Theory

13
THE CONSUMPTION SET

14
AXIOMS OF INSATIABILITY AND CONVEXITY

15
THEORY OF CONSUMPTION

Part 4   Economic Systems

Part 5 Production Theory

22

THE CONCEPT OF COST

Part
1
General
Choice Theory

1
ECONOMISTS
AND
THE SCIENTIFIC
REVOLUTIONARIES

. . . they are men so young or so new to
the crisis-ridden field that practice
has committed them less deeply than most of
their contemporaries to the world view
and rules determined by the old paradigm.

Thomas S. Kuhn
The Structure of Scientific Revolutions

Science, of course, belongs naturally to the young. But particularly is this true of scientific revolutions. The field we are about to enter will serve as an example of the new science, and some of its brilliant young practitioners are beautiful examples of the scientific revolutionary. This statement could do with some explanation.

This book is a contemporary introduction to pure economic science. For most of its length it will stick to being nothing more (nor, I hope, less) than just precisely that. It so happens, however, that these days one cannot really introduce economic theory without—if one is success-ful—giving an insight into a wider phenomenon: a key aspect of our contemporary scene.

The structure of choice theory (which is the core of the pure science in economics) and the characteristics of the men who are taking it furthest are, respectively, typical of the new science and the new scientist.

I am claiming that, by looking into the character of economic science as it is today, you will get an introduction to choice theory itself, plus some insight into a wider characteristic of our times—more especially, of our future.

The justification of this claim, of course, constitutes the whole book.[1] But some hints may still be in order. Of course, it would be best if you did not think in stereotypes at all. But at least don't unconsciously cling to old, out-of-date stereotypes of the scientist. Don't think of him as an old boy in a white coat who makes explosions and smells in a lab: a sort of glorified engineer, narrow, technical, destitute of human culture and political concern; a morally moronic maker of bombs. As stereotypes go, this was never a fair picture, but it is particularly misleading now.

Almost by definition, the new scientists are young. Youth is more than a matter of chronological age with them, it is a quality of spirit—they have the wings of the morning. If we must have a name for these scientific revolutionaries, I shall adopt one that is going around and call them the "Young Turks."

I cannot give a list of characteristics that any Young Turk would necessarily possess; but I can sketch some typical qualities. They tend to be mathematicians, which accounts for part of their elegance and style—and indeed for their artistic streak, since it is well known that mathematicians always were noted for this characteristic. They are mathematicians of the new kind, preoccupied with issues of form, which are largely involved with logical structure and are in a sense sometimes philosophical.

They are devastatingly successful, but they do not worship the bitch goddess success. Of course, they do not need to. They are the first generation of American academics not acquainted in their own lives with problems about money. A Young Turk may drive a Ferrari or a Volkswagen, but he will choose his car because it suits him and not because he needs to keep up with the Joneses (or even with the Armstrong-Joneses). And he is likely to be dressed in a way that makes cops hostile, unless he is dressed very well indeed by a Carnaby Street tailor—and that could make cops hostile too.

[1]Not to speak of the beautiful formal literature, which I hope you will go on and read.

He could be the young man from whom you take over the wheel of an ocean racer or the young man who links arms with those he loves in resisting evil. He could be any young man who walks into a lecture escorting a teen-age girl—you could never tell, if you did not know, that he was the one who was going to lecture. The Young Turk's dignity is the dignity of science; he lectures simply because he has something to say.

Some of the Young Turks are economists. Some of what is revolutionary in science is being done by economists. This is clearly very new: under the old regime, economists never made it as scientists. But revolutions in science in general, and in economics in particular, are making economics the kind of thing a Young Turk is likely to do.

Of course, economists always *wanted* to be taken seriously as scientists. In the old days, however, things were hard for them.

On its empirical side science meant, above all, laboratory experiment—and how could economists do this? And then, on the mathematical side of science, the model for the scientific use of mathematics was the physicist's use of the calculus. And that, while it was *made* for the physicist, was in a way (as we shall see) rather a temptation to the economist. The latter's early mathematical efforts took place in an atmosphere that just wasn't his *kind* of mathematical scene. It led him to assuming that things could be treated as continuously divisible when this was misleading and into hoping that things could be measured when they couldn't be—and when, anyway, measuring them wasn't the point. What was needed, as we shall see, was (among other things) the ability to subdivide sets of possibilities into certain significant subsets and to discover and define certain kinds of orderings.

Some of the new mathematics, however, is proving to be just what the economist wants, and parts of it have indeed been constructed by persons who are interested in economic science. Moreover, economics is only one of many sciences for which nowadays the computer overshadows the laboratory as a testing ground.

Economics is in no way unique in all this—June, so to speak, is bustin' out all over. However, the very (admitted) weaknesses of economics as a science in the old days make its new strengths all the more glaring examples of what is new on the scientific scene in general, as compared with the new developments in any science that was doing very well, thank you, under the old regime.

If you want to study the newly rich, the more nouveau a group you pick the better. Even a short time ago, the most startling things in science were the things it could physically *produce*—what has been called "hardware."

So the old sciences, the strictly physical sciences, were still what people looked at even when they considered "scientific revolutions."

Gradually, however, even at the most popular level, attention has been shifting from what can be physically made to what can be optimized—handled so that it makes for the best. Attention has been shifting from the lab and its ultimate physical products to the computer and the ultimate products of its successful use: information, and optimal use of systems, the optimal attainment of goals— not the physical production of *things*. We feel that men know (or soon will know) how to produce almost anything. Our interest has shifted to the question of how to be sure we are choosing the best that is possible.

It is not an accident that economic science in its contemporary form—the mathematical theory of choice—should serve as a good example of the new science or that its young devotees should exhibit the characteristic strengths and weaknesses of the Young Turks to whom these sciences have given their unmistakable stamp.

2
THE
CHOICE
SET

For reasons that will become vivid as we progress, I want
to introduce the fundamental notions of choice theory in a
context deliberately swept free of certain associations.[1] To
begin with, I wish to avoid any situation that might ordinarily be expected in a work on economic theory. But I
also want to avoid for the moment emotionally charged
human issues, since in the first part of this book the structure of choice *as such* is our concern. So we are going to
have to take a (short) vacation. If we are to avoid involve-
ment we had better leave America, and I cannot think of
a more suitable place to go than to the South of Spain, since

[1]In this chapter, which sketches a finite model for choice
theory, the word "set" and certain notions about sets will be used
naïvely. General choice theory itself will be axiomatized, in Chapter 9, within first-order logic.

no one there is committed to anything or really thinks about anything. For a young American, this should be a total change. So there we go.

Suppose we are sitting in a little group at a table in a restaurant by the beach, somewhere on the Costa del Sol. It is a mixed group of, say, five men and five girls; but no one exactly has a date, because as one's hostess had pointed out significantly during the first few days at her villa, one simply does not make dates in advance in the South of Spain—not even by the end of a protracted late lunch for that same evening. Yet, by the time everyone has drifted up from the beach and dropped into the bar to survey coolly the *frisson* of the evening as it flows quietly by—at least by the time people are ready for dinner to be followed by a general movement in the direction of the favored discotheque—it is somehow clear that things have solidified to a degree. By dinner time, each of the young men has an idea with which of the five Swedish girls he is to stay. To give the simplest possible picture of choice theory, we are assuming that no one leaves or joins the group, also that each young man must choose at most one girl.[2]

So, on these assumptions, your[3] choice must be one of these five Swedish girls. Let us call them the "choice set." This term delineates the set or collection of those among whom one might conceivably choose.

THE UNIVERSAL SET   In any scientific discussion, one hears the phrase "universe of discourse," which defines the widest sphere within which in any argument further distinctions will separate out parts or elements. A zoologist talks about animals—they are his universe of discourse. But he may concentrate now on this animal, now on that. If he stops talking about animals in general or about lions in particular to discuss the wines of Bordeaux, he has stopped being a zoologist for the moment (he is having an important conversation with the wine steward). Mathematicians use the

[2]To give this assumption an aura of realism, I have elected to set this chapter in a rather old-fashioned European scene. In Chapter 16, where we are ready for a more complicated structure and this restrictive assumption can therefore be dropped, my illustrative example concerns young contemporary Americans.

[3]Girl readers may substitute five Spanish youths.

term "universal set" for the set that includes as subsets whatever is relevant to a particular argument. In our situation on the Costa del Sol, the universal set is just exactly the five Swedish girls, since it is among those five at most that a choice must be made, and we are concerned entirely with choice.

In economic choice theory, it is usual to give the universal set with which we are concerned some such name as "choice set" or "action set" to indicate that we are always interested in sets of choices or perhaps actions and to draw attention to the fact that we are not just talking abstract set theory but rather are applying the latter to the problems of the nature of choice.

Let us return to our little scene by the shores of the Mediterranean. As the evening progresses, it becomes clearer how many of the five girls are possibilities. It turns out that two are committed, are already lost to you. We express this by saying that three members of the choice set are in the attainable set and the other two are (alas) in the unattainable set.

We say that the attainable and unattainable sets are "proper" and "exclusive," or "disjoint," subsets of the choice set. They are "proper" subsets because neither of them alone is the whole of the universal set—you will recall that there are three girls in one subset and two in the other—and "exclusive," or "disjoint," because, when the moment of decision comes and the chips are down, no girl is a member of both subsets at the same time from the point of view of the same young man. They are members *either* of one subset *or* of the other. A division of a set into two subsets of this kind, where there is no overlapping, where the subsets have no members in common, is often called a "partitioning" by mathematicians. I think that is a good, vivid word, and I suggest that we use it. Partitions have their uses. We may illustrate these notions by means of a diagram (Fig. 2-1). The whole rectangle is the choice set. The smaller, shaded area that is included in the larger is the attainable set, which is labeled "A." The part of the choice set that is not included in the attainable set is the unattainable set, which is, of course, the unshaded remainder of the rectangle, labeled "−A." All this can be expressed more briefly and

ATTAINABLE AND UNATTAINABLE SETS

FIGURE 2-1
Attainable and unattainable sets

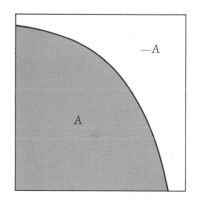

elegantly in notation, which is offered later in the book, but for the moment I want to rely on symbolism as little as possible.

Suppose that the time has come when you have partitioned the choice set and know which three members are in the attainable set. If we are to get any further, we now need a crucially important notion: the concept of an *ordering*.

You must, if you are to choose, be able to rank the members of the attainable set in some kind of order.

ORDERING

The simplest situation for choice theory (and for life) is one in which we can say that we have some simple order of preference among the members of the set. Suppose that you feel that in your attainable set Marina stands highest, then Karen, then Inge-Britt. If you feel like this (and in life one certainly *sometimes* does), you have what has been called a "strong"[4] or a "simple" or a "complete" ordering. The diagram of Fig. 2-2 illustrates the notion of a strong ordering. Let the letters, M, K, and I-B stand for the names of the three girls. We represent the ordering by a chain of linked circles in ascending order of preference. Clearly, M stands highest, K is next most preferred, and I-B least. Again, notations exist for elegant manipulation of these ideas—and much more complicated ones derived from them.

In later chapters we shall consider situations in which one does not have a simple ordering of this sort. But for the moment let us content ourselves with this case. Simple as it is, it suffices to give a thumbnail sketch of the very purest and most general choice theory. It boils down to this: Choose the most highly ordered (say "most preferred," if you like) member of the attainable set.

Underlying this sketch is an assumption which we must now unearth. (Aficionados will spot many others, but they can wait.) The assumption is that if you prefer

FIGURE 2-2

Strong ordering, showing preference

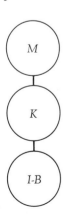

---

[4]This was Kenneth Arrow's term (see *Social Choice and Individual Values*, 2d ed., John Wiley & Sons, Inc., New York, 1963, *passim*). The concept was not new to mathematicians, but he introduced it into economic science, together with much else in the apparatus of what has become our contemporary choice theory. Arrow was one of the founders of the axiomatic, formal approach to choice theory.

Karen to Inge-Britt and Marina to Karen, it follows that you prefer Marina to Inge-Britt. The preferences are thus assumed to show a thread of consistency—a property called "transitivity"[5] by mathematicians.

Preference is said to be a "transitive relation." Concepts may be related in many ways, and it always helps to know exactly how they are related. For our present purposes, however, all we need is the distinction between transitive and intransitive relations. "Larger than" is a good model of a transitive relation. As for an intransitive relation, consider "in love with."

PREFERENCE AS A TRANSITIVE RELATION

It seems reasonable to assume that the relation of preference used in our sketch of the simplest general choice theory is a transitive relation. If we wanted to be formal, we would have to build this assumption into an axiom, as we shall do in a later chapter, but here we are speaking informally about things that can be made very formal indeed.

Given transitivity of preference and given the attainable set, Marina is the choice.

In more complicated models, we do not assume that preference is the only relation existing between the objects of choice—the agent may be indifferent between two members of the attainable set. No more will be said about this now—we need more equipment.

I doubt that too many young people in the South of Spain need a formal choice theory to lead them to the highest ordered elements in their attainable sets. Machines, however, dealing with rather more complicated optimizing problems, are not so happily situated. Let it be borne in mind that concepts capable of the most complicated uses are often best introduced in their very simplest and most obvious form.

One may even describe—in the style of a cookbook recipe—an elementary procedure for solving a problem of choice: Determine the choice set. Partition it and extract the attainable set. Order the members in the attainable set. Pick the most highly ordered member. Bake till brown all over, as it were, and hope for the best.

[5]Again, Arrow did much of the pioneering work in introducing the concept into economic science. A good deal, of course, has been added since by others.

QUESTIONS

1. What is meant by the expression "universal set"? Give some examples of universal sets, relating to different fields of discussion. How would you draw the frontiers of such a set? What criteria would you use? Illustrate.

2. What are the characteristics of "choice," or "action," sets? What sorts of things can be included in such sets? Can you think of things that could *never* be members of such sets? How would we decide what to include in the choice set for a particular problem?

3. What are "attainable" and "unattainable" sets? Why is the distinction important to the analysis of choice? What would happen if you did not know what were the members of the attainable set? How are attainable sets related to choice sets?

4. Is there a set whose members belong to the choice set but not to either the attainable set or the unattainable set?

5. What is "partitioning"? Can the set of sailors be partitioned into the set of drunken sailors and the set of Irish sailors?

6. What is a "simple," or "strong," ordering? Can you apply this concept to some things among which you currently choose? Give examples. Suppose the following were members of your attainable set: Miss Denmark of 1970, a Nobel Prize in physics, a villa near Marbella. How would you order them? Can you think of situations in which the concept of a simple ordering is not enough to express our choosing processes? Give instances that you feel raise difficulties.

7. What are "transitive" relations? What is the significance of transitivity in choice theory? Why do we not regard "in love with" as a transitive relation? Can you think of circumstances where it would be?

3
CONCEPT
OF
SCARCITY

*. . . when time and the means for achieving ends are
limited and capable of alternative application, and
the ends are capable of being distinguished in order of
importance, then behavior necessarily assumes the form
of choice. . . . It has an economic aspect.*

Lord Robbins of Claremarket

An Essay on the Nature and Significance of Economic Science

We must now build on our scaffolding the full structure.
We must solidify the hard *form*, as it were, of a crystal,
complex yet bright and sharply edged: the structure of pure
economic science. We have, in simplified form, all the
abstract concepts we need. Yet as a matter of history, this
structure has proved as elusive as the Holy Grail.

Only recently have economists begun to understand
consciously that the theory of choice is the core of the pure
science (as distinct from the engineering) in economics.
And even today, when one points out some of what this
fact implies, there are people—including some in high places
—whom one can still startle.

Scientists, particularly in the creative age bracket, are
not much given to ancestor worship. In the more developed
sciences, a student learns how things are done now (or at

least until quite recently) and not how they have evolved from the nineteenth century—except, of course, in lectures explicitly on the history of the field.

But in our science, if we introduced no ideas older than those of Chapter 2—if we stuck to a treatment wholly in terms formalized only in the past twenty years or so—we would, I believe, suffer two grievous losses. First, we would miss the chance to throw the sharp cold light of history on the emerging structure of pure economic science. Second, we would not introduce the subject fairly, because we would render unreadable—or at least would offer no help in understanding—much still-important literature. And there is no provincialism so vulgar as provincialism in time, nor half so pathetic, one imagines, to the smiling gods.

Therefore, our search for structure must be partly a journey in time. In fairness, I must immediately warn you that it will fail, in two different senses, to be fully historical.

To begin with, I shall not attempt to trace the concepts with which we shall be concerned back to their true roots, simply because of your lack of time. And then, my purpose is—unashamedly—to explain contemporary economic science, and a historian may thus legitimately raise an eyebrow.

THE CONCEPT OF SCARCITY

For our purposes, we may say that consciousness of structure in pure economic theory begins with the *self-conscious* development of the concept of scarcity. This conception, as far as its implicit use is concerned, had a long slow growth and could be traced by a historian well back into the nineteenth century. But for us there are sound reasons for starting with the famous essay quoted at the beginning of this chapter.

Lord Robbins was not the first to *use* the concept of scarcity (as he was at pains to point out in the first edition of his *Essay*).[1] However, he made, in terms, a very special, explicit claim about this concept; namely, that the *scope* of the effects of scarcity and the *scope* of economic science are crucially related—that the structure of economic science is such that the concept of scarcity, properly understood, is precisely definitive of it.

[1]An *Essay on the Nature and Significance of Economic Science*, Macmillan & Co., Ltd., London, 1932.

For several reasons, the staggering nature of this claim was not at all understood at the time. To begin with, economists of the 1930s and 1940s were not in the habit of thinking choice-theoretically; and, as we shall see, the full bearing of the noble Lord's contention becomes vivid only when one uses the kind of analysis introduced informally in Chapter 2. Then, as a matter of engineering, economists in those days did not look toward computer science. Above all, the idea of vast areas of applicability for economic science, quite apart from the explanation of prices in a market, did not occur to them. The significance of claiming that wherever you ran into the manifestations of scarcity you might be able to apply economic concepts was therefore lost on them.

Over the years, many of the introductory texts, both here and in Britain, paid lip service to the *Essay* and to the concept of scarcity. If you look at them, you will find that each states in an early chapter that economics is needed because resources are scarce in this world. If we could all have everything we wanted without effort, who would have to economize? Put like that, the point does not look too profound. One supposes that Robbins must have had something rather more in mind.

Let us try to unravel what is nontrivial about scarcity as a concept. Robbins took some pains to distinguish an analysis of the structure of pure economics in terms of the notion of scarcity from what he called the "materialist" view. By the latter, he intended the view that economics was concerned with the analysis of something called "material satisfaction" or "material well-being."

This analysis was thought too esoteric for inclusion in the introductory books, and even in the scientific journals it caused some puzzlement. The general attitude was that everyone understood, of course, that material objects were not the only things that could be scarce and therefore need to be economized. Services, after all, were not exactly material things, yet they were in short supply and needed economizing. Both goods and services, however, could be priced; and economics existed to explain the formation of *prices*—so why the big fuss about *scarcity* applying to immaterial states of affairs? Economists were practical people, like engineers, and they felt that their time was being wasted. At best they would grant Robbins a philosophical victory, with the open hint that it had merely wasted their time.

But if history is often unkind to the "practicality" of would-be practical people, the history of science is especially likely to be so.

I shall present here, in our contemporary language, what I believe to be the core of the *Essay's* scientific message—a message, by the way, of highly practical significance.

THE STRUCTURE OF ECONOMIZING

Start with the word "economizing" in ordinary English. We use this word typically in two ways. If someone offers us a nameless whisky, and if he is a good friend, we may kid him, saying, "God, you *are* economizing, aren't you? No J & B?" For the purposes of science, we may dismiss this usage.

We also use the word "economizing" simply to indicate any activity aimed at making the most use of something that is available in limited supply. We economize whatever is scarce. To be scarce is not the same as being a finite quantity or number. There are a finite number of bad eggs in existence at any moment; but they are not scarce, except at an old-fashioned Irish election. To be scarce is to stand in a relation—and whatever is wanted by someone stands in that relation.

Of the set of all wanted things, a proper subset (probably becoming less and less significant at more and more advanced levels of economic development) *may* be said to be "material," if it makes you any happier. Linus' blanket is material. But love is not. Nor is information, of all sorts and kinds, needed by different persons or systems— including information about love.

To have wants is to be affected by scarcity—to have to economize or, as we say nowadays, to optimize, that is, to choose the optimum position from those attainable. To have to find the most highly ordered member of your attainable set and choose this, is to have to economize.

The agent may be a person in private life (or love) or in public office or in secret service. It may be a group acting in unison, such as a guerrilla band, a planning board, a directors' meeting, or a body of strategists. The agent could be Bond at the tables at Blades' or a machine programmed to scan certain possibilities for a certain sort of solution to a certain sort of problem: the economic problem.

Observe that what is wanted, what is scarce, may be anything whatever: satisfactions, experiences, actions, chances, the possible adoption of certain policies, the passage of certain laws, money, striking power and defensive umbrella coverage, high chips, certain sorts of information.

The structure of economizing is independent of whatever in the concrete situation is being economized: *all* economizing has a common formal structure that can be exhibited and can be formalized mathematically, without concern for particular goals or their objects. Even more significant, a machine can be programmed to optimize irrespective of the type of concrete (material or immaterial) thing it is optimizing.

The core of economizing is choosing; thus the core of pure economic science is the general theory of choice.

As for the engineering applications: The explanation of prices is only one of many concrete applications of pure choice theory, although historically it has been the most important one. Looking toward the past, we can understand that the critics of the *Essay on the Nature and Significance of Economic Science* were within their rights to dismiss as trivialities or as philosophical subtleties the whole notion of unexplored areas of the economic effects of scarcity. But we must live in the present and must look toward the future. Every indication of the tenor of the science shows the old price-theoretic application of choice theory being more and more overshadowed by applications to systems, which may be in the public or the private sector and which are concerned with communication, optimizing, men, or machines.

QUESTIONS

1. What did Lord Robbins mean by scarcity? What sorts of things can be scarce? Can the absence of a mother-in-law be scarce? Can the number two be scarce?

2. Why did conventional mathematical economists in the 1930s and 1940s regard the concept of scarcity as a philosophical abstraction, of no practical importance in economic science? What changes in science, mathematics, and the world would lead us to take a different view today?

3. What is meant by "economizing"? How is this concept related to that of scarcity? How are both the former concepts related to the notion of an unattainable set and the notion of an ordering?

4. Why would it matter if economics confined itself to the study of scarce material things? What insights would we lose? What areas of application for the science would be missed?

5. Can you think of reasons why early economists concentrated on the study of the scarcity of material things?

6. Do we know the formal structure of a science if we just know some of the sorts of facts with which the science can deal? If not, why not?

4
NEOCLASSICAL UTILITY THEORY

It is clear that the indiscriminate use of methods and ideas which are palpably without logical foundation is not to be condoned. Such logical basis is, of course, ultimately to be sought in order to avoid hopeless confusion . . . ; but pending the final establishment of this, the banishment of suggestive views is a serious mistake.

Carl B. Boyer
The History of the Calculus

How much of the content of the usual introductory texts is in fact implicit choice theory? How much should be retained in a contemporary treatment? The key word is "implicit." Quite a bit of general choice theory can be dug out of the conventional texts, if you know exactly what to look for and how to sieve it free of sand.

If you have a canny eye, one of the first nuggets you should spot in these books is the concept of utility. It is, in a certain sense, still important today. We must now sift it out and discover what about it is still significant. To do this, we must again look into the past.

The concept of utility has a long history in philosophy, and its use, even specifically, by economists can be traced well back into the eighteenth century. It did not gain wide

THE USES OF UTILITY

acceptance among the economic establishment, however, until toward the end of the nineteenth century. When it did become accepted it had a particular form, which became virtually standard. It is in this finally established form that we shall study the concept here. (The history of the early development is fascinating, but it is work for professional historians.)

Certainly by the 1880s, if not earlier, had you asked any typical English or American economist[1] how we arrive at our choices, he would have answered that we choose in such a way as to maximize utility.

What exactly did this mean? Notice that the economist's use of the word "utility" had almost nothing in common with our use of that word in ordinary speech.

The word "utility" in common speech has a narrow range of uses. We normally speak of a good solid work bench as having utility, and the phrase "utility furniture" was once common. A Jeep or a truck might, without violence to usage, be described as giving its owner utility.

Suppose someone familiar with usage in economic theory were to tell a friend who lacked this knowledge that he had just bought a new car from which he expected to get great utility. His innocent hearer might ask, "What is it, a Land-Rover?" Suppose he replies, "Oh, dear, no—a Ferrari."

The innocent (of economic theory) friend may now get the point and remark, "If that's what you mean by 'utility,' you won't do so well, not round St. Tropez. These days you'll find forty Ferraris chasing the same Bardot *manqué*."

Now anyone can see that, whatever else is going on, the word "utility" is being used here in a very unusual way. To ram it home: The economist who adopted the usage at issue could not consistently have denied that a Bentley Continental, a delightful little piece of Chippendale, a Romanée-Conti 1964, a first edition of *Alice in Wonderland*, a lover, the availability of religious liberty, a knowledge of mathematical analysis—all might correctly be said to give utility to anyone who wanted one, or some, or all of them.

Clearly, this needs looking into. As a matter of simple historical fact, the economists in question took over their

---

[1]Economists on the Continent of Europe and at Trinity College, Dublin, had seen this much earlier.

usage of the word "utility" from a group of nineteenth-century English philosophers known as Utilitarians. "Took over" perhaps understates the case. Some of the economists in question were themselves believers in utilitarianism. So they simply took a concept that they accepted in one field of thought and applied it in another. This was not necessarily an intellectually disreputable thing to do, nor were the utilitarian economists the only people to do it: look at the use of concepts borrowed from abstract set theory in the formulation of contemporary economic choice theory. The advice "Neither a borrower nor a lender be" is scientifically unworkable and has been throughout history. The question must turn on whether the particular piece of borrowing is legitimate.

UTILITARIANISM

The trouble was that the concept of utility, thus transplanted, was a philosophical concept, which had been constructed to do philosophical jobs and had deliberately been given properties that enabled it to do exactly those jobs. These tasks were not necessarily identical with—or even consistent with—those of economic science.

This did not occur to or worry the original borrowers. They were convinced of the truth of utilitarianism, and they did not mind if its supposedly general truths were taken for granted by the special science of economics. Later economists *did* begin to worry, because they knew that philosophical utilitarianism had quite definitely had its day.

The stately homes of England are not what they were, and the stately concepts of utilitarianism are in even worse disrepair. The economists who inherited these concepts found themselves burdened with philosophical debts which they neither could nor were willing to pay off.

In order to understand both the uses of the concept of utility by economists and also their growing embarrassments about it, we are forced to ask: What was the character of the concept when economists first took it over?

Part, at least, of the gist of the utilitarian position had been that *all* action—whatever the agent might claim as his motive—was in fact undertaken in the attempt to maximize something called "utility."[2] Observe that it was

---

[2] Some utilitarians wanted to say also that all action *ought* to be so motivated. But if all action *is* so motivated, it is unclear what can be meant by adding that one *ought* so to act.

a matter of *all* action, of *every* choice whatever.[3] Joan
in agony at the stake, Antigone determined to bury her
brother, Hamlet in the despair of indecision, and Virginia
Woolf's heroine who was never "wholly unconscious of
the cheapness of eggs" are *all* supposed to be trying simply
to maximize *utility*.

This is clearly quite a tall order. What can they have
meant by "utility"?

**PLEASURE
AND SATISFACTION**

It was sometimes suggested that words like "pleasure"
or "satisfaction" would do as translations—or at least as
approximations—to what was intended by "utility." As
regards "pleasure," obviously this is nonsense. Unless the
word is to be used in ways in which it is never normally
used, it cannot indicate half the range of the concept of
utility. And if we give "pleasure" these new uses, it stands
in as much need of explanation—being no longer the familiar word we are used to—as does "utility" itself.

"Satisfaction" is not much better. Consider a man who
maintains and lives with a wife whom he hates, simply
from a sense of duty.[4] One may, of course, say that he
does this to get masochistic "satisfactions." Indeed, this is
the only move open if one is to stretch the concept of
"satisfaction" enough to make it cover the case. But anyone
who knew the man might think it simply absurd to interpret
his behavior this way. As Masoch, I seem to recall, said,
one can go only so far.

As with "pleasure," by the time one has done all the
necessary stretching, "satisfaction" has itself been removed
so far from its familiar uses that it stands in as much need
of explanation as the concept of utility itself.

HAPPINESS

The most plausible identification was that of "utility"
with "happiness"—because the latter, after all, covers a
multitude of sins.

However, consider a dour Scots engineer named

[3]Thus utilitarianism implies a *general* theory of choice. Textbook writers have lost sight of this fact.

[4]The example is from I. M. D. Little, *A Critique of Welfare
Economics*, 2d ed. (Oxford University Press, Fair Lawn, N.J.,
1957), where there is a lively and strongly argued discussion of the
concept of "satisfaction." See pages 15 to 37.

McTavish, who chooses a certain steel alloy over a certain aluminum alloy for a particular aircraft component on grounds of the supposed technical superiority of the former for the job. You need only look at McTavish to see that he never felt happy in his life. To suggest to him (even in private) that his choice had anything to do with happiness—his or anyone else's—would scandalize the good soul to the roots of his being. He chose the particular metal because his training told him it was the best available for the job—and on this he is prepared to defend himself to the directors if need be. (In our notation we would say that the metal he chose was the highest-ordered member of his attainable set of metals; and I feel sure that if we explained what our notation meant in terms of simple ordering, he would accept our formalization without scandal or protest.)

It boils down to this: When people believed that all action could be explained in terms of the search for the greatest utility and the word "utility" could be given a rich, vivid context by appealing to key words of the emotional vocabulary, like "pleasure," "satisfaction," "happiness," and the like, it naturally seemed to economists that they could legitimately borrow this happy notion and use it to explain economizing as simply the ways in which people went about maximizing utility.

The economic uses of the concept of utility were brought before a British public which, at the end of the nineteenth century, was already habituated to thinking in terms of this idea throughout philosophy and psychology. It was presented with the inescapable force and cogency of mathematical argument by William Stanley Jevons.[5] It was played upon by the Pan pipes of the fey Anglo-Irish genius of Francis Ysidro Edgeworth. It was finally conse-

[5]Bitter at the initial neglect of his ideas, Jevons wrote to a friend that he was thought a fool by some and unoriginal by others. He had discovered that the German Hermann Heinrich Gossen (who died unrecognized) had written up the main lines of an economic theory of utility in the 1840s. But the history goes back to Mountiford Longfield, first holder of the Chair of Political Economy at the University of Dublin, in the 1830s, and his patron and friend the Earl of Lauderdale. And beyond them, back to the France of the *ancien régime*: it is to be found in Condorcet, Condillac, and the others of that brilliant circle. It is an irony of history that the theory was to end up described as "Marshallian."

crated as the cornerstone of the neoclassical economic establishment through the writings and the vast verbal influence of Alfred Marshall. So the concept of utility became the core of economic theory from the 1880s until the late 1930s at least.

Thus things remained until the "Hicksian revolution" in terms of the indifference curve. When the concept of utility entered economic theory many men of substance in the field were believing utilitarians. Long before the notion came under final attack from Sir John Hicks and R. G. D. Allen in the thirties, the intellectual temper of the times had changed so that you could hardly have found a utilitarian under a flat stone.

The philosophical debts of the concept of utility have been sufficiently brought home in giving an account of its origins and character. The manner of the final revolt from it on behalf of the economic establishment will be the concern of Chapter 6, which introduces the Hicksian use of the indifference curve.

We are now ready to begin the consideration of how much of the work of the utility theorists bears on contemporary choice theory. To do this, we must lay bare the technical mechanics of their analysis of choice in terms of the maximization of utility.

THE UTIL

It was assumed, then, that there was this something, which in the formal theory is simply called "utility." This utility is supposed to be in some sense measurable—at least in principle—so that it makes sense to speak of quantities of it (they actually spoke of so many "utils"). One could thus legitimately say in this language that one got 2 utils from a shot of Jack Daniels and considerably more from an evening with Marina.

This is surely a staggering idea. The introductory texts usually water it down—expurgate it, so to speak. But I think that doing so is a serious mistake: if you emasculate it you prevent people from seeing the stark, simple daring of the idea. Even in Marshall's *Principles* (which sold the theory to the economic profession), it is presented with the woolly reasonableness—that willingness not to press the logic of the thing—that is a dangerous characteristic of British empiricism, the complacent belief that without much ado we can all muddle through.

To see neoclassical[6] utility theory in its pure form you must go to Edgeworth's brilliant, delightful, haunting book, *Mathematical Psychics*. There you will find, bathed in the splendor of their Celtic twilight, the march of the utilitarian gods.

Edgeworth really believed in the ultimate possibility of a science, of an actual calculus, of pleasure and pain.[7]

Forgive a slight detour into science fiction. If you went to Mars, you might find the Martians talking like this: "Have another drink?" "No, really—I've had enough, I only got 1 util from the last, honestly." If they all did this—and weren't just pretending—and gave every sign of understanding and agreeing with one another, then of course they could regard Edgeworth's analysis as practical and applicable science.

Suppose the Martians could not discriminate finely between musical notes—were all tone-deaf. They would then find your accurate musical ear as outstanding as you found their "nose" for utility.

That we on this earth do not have this nose is simply a matter of *fact*. We know that we can sometimes form a simple ordering: preferring Marina to Karen, and Karen to Inge-Britt.[8] But if I ask you how many utils you would expect from one of them—?

In approaching our discussion of the mechanics of neoclassical theory, however, I ask you for the moment to swallow the business of utils. Exercise, if you will, what Coleridge called "the willing suspension of disbelief." We then get the law of diminishing marginal utility.

The gist of diminishing marginal utility is quite simple. The beginnings of some consumption give great utility, many utils—that first drink when you come ashore

DIMINISHING MARGINAL UTILITY

[6]The term "classical economist" is used by historians for the school of English economists founded by Adam Smith and David Ricardo. The term "neoclassical" is used to differentiate William Stanley Jevons, Alfred Marshall, and their followers who adapted the classical tradition so as to use the concept of utility.

[7]*Mathematical Psychics*, in 1881 (Kegan Paul, Trench, Trubner, & Co., Ltd., London, reprinted by Kelly & Milman, New York, 1954), was perhaps the first book by an economist to present a fully self-conscious general choice theory—of course, it is done on utilitarian assumptions.

[8]Even this assumes transitivity.

off an ocean racer. Subsequent units yield additional utils but in declining quantities. The marginal unit is the last unit consumed, so the law of diminishing marginal utility amounts to the claim that each unit consumed yields less utility than the one immediately preceding it. As presented in particular by Alfred Marshall, this idea has a cozy plausibility. He asks you to picture a small boy eating berries. Many utils from the first few berries, declining steadily. Finally, sharp disutility. So there, Charlie Brown.

This is not nearly so innocent as it looks. The boy-and-berries sort of story suggests that *marginal* utility (the utility added by the consumption of the last berry) diminishes gradually as he eats more berries. But suppose we are consuming something addictive, like a habit-forming drug or difficult music, for which we develop a taste, or the great wines of France, which one grows to appreciate more and more as he educates his palate?

The immediate reply always was that the concept of diminishing marginal utility was not to be regarded as depicting a gradual process, spread out over time, so that tastes and capacities for enjoyment might change. It was to be regarded as a way of expressing something that was, strictly, timeless. That is, if we choose a larger quantity of something rather than a lesser, the number of utils we would receive would be greater, but not *proportionately* so.

Notice that this last formulation has none of the homely plausibility and familiarity of Marshall's boys and their berries.

Even in this arid, timeless form, however, as a proposition about the number of utils associated with different choices, the law of diminishing marginal utility will not stand up. One is not sure what the neoclassical economists imagined to be the status of this "law." But it is surely obvious that (supposing there were such things as utils) it is simply a question of *fact* whether two glasses of J & B yield twice as many utils as one glass or less than twice (as the law of diminishing utility requires) or perhaps *more* than twice as many.

DISUTILITY   There are important situations in life in which very small quantities of some experiences are worse than useless —to be taken half the way is not to have gained more than half of the utils but rather more likely to have gained none at all, if not to suffer positive disutility.

Clearly, if there were utils or if we should ever be taught by Martians or others how to measure them, there are good reasons to suppose that, at the margin, one will find utility increasing or constant, rather than uniformly diminishing, over some ranges of quantity chosen.

Furthermore, as we shall see throughout this book, there are some important choice situations in which the object of choice must be available in just exactly one form to be *any* good at all—where the idea of slightly more or less just does not apply.

This can be so even when the thing chosen happens to be a physical thing which is finely divisible, like a chemical. Most of the drugs prescribed by physicians are highly divisible. Yet it is a matter of common practice that what he prescribes is some exact dose; quantities less than the right one may be useless and greater ones may be fatal.

We have uncovered one of the salient characteristics of the doctrine we are examining: It assumes virtually the continuous divisibility of all the objects of choice. The very notion of utility at the *margin* is of the essence. The bloodlines of neoclassical utility theory are clear: It is by the differential calculus out of philosophical utilitarianism.

The neoclassicists were aware, of course, of what they called the "problem of indivisibilities." But their approach to this problem was that of the ugly sisters confronted by Cinderella's slipper: chop the offending indivisible foot down until it would fit the slipper.

Contrast our contemporary concepts. In Chapter 2, we saw that the members of the choice set can be highly indivisible concrete entities without its mattering an iota to the applicability of contemporary general choice theory. Houdini demonstrated that one can saw a woman in half, but one hates to think of girls being divided into infinitesimals or even into very small parts. Of course, one may try to save the old continuity scene by saying that *time* spent with any member of the choice set *can* be so divided. And how true this can prove. But then, again, how false it can also prove, as Antony found out too late—one can be betrayed by the assumption that one can always take or leave something in small quantities. Some systems are simply either on or off, and there are thus choices that require one to accept or to forgo something as a whole.

By the very nature of its ancestry and characteristics, neoclassical utility theory was not good for handling these situations. As we have seen, the neoclassicists had ways around this difficulty, but these expedients unfortunately depend on making the discontinuous and different kind of choice look like the ordinary divisible kind, thus drawing attention away from what was special and important about it.

But, it may be asked, can our contemporary theory handle all the choice situations that could be handled by the old? Well, if there are three members in the attainable set and someone tells us that the first is worth 138 utils to him and the second worth 60 utils and the third worth only 20 utils, a machine could handle this problem on general contemporary choice-theoretic principles if it is simply programmed to treat a higher cardinal number as indicating a higher place in the optimizing agent's ordering.[9] If there are utils, they can be handled; but if there are not, we do not need them.

THE CURVE OF MARGINAL UTILITY

We are now ready for a little of the formal language of neoclassical theory. So let us look at the curve of marginal utility.

In a two-dimensional space, measure quantities of a (supposedly continuously divisible) commodity along the horizontal axis. Measure the increments of utility resulting from increments of the quantity consumed—making these increments as small as you will—up the vertical axis. On the continuity assumptions, a smooth curve appears showing the functional dependence of utility upon quantity of commodity. The curve is usually shown somewhat as appears in Fig. 4-1.

The curve has been drawn to embody the usual neoclassical assumption of diminishing marginal utility—its shape would have to be changed for the situations we have been discussing in which this assumption does not hold. No more will be said about this. A number of new objections can, however, now be made.

These objections become vivid as one looks at the construction in Fig. 4-1. Yet the objections are concerned

FIGURE 4-1
Diminishing marginal utility

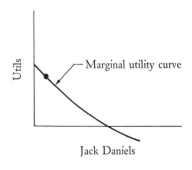

Jack Daniels

[9]I have ignored indifferent positions, for simplicity at this stage. But there is always available an induced simple ordering of the indifference sets, as we shall see in Chapter 5. I have also ignored the need for cardinal estimates in situations of uncertainty. But as everyone knows, the cardinality we ask for (and get) does not establish or require the existence of utils. See Chapter 7, "Contemporary Utility Theory."

not with mathematical properties of the marginal utility function but with further troubles about the concept of utility, which the curve (or its symbolic expression) merely brings to our attention. I shall confine my comments to these difficulties with the concept of utility, which come to our attention as we look at that curve in Fig. 4-1.

Infinite versus finite utility   First, notice that at the upper left-hand corner of the diagram the curve has been allowed to go to the vertical axis. This implies that the first increment (as small as you will) of the commodity gives us only a finite quantity of utility. Suppose the commodity is something without which, in some minimum amount, we should die. Is it very happy to say that we derive only a finite quantity of utility from being alive?

On the other hand, if we postulate that the necessities (or the luxuries) of life give us infinite utility, I can see an old-fashioned, sound, experimental scientist looking up from his claret at High Table, white eyebrows faintly arched, remarking, "Infinite actual quantities of utility, my dear chap. Do tell me, how did you ever *find these out?*"

Either decision—that there are or that there are not—such infinite utilities is embarrassing for a scientist. However, it is not a *mathematical* embarrassment. The problem is implicit in the concept as it was taken over from the philosophical utilitarians. It can arise only for someone who believes that there is actually something called "utility." If there *is* such a thing, obviously it either can or cannot appear in infinite quantities.

On the other hand, if all one is trying to do is to express an order among the elements of a choice set, he can let a finite cardinal number, say 138, be the name of the highest-ordered member of the attainable set—as long as the less-preferred members have as names successively smaller and smaller cardinal numbers. We are not claiming to be aware of how much of some supposedly unique experience the elements of the choice set give, nor are we claiming that there is any one *experience* that can in fact be derived from all of them. They might be radically different sorts of things; all we ask is an ordering.

Jevons, by the way, apparently was aware of this difficulty about the upper left-hand corner of the diagram. In this, as in so much else, he shows the delicacy and subtlety of his mind. He suggested that it might be better not to carry the curve right up to the vertical axis, stopping it, say, at the dot near the vertical axis (Fig. 4-1), on the ground that we can attach no clear meaning to the remaining stretch.

Disutility   Now, a favorable comment on the utility curve. Notice that at its bottom right-hand end the curve cuts the horizontal axis and continues downward. This implies that amounts of some desired thing that are greater than some optimal amount bring disutility rather than utility. Disutility is to be measured vertically downward from the horizontal axis, which introduces a notion that is still of fundamental importance for contemporary choice theory. This notion, of course, can now be expressed in ways that do not depend on neoclassical utility theory.

Maximization and optimization   The notion may be expressed as the distinction between maximizing and optimizing. You can have too much of a good thing. Acting rationally is choosing just the *right* amount, which is not necessarily the physically greatest. In a poor society, everyone has so little of everything that improvement presents itself naturally as the effort to maximize, in order of their importance, all physical outputs. In an affluent society, and more and more as the scientific revolution comes upon us, problems of rational choice present themselves as problems of *optimization*.

Clearly, the distinction between decreasing utility and increasing disutility embodies quite well the distinction between optimizing and maximizing.

Ironically, when economists revolted against neoclassical utility theory and replaced it by the language of indifference curves[10] (as we shall see in Chapter 5) in the 1930s, they ended with a notation that quite failed to make vivid in its symbolism this vital optimization/maximization distinction.[11] In this respect, at least, the "Hicksian revolution" was hardly an advance on existing ideas.

[10]An indifference curve is a geometric representation of a set of positions, about any of the members of which the choosing agent is indifferent. These curves form part of the subject matter of Chapter 5.

[11]Despite the curious fact that, as it happens, a device for doing this, the closed indifference curve, had existed in the literature for a long time, and had been written up even by R. G. D. Allen himself. Possibly the temper of the times was against their seeing the importance of the distinction. The question will be taken up again in Chapter 5, when we come to discuss the properties of indifference curves.

The neoclassical account of optimizing is quite clear and reasonable—if you accept the util, of course—and in general terms runs like this: Simply choose a particular combination of the objects of choice that makes it impossible, by any *marginal* change in the quantities of these objects chosen, to increase the number of utils enjoyed.

Clearly, one would not carry the acquisition of any one enjoyment beyond the point where the curve of marginal utility for it cut the horizontal axis. Given competing wants and scarcity, one would not push any one thing even this far, since before marginal utility from it became zero, it is to be expected that there would be higher numbers of utils available from diverting one's scarce resources elsewhere. Since all quantities are assumed in the theory to be continuously divisible, a neat solution appears, with the last increment of any one chosen thing yielding an amount of utility that exactly compensates for any possible loss elsewhere from going without a forgone alternative.[12]

To what extent is this neoclassical theory, at least by implication, a general theory of choice?

From our point of view, the most striking thing about this theory is surely the implication, which comes down from original philosophical utilitarianism and is never wholly abandoned, that a theory of *utility* is a theory of *all* action. Whatever we do, we are supposed to do it in order to increase utility. Remember: To *maximize* utility is to optimize—since one stops short of disutility. Maximizing utility is not like maximizing blackberries.

The neoclassical economists talked a good deal about utility theory being an explanation of the formation of prices. However, the choices people make in a market are only a subset of all human choices, and the notion of utility was originally designed as an account of the latter.

The fascinating question thus arises: Did the neoclassical economists intend to produce a completely general choice theory? And, even if they did not so intend, was such a theory the result of their efforts?

It depends on whom you read. If you read Marshall, as most people have always done, the answer to both questions is surely No. "Utility," for Marshall, is used to explain market behavior, and far-reaching implications of the idea are to be left, like sleeping dogs, to lie.

A GENERAL THEORY OF CHOICE

[12]Total utility curves and utility surfaces have not been forgotten. They will be introduced in Chapter 5.

But if you read Jevons—and particularly if you read Edgeworth—the case is altered. The very title of Edgeworth's amazing book, *Mathematical Psychics*, expresses the hope of a possible science of all pleasure and pain, of a mathematical calculus of happiness. This book was not written for men just going about what Marshall called the "ordinary business of earning a living."

The poet Yeats wished to dine at journey's end with Landor and with Donne. Not disagreeing as to the charm of that evening, I should, however, like to dine with Edgeworth and with Jevons. I should like to ask them both, but particularly Edgeworth: "Had you any idea what you were starting?"

Until that small dinner party, there is, in a sense, no way of knowing. A historian might go a certain distance with textual criticism and letters—I cannot myself say how far. I await my dinner invitation. By the way, Jevons, who was a pioneer in mathematical logic, built one of the first working logical machines—computers, if you wish. It may be seen, I believe, in a museum at Manchester University.

Since we are neither historians nor yet at the wharf of Lethe waiting, let us ask how much of a general choice theory one can get out of their utility theory, if he really tries.

The way to give this a run for its money is to waive all objections to the concept of utility. Suppose we play Alice in Edgeworth-land, *where we have utils, and continuity and all that going for us.*

A set of possibilities may certainly be ordered by stating the number of utils one derives from each—if one can do this. If one said, "Marina 138, Karen 73, Inge-Britt 30," we could translate this into an ordering.

Consider a suggestion: Anything that can be expressed in Edgeworth-land can be translated into contemporary choice-theoretic terms. (It will take chapters to justify this statement.) Does it follow that anything that can arise in contemporary choice theory can be made to arise in Edgeworth-land?

I cannot give more than a *hint* of an answer here, since anything more would take us into some of the newest and most uncharted waters of current mathematical choice theory.

However, first, we would somehow have to regard all choices whatever as simply matters of relative quantities of utility (remember McTavish?). Second, we would be embarrassed by choices that had to be made between things that cannot sensibly be regarded as divisible without limit. Take girls—they give rise to situations that are, to use computer language, either on or off. Strategic decisions and the highest-level decisions in industry and in optimizing by systems are often, though not always, of this kind.

Lastly, there is an issue that takes us to the very frontiers of contemporary choice theory. If we lived in Edgeworth-land, we would find that every pair of possible choices had the following characteristics: Either both choices would yield equal utility or one would yield more than the other. As we roved among our possible choices, altering things ever so slightly, this would always remain true for every pair of possibilities. There would be no two things such that they could not be directly compared and their respective value in utils calculated.

A moment's reflection will show that (problems of the measurement of utils aside) life simply is not like this.

How much distinction as a soldier is comparable to a given level of celebrity as a pacifist protester? How much attainment as a member of a contemplative order is equivalent to rounding St. Mary's turn like Stirling Moss? Women have always known these things: Ask any woman if there are not experiences that cannot be compared.

Choice theory, however, began only recently to introduce the notions necessary to take these obvious facts of life mathematically into account. And it certainly cannot be done within the language of Edgeworth-land (nor, as we shall see in Chapters 5 and 6, within the terms of reference of the Hicksian indifference language).

It is a curiosity of the history of science that some of the most obvious and immediate of human experiences seem to require the very newest kind of formal expression. It must always have been obvious that there are things that cannot be compared. It is equally obvious that of any two such things it can correctly be said *neither* that they give the same amount of utility *nor* that one gives more. Likewise, it can be said *neither* that one is indifferent which one gets *nor* that one has a preference ordering between them. Yet the formal embodiment of this obvious truth is only now, as I write, taking place at the hands of certain young American choice theorists.

It may be said that this is because the kind of mathematics needed for the job required a revolution in thinking. This may be true. What is striking and important, however, is that once the issues have been tackled from the new point of view, the upshot can be stated with the aid of very few and very simple notions.

For the moment it is enough to see that for neo-classical utility theory the whole question cannot exist: Every two elements in the universe of an optimizing agent have either equal utility (or disutility) or one has more.

Let me end on a practical note. It may be admitted that the life of spirit and sensibility offers strong evidence of the existence of incomparable states of affairs. "Shall I compare thee to a summer's day?" It may nevertheless be questioned whether, for its practical uses, choice theory need adapt itself to such problems.

Let me reiterate that a science does not reformulate its axiom system or alter its theorems only when to do so would lead to obviously and immediately practical advantage. It also changes its structure when parts of that structure turn out to involve either serious factual untruth or formal inconsistency with other parts of the structure, and there is available an alternative theoretical structure that is free from these problems.

It is well known, however, that there have been, in this century, changes in pure science whose practical applications were not foreseen at the time but which had, later on, explosively practical consequences.

As it happens, however, in our case one can indicate some of the possible applications even now. Curiously, I think this can be most vividly seen by considering instances in which the actual engineering would pose formidable complexities in detail. Consider a vast system, in which optimizing is done with the aid of computers. If this system does not have a "policeman" computer that is programmed to recognize the development of structures that will lead to incomparabilities, these incomparabilities may not be revealed before information is fed to the supreme decision center.

Admit that incomparabilities may exist in the states of affairs the system is trying to handle. It immediately follows that two distinct kinds of indigestion will arise in the system. First, no steps will be automatically taken to see if the incomparabilities that are developing can be diverted in some way that heads off their escalation toward ultimate conflict. Second, there will be no mechanism for passing on to the nerve center of optimizing decision the crucial warning that the decision-making process ought to be halted until the situation that has led to the development of incomparabilities in parts of the system can in some way be overcome or bypassed.

1. How does the use of the word "utility" by economists compare with the uses of this word in ordinary speech? Give examples of each usage.

2. In what way did the utilitarians explain human action? How did they use the concept of utility?

3. Criticize the claim that the concept of utility meant for the utilitarians something equivalent to what is meant by "pleasure" or "satisfaction" in ordinary English.

4. Does a consistent masochist maximize utility?

5. Why are McTavish's choices a stumbling block for utilitarian theory?

6. What is meant by the notion of a util?

7. Give an account of the concept of diminishing marginal utility. Need it have been supposed that utility would always diminish consistently at the margin? Suggest counterexamples.

8. What can be said about marginal utility in the case of things like medicines, where only an exact dose will do? Contrast the capacities of marginal utility theory and contemporary choice theory for dealing with choice among indivisible entities.

9. Draw a marginal utility curve and describe its properties. What problems arise over infinite utilities? How did Jevons avoid these in his treatment?

10. What is meant by "disutility"? How did the marginal utility curve embody this idea? Is there a sound insight behind the notion of disutility? Can you think of illustrations? How is this notion related to our distinction between maximizing and optimizing?

11. Is there a general theory of choice implicit in neoclassical utility theory? What characteristics of utilitarian thought suggest that there is? Describe some of the problems involved in constructing a general theory of choice on utilitarian lines.

QUESTIONS

5
INDIFFERENCE
SETS

Let us return for a moment to the shores of the Mediterranean. I want to introduce a new element into the scene in Chapter 2: one more girl. You will find that this addition is enough to make the simple choice theory developed earlier much more powerful and much closer to life. It will also give us all the equipment we need to evaluate a supposed revolution that took place in economic theory in the late 1930s, when Sir John Hicks and R. G. D. Allen adopted a concept of indifference in an attempt to banish from economic science the utilitarian notion of maximizing quantities of utility.

So back we go. When we left, there were five girls, three of them in the attainable set. We were able to order these three simply, in terms of the preference relation. If you recall, I enforced the assumption that no one left or joined the group. Suppose we relax this assumption and allow another member in, and further assume that this new member is in the attainable subset of the choice set. Call her Marie. Once we see Marie, we know immediately that she stands above Karen and Inge-Britt, but that she and Marina are, as it were, on a par.

Mathematical economists have long expressed this by saying that between Marina and Marie we are indifferent, but it is important to understand the force of the term. We may be sure these economists do not mean that we are unconcerned. What they mean is that between these two members of the attainable set the preference relation does not hold in either direction. Both members are equally ranked in our ordering. We could now express this as in Fig. 5-1, which is an adapted form of Fig. 2-2.

I am writing "M_0" for Marina and "M_1" for Marie. Placement of the circles containing "M_0" and "M_1" at the same level represents the indifference relation.

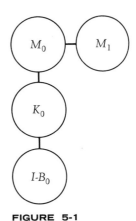

FIGURE 5-1

Weak ordering, showing preference and indifference

FINITE AND TRANSFINITE INDIFFERENCE SETS

Our little scene now contains, in its simplest form, the notion of an indifference set. An indifference set contains simply those members of the choice set that have the same preference ranking. It does not matter how many elements belong to an indifference set. It can, for instance, have a pair of members, or three, or many, or an infinite number. Here a little slightly more formal notation is very useful.

If we wish to refer briefly to a set as a whole we write, for the set of all x's, capital "X." If we wish to spell out the elements we write them out like this, between braces: "$\{x_0, x_1\}$" if there are just a pair, as in the case of the indifference set composed of Marina and Marie, which we may now write either as "M" or as "$\{m_0, m_1\}$." If there are more elements in the set, these simply appear as more lowercase letters with subscripts when the set is spelled out at length between braces: "$\{x_0, x_1, x_2, x_3\}$." Where there is a large finite number of elements in a set and we are too lazy to spell them all out, we may write "$\{x_0, x_1, \ldots, x_n\}$," where n is the number of elements. Finally, we may indicate the fact that X is an infinite, or transfinite set, by simply writing "$\{x_0, x_1, \ldots\}$."

Notice that in all of these cases the set as a whole may be written simply "X." For certain important purposes, it is equally easy to manipulate sets of indifference sets whether the indifference sets have a pair of members, a large finite number, or are infinite sets. We may know that the set M is preferred to the set K, which is preferred to the set I-B, without having to inquire how many elements are in each, as it were, box.

Induced simple orderings   Look again at the ordering in Fig. 5-1. Observe that compared to the simple ordering of Fig. 2-2, it is rather inelegant—that is to say, it is complicated. Some of the members are related by preference, but Marina and Marie are related by another relation, that of indifference. The whole attainable set is not ordered simply in terms of one relation. The ordering is what has been called "weak,"[1] "incomplete," "partial." But now suppose we form indifference sets. We may write them as

$$\{m_0, m_1\}$$

$$\{k_0\}$$

$$\{i\text{-}b_0\}$$

I have treated "$\{k_0\}$" as the indifference set whose only member is Karen and $\{i\text{-}b_0\}$ similarly for Inge-Britt. Once we think of indifference sets as boxes that simply contain however many members of the attainable set have identical preference ranking, we realize that obviously an indifference set may contain just one member, or two, and so on. But now we have restored the simplicity of the ordering in Fig. 2-2, since between the indifference sets simple preference holds. This becomes vivid if we write these sets as "M," "K," and "I-B." We can now reproduce Fig. 2-2, except that "M," "K," and "I-B" are the names of sets instead of elements (Fig. 5-2).

If we group the indifferent elements into indifference sets, we can always induce a simple ordering by preference. Notice that we say "induce"—the attainable set as such does not *immediately yield* a simple ordering, since some elements in it are ordered by preference and some by indifference. We must partition the attainable set into indifference sets, then order the latter. The indifference sets, of course, can be ordered simply by the relation of preference. Such an ordering over the indifference sets will therefore be referred to as an "*induced* simple ordering," to distinguish it from the situation in which there are no

FIGURE 5-2

Inducing order by preference

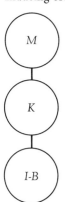

[1]Arrow's term.

indifferent elements in the attainable set, and the latter can immediately be simply ordered by preference.

Notice that the operation of separating out the different indifference sets is a *partitioning*: there are no elements in the attainable set that are in both of two indifference sets.

Rational decision for attainable sets that partition into indifference sets The question may be asked: How do one's rules for rational decision need to be modified when indifference exists? The answer is that once one sees that indifferent elements can be treated as we have done, the decision process can be shown to be virtually as simple as before.

Suppose that M and K stand for indifference sets, with no specification of how many girls are in each. Suppose that we are told (assume it is on good authority) that the set M is to be found in Pedro's, whereas the set K is to be found in the Bar Central on a particular evening. Given that M is preferred to K the decision rule is: Go to Pedro's and allow chance to determine which member of M you become attached to.

The same instructions could, obviously, be fed more formally to a computer. It could be programmed to rank the indifference sets, find the most highly ranked set, then deliver any element at random from that most preferred set. To say that there is one element more preferred than any other is to assert implicitly that the most highly ordered indifference set contains only one member. If it contains two or more, the computer is free to dish up any one of them.

We must clearly understand and remember that to say that we are "indifferent" among a set of choices is to say that we don't care *which* of them is offered. We exhibit this willingness by allowing the result to depend on a toss of a coin or on a selection by some random process.[2]

Romeo and Friar Lawrence have some arguments in which Friar Lawrence is hoping to make Romeo admit that Romeo's most preferred set—call it "J"—may contain more than one member. (As a friend, the Friar is deeply concerned that the only so-far-discovered member of Romeo's set J is diplomatically embarrassing.) Romeo, however,

[2]This operational view of indifference was suggested by William Baumol in a personal letter.

insists on Juliet's uniqueness, which amounts to saying that for him the most preferred, or maximal, set J contains only one member. This does not entail that sets less high in his ordering also are limited to one member—indeed, quite the contrary.

Geometrical mappings of indifference sets   As early as 1881, Francis Edgeworth was interested in the notion of indifference, and he developed a geometric device for its analysis.[3] His concept was to have a chequered career and to become the chosen battleground of would-be scientific revolutionaries; its importance has not disappeared even today. His device was called the "indifference curve."

Let us approach this notion by asking if we can find a geometric translation of some of the concepts of this chapter. In a sense, we shall be asking a question that goes back to Descartes (if not much further!), namely: What translations are possible between certain abstract mathematical concepts and the spatial structures of geometry— what sorts of maps can geometry make for us of our abstract notions?

In one respect, we shall indeed be living in Descartes' world: The geometry used by Edgeworth was traditional, and we shall follow him in this for the moment.

Suppose we lived in a world in which there were only two sorts of things among which we could choose. Robinson Crusoe on his island might have been able to choose only between devoting his energies to knocking down coconuts for food, or skindiving for bottles of J & B, which we may suppose to be intact in their cases in the wreck, conveniently imagined to be within skindiving range. Of course we know that even he could choose other actions: He could build a hut, do pure mathematics, or just lie in the sun. But if we are to follow Edgeworth and use Cartesian geometry, we must suppose that the attainable set of actions can be partitioned into two[4] subsets and that each of these can be treated as one kind of action. Crusoe's possibilities may then be represented as follows.

Geometrical representation of indifference   In a two-dimensional system such as that in Fig. 5-3, measure

FIGURE 5-3

Two-dimensional representation of indifference

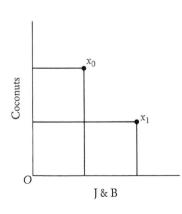

---

[3]By the 1880s, Irving Fisher in America had the same idea, and Pareto followed about the turn of the century.

[4]Three, if we are willing to use three-dimensional geometry.

up the vertical axis quantities of coconuts and along the horizontal axis quantities of J & B. Strictly speaking, we know that J & B and coconuts both come in minimal units, but for the purposes at hand we have to suppose them to be continuously divisible.

Now consider any pair of points in the space between the axes such as x_0 and x_1. These points are the geometric representation of a certain quantity of coconuts and a certain quantity of J & B. If we drop perpendiculars, as Euclid would have said, to the axes we can see this: The distance of x_0 from the horizontal axis mirrors the amount of coconuts and the distance from the vertical axis, the amount of J & B.

Now observe that at x_1 Crusoe has a different mixture of the two objects of his choice than at x_0: He has more of one but less of the other. He has what has been called a different "bundle" of the two things at x_0 and x_1. Now consider any point such as x_0 and suppose that there is at least one other point, call it x_1, such that the bundle represented by the latter would exactly compensate him for the loss of the bundle represented by the former. We then have a geometric representation of a case of the indifference set $\{x_0, x_1\}$. In the case where the indifference set I is a transfinite set, which we write $\{x_0, x_1, \ldots\}$, this will show geometrically as a smooth curve.

As we shall discover in later chapters, the curve may assume many shapes, but in general it will be convex to the origin as it looks in Fig. 5-4. This convexity reflects the assumption that as J & B is given up, larger and larger quantities of coconuts are required to leave Crusoe indifferent to successive losses of J & B, and vice versa.

This sounds reasonable. If we have two interests, we will relinquish some of one normally only if we are offered more of the other in exchange. Edgeworth, who believed in utils, thought of an indifference curve as tracing the loci of those points on the space that would yield equal amounts of utility to the chooser. Our indifference curve simply shows the set of all points that represent combinations of amounts of two things, such that the chooser is indifferent between any two such points.

Notoriously, however, maps can have their shortcomings: A map of the world, on a two-dimensional space, is bound to distort it in one or more of a number of ways, since the world is rounded and the map is not. Pictures

FIGURE 5-4

Indifference set as a transfinite set

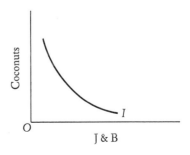

mislead; cameras in fact lie; images, projections, reflections can, like shadows, lead one badly astray. Narcissus was probably not the first to be mislead by a reflected glory, and the poet Yeats admits that

> Players and painted stage took all my love,
> And not those things that they were emblems of. . . .

How about indifference curves as mappings of indifference sets? It will appear on reflection that the case of indifference that appears most clearly in the geometry is in fact highly restricted in two different senses. Mathematically, it is a special case; empirically, it depicts a pattern of indifference most unlikely to be found in real life. This must be explored at length.

Restrictions of the indifference curve   Some of the things among which we choose in ordinary life have the property that they can be divided and measured in ways that tempt one to represent them mathematically in terms of the concept of continuity. Sugar and flour are like this, but girls, airline tickets to Tangier, and plans to open a European subsidiary company (of a certain minimum effective size) are emphatically not.

We saw this problem arise in the case of the neoclassical concept of utility, and it arises with equal force over the concept of the indifference curve. The whole seductiveness of the curve requires continuity: If you have only indifference sets containing a couple of elements, say $\{x_0, x_1\}$, why bother to try to represent this geometrically? As we shall see in later chapters, all the elegant passes with the, as it were, cape, all the exquisite classical bullfighting of formal indifference-curve analysis calls for and gets the assumption of continuous curves.

However, set-theoretically, the case of a transfinite indifference set is a limiting case, and practically, in how many decision situations are we concerned with infinite sets of indifferent positions?

There is, however, a more damaging property of the indifference-curve geometry. Since we are compensated for having less of one thing by being given more of another, *physical quantity* of each of the two things is of the essence of the structure. Thus preference is shown in Fig. 5-5.

Of any two indifference surves I_0 and I_1, I_1 is called the higher, and the higher (or farthest from the origin) of

FIGURE 5-5

Physical quantity and preference

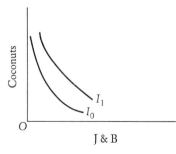

J & B

any two curves is said to be preferred. That is to say, any point on I_1 is preferred to any point on I_0. The only property that distinguishes any point on I_0 from any point on I_1 is that the latter represents a larger physical quantity of one or both of the two things being chosen. The geometric representation of the relation *preferred* has to be simply *larger*. But, if you remember Chapter 2, although Marina was preferred to Karen and to Inge-Britt both, nobody said she was the largest girl.

The geometry can serve as a valid mapping of sets of ordered indifference sets, only if the relation "is preferred to" can be represented by the relation "is larger than."

Generality of the concept of a set of indifference sets   Not only is there no need for the members of an indifference set to be divisible, but also there is no need for them to bear any physical resemblance to one another. To say that two choices are members of the same indifference set is to say nothing about their physical character; it is simply to say that the chooser is indifferent which he has. Any collection of things *might* all be members of the same indifference set. They may be written $\{x_0, x_1, x_2\}$. The fact that we use the notation of lowercase x with a subscript in no way implies that they are different quantities of some physical thing or some combination of quantities of two or more things. All it implies is that they are elements in the indifference set X. A day with a favorite lover, a chance to avoid a hated relative, and an evening dining with three beloved old friends might all be members of the same indifference set. Likewise, of course, they might be members of different indifference sets.

Thus neither the indifference sets as a whole nor their individual members need have any of the properties necessary for their representation by the use of indifference curves.

QUESTIONS

1. What is the minimum that one must add to the simple model of choice in Chapter 2 in order to introduce indifference?

2. What are indifference sets? How many members need they have? How are they expressed in notation?

3. What are induced orderings, and how are they related to the simple ordering of Chapter 2?

4. Can the one girl Karen be treated in terms of the concept of an indifference set?

5. What are the rules for rational decision where indifference exists? Could a computer follow these rules? Could a Scotsman follow them?

6. How do you demonstrate operationally that you are indifferent as to which of two members of your attainable set you obtain?

7. Do all the indifference sets in Romeo's attainable set have more than one member?

8. Describe a two-dimensional representation of indifference.

9. What are the limitations of indifference curves?

6

THE
HICKSIAN
REVOLUTION

We are now ready to describe and to evaluate the Hicksian revolution referred to at the beginning of Chapter 5. Using the indifference curve of Edgeworth, Hicks and Allen fought an action so successful that they changed the whole technical face of microanalysis to such a degree that intermediate and even introductory texts acquired a look which they have not lost to this day.

At the beginning of the 1930s, and particularly at the London School of Economics, the neoclassical concept of utility was dying on its feet. In the *Essay on the Nature and Significance of Economic Science*, Lord Robbins remarks that he is avoiding philosophical refinements as being outside the field in which he has any claim to technical competence. Nevertheless, the fact remains that the

INDIFFERENCE MAPPINGS
AS AN ESCAPE
FROM UTILITARIANISM

view of economic science as a structure of abstract relations between scarce means and ranked preferences which
emerges from his book neither needs nor offers any support
for the lingering remains of psychological utilitarianism in
economic theory.

And then there was the whole spirit of the age: The
thirties looked askance at other metaphysical notions than
that of utility and devoted its energies to the debunking
of great Victorians other than the English Utilitarians. A
new spirit was abroad, the spirit of logical positivism.

**THE SPIRIT
OF LOGICAL POSITIVISM**

The new logic, which was later to merge with the
new mathematics, did not have the practical applicability
to reshape the world that it was to acquire when the computer became its powerful slave; but it was already a
strong acid, eating away the faces of the graven idols of
traditional philosophy.

In its turbulent youth, the new logic generated a
philosophical point of view as hostile to utilitarianism as
anything could possibly be. Hammered out as a fighting
program by men who were scientists and logicians first and
philosophers only secondly, emanating from the Vienna
circle and taking England and America by storm, the
movement spoke with particular force to those, like economists, who craved admission to the halls of science and
who most feared the contemptuous dismissal of its advo-
cates. In Britain, they were known as "logical positivists";
in America, often as "operationalists." We shall find that
in economic theory their influence has lingered long after
mathematical logicians, philosophers of science, and members of the more developed sciences had seen the errors
of their youthful excesses.

For the logical positivists, only two sorts of utterance
were admitted as scientifically meaningful. One they called
"tautologies," which was their word for truths such as those
of mathematics and logic. The other approved class of
utterances were "empirical statements," whose truth could
be tested, like "There is a cat on the mat." The latter could
be tested by kicking the cat or, if that sounds inconsiderate,
by rolling it over, feeling it, and so on. If the object on the
mat is a girl's muff, or a toy cat, one soon finds this out.
Science, properly so called, was supposed to be constructed
solely from tested observations and mathematical analysis
of their structure.

Obviously, the neoclassical curve of diminishing marginal utility does not offer a mathematical analysis of a series of tested observations of something called "utility," since quantities of utility—and even the very idea itself—are never open to test in the way in which, say, the behavior of a gas is.

Like the neoclassical economists before them, the indifference-curve critics of utility were children of their philosophical age: As the men of utilitarian days had been predisposed to accept the idea of utility, the men of the thirties were predisposed to reject it. In an early chapter of his great book *Value and Capital*, Sir John Hicks states the newer point of view succinctly:[1] "If one is a utilitarian in philosophy, one has a perfect right to be a utilitarian in one's economics. But if one is not (and few people are utilitarians nowadays), one also has the right to an economics free from utilitarian assumptions."

Hicks and Allen did not invent the indifference curve; as we have seen, Edgeworth and others had it much earlier. What they noticed was that it could be used to give an account of choice wholly in terms of the two relations of indifference and preference. Edgeworth had treated points on the same indifference curve as points of equal utility, but clearly, all one needs to say about any two such points is that neither is preferred to the other. Also, any point on a higher curve is preferred to any point on a lower.

ECONOMIC CONSEQUENCES OF THE HICKSIAN REVOLUTION

It is a little hard to see today how exciting this must have seemed in the thirties. From our point of view, the set-theoretic account of choice in terms of an attainable set of choices, partitioned into indifference sets and ordered by the preference relation, offers a general account of decision making completely free from utilitarianism. True, the indifference curve offers this freedom from utilitarian assumptions, but it restricts the account of choice to highly special cases, as we have seen in Chapter 5.

Edgeworth introduced indifference curves to study special cases of choice, as Hicks himself notes in *Value and Capital*. In this, contemporary theory supports Edgeworth: As we shall see, here and in later chapters, such curves are useful in special cases. But for Hicks and Allen, this special

[1]J. R. Hicks, *Value and Capital*, Oxford University Press, London, 1939, p. 18.

mapping seemed a universal and necessary mold into which all microeconomic argument must be cast if it was to escape the taint of utilitarianism.

Ironically, the Hicksian revolution did not have its full effect on the format of texts until well into the 1940s.[2] By 1951, a fully general account of choice theory in terms of ordering relations was available, in the first edition of Kenneth Arrow's *Social Choice and Individual Values*. Had utility theory struggled along for another few years, it might have been replaced in the texts by what we would recognize today as a contemporary choice theory. However, the texts from the mid-forties through today exhibit a total concentration on the indifference curve, which looks odd to our eyes and would probably look equally odd to Edgeworth were he alive and with us today. From these humble materials grew the towering intellectual structure of the Hicksian revolution.

HICKSIAN VERSUS CONTEMPORARY USES OF THE INDIFFERENCE CURVE

It has already been remarked that contemporary choice theory can sometimes make use of geometric representations of an Edgeworthian type to illustrate special cases. I am about to give a preliminary account of the sort of geometric structure normally used today. The moment I do so, however, a further historical irony will appear; that is, the version of indifference-curve geometry adopted by Hicks in *Value and Capital* and followed by virtually every undergraduate textbook written since then[3] is *more restrictive* (and of much less interest today) than earlier versions, some aspects of which go back to Edgeworth.

To make this vivid, I shall first offer a very elementary contemporary use of geometry to represent choice-theoretic concepts, then present a brief account of the straight Hicksian version.

A CONTEMPORARY MAPPING IN AN EDGEWORTH BOX

If we are to use two-dimensional geometry we must, as we have seen, place highly restrictive limits on the kinds of choices we can illustrate: Decisions must be between bundles, made up of different amounts of *two* continuously divisible objects of choice. Within these restrictions, however, certain interesting things can be shown. Let us begin

[2]Hicks' *Value and Capital* came out in 1939, and was the beginning of wide acceptance of the idea. Hicks and Allen had been writing articles on their ideas from the early thirties.

[3]With the exception of the work of Kenneth Boulding.

by constructing a very old device—an Edgeworth box. This can be done very conveniently for the Crusoe situation. Let the horizontal sides of the box represent the total stock of J & B in the sunken wreck and the vertical sides the total supply of coconuts in the island trees (Fig. 6-1).

Anyone who is at 0, which is treated as the origin, has zero coconuts and zero J & B. Movements along the vertical side of the box in the direction of the arrow, from 0, indicate increasing quantities of coconuts, with the top left-hand corner indicating possession of the total quantity on the island. Movements along the horizontal axis in the direction of the arrow likewise indicate the possession of larger and larger amounts of J & B, with the bottom right-hand corner indicating possession of the total stock in the wreck. Any point within the box such as x_0 indicates possession of a bundle made up of some quantity of each of the two things. To find out how much, drop perpendiculars to the axes. Finally, to be at the top right-hand corner, diagonally opposite from 0, is to possess the island's entire stock of both J & B and coconuts.

Notice that the box thus defined exactly maps the choice set, on the assumptions that Crusoe chooses only between coconuts and J & B, that he is confined to his island, and that nothing there changes. Further observe that, as long as we assume continuity,[4] there is no limit to the set of points such as x_0 that can be found within the box. Thus the Edgeworth box offers *within its limits* a strikingly vivid picture of an infinite choice set. This mapping of the choice set will be called the "choice space." It is a *particular* model for the theory of choice, which involves continuity assumptions.

The next concept to be represented is clearly the attainable set. This appears in the present model as an area, called the "attainable region." Its frontier is determined in the following way. Suppose we are trying to determine what choices are open to Crusoe as a result of his working during some time period, say a day or a week. If he concentrates all his energies on knocking down coconuts (an extreme decision!), we may indicate how much he can attain by marking some distance from 0 up the vertical side of the box. Likewise, if he devotes himself solely to

[4]Remember that any use of indifference curves involves this assumption.

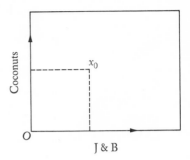

FIGURE 6-1
An Edgeworth box

THE ATTAINABLE REGION

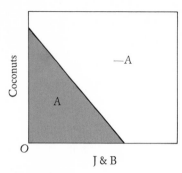

FIGURE 6-2

Maximum possible combinations

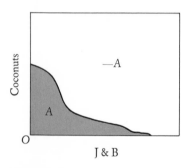

FIGURE 6-3

Brendan Behan's frontier

skindiving, we may indicate his successes by some distance along the horizontal side of the box away from 0 (this decision approximates to that made by some famous Irish playwrights).

Clearly, however, Crusoe may divide his energies, and, assuming continuous divisibility, we may draw a line indicating all the maximum possible combinations of J & B and coconuts open to him—maximum in the sense that he can only have more of the one by having less of the other (Fig. 6-2). This line forms the frontier of the attainable region, which, on present assumptions, is a mapping of the attainable set.

Here we can immediately draw attention to an interesting property of the geometric version. A region has a frontier, and a frontier has a visible shape, which can be directly seen. In Fig. 6-2, the frontier shows as a straight line. But this is only because I assumed that no matter how Crusoe allocated his energies, his effectiveness in the two activities remained unchanged. Had Brendan Behan been shipwrecked on an island in Crusoe's circumstances, his frontier might have looked like that shown in Fig. 6-3. This frontier is constructed on the assumption that the noted playwright would have become less and less effective as he concentrated more and more on coconuts, but more and more lively as he concentrated on fishing up J & B.[5]

Observe that *general choice theory* puts no restrictions on the shape of the frontier. No geometric shape is ruled out as a possible frontier of an attainable region of some choice space. When choice theory is *applied* to describe the possibilities open to different kinds of choosing agents, the frontier relevant to each kind of agent will be determined, as it were, by engineering considerations—the technical possibilities of the agent's particular situation.

**CLOSED CURVES
AND AN OPTIMAL REGION**

We already know that indifference sets ordered by preference will appear in this model for choice theory as higher and lower indifference curves, but there is considerable freedom as to exactly what form these will take.

In the Edgeworth box in Fig. 6-4, the indifference curves are what has been called "closed curves." I have lettered significant sections of them, whose properties I now

[5]This concept of variable returns has been known for a long time and is to be found in neoclassical theory.

want to discuss. From a_0 to b_0 the curve bears the now familiar interpretation. As we give up coconuts we require larger and larger quantities of J & B to compensate us.

But what about the stretch going from b_0 to c_0? Here we are getting larger and larger quantities of coconuts for every given increment in J & B. The interpretation of this section is that J & B has become redundant (Behan would have refused to accept this, even as a logical possibility, but I ask you to) and we are having to be *compensated* for taking more J & B. Briefly, to remain indifferent, we need more food if we are to accept more drink.

Between a_0 and d_0 the same sort of relation holds, only here we need to be given more drink to compensate us for additional food. Finally, consider the curve from c_0 to d_0. This is like a conventional open indifference curve —that is, like the stretch going from a_0 to b_0, except that *both* J & B and coconuts are now in redundant quantities. Imagine a situation in which you are offered two things, both in embarrassingly large quantities. You will remain indifferent to having more of one of them only if you can take less of the other, and vice versa.

You might see this best by turning the box around and looking on 0_1 as the origin. Then the stretch of curve from c_0 to d_0 appears as a normal indifference curve, except that we know that it shows how much *avoidance* of one excess will keep us just compensated for additions to the other excess.

"Higher" indifference curves might now be better described as "inner": I_1, which lies inside I_0, represents an indifference curve preferred to I_0. The section from a_1 to b_1 on I_1 represents positions preferred to those on the section from a_0 to b_0 on I_0 for the usual reasons that hold for open curves, namely, they represent more of one or both of some desired thing. Other points of the closed curve I_1 are preferred because they represent *less* of some one or two redundant things. The curves will close about a core, which may be either a point or an area. This is the geometric mapping of the maximal set. It can be a point if this set contains only one member; if the set is transfinite, it can be an area, which we call the "optimal region."[6]

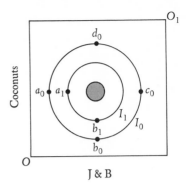

FIGURE 6-4

Indifference (closed) curves in an Edgeworth box

---

[6]"Optimal" is better than "maximal," since it draws attention to the fact that what is at issue is a matter of the right proportions of two things, not just of getting as much as possible.

**TANGENCY AS A
GEOMETRICAL
REPRESENTATION
OF OPTIMIZING**

In the situation shown in Fig. 6-5 the optimal choice will be the bundle indicated by the point x_0 in the choice space. Let us explore the implications of this. At x_0, the indifference curve I_2 is just tangent to the frontier of the attainable region. Then x_0 must be the best attainable choice for the following reasons. We cannot choose any point on an inner curve, such as I_3, since such a curve nowhere even touches the attainable region. On the other hand, there is an infinite set of points we could choose on an outer curve, like I_1, since a whole segment of the curve I_1 lies within the attainable region. But because it is an inner curve, any point x_0 on I_2 lies closer to the optimal region than any point on any outer curve such as I_1. So x_0 on I_2 must, under the present rules, be preferred to any point whatever on I_1.

When preference is mapped in terms of the properties of an Edgeworth box with closed curves, any point on an inner curve is preferred to any point on an outer, since any point on an inner curve represents a bundle closer to the optimal ones in the optimal region. The situation is analogous to the one we face in shooting at a target with a rifle. A hit at any point on an inner ring is preferable to one at any point on an outer ring because the former is nearer to the bullseye.

An interesting result follows from this: As long as the frontier has the sort of shape shown in Fig. 6-5, the decision-theoretic rule is always simply to find the tangency. Whether we are speaking of men or of machines, they have economized if and only if they are at the point x_0. Clearly, in all such models for the theory of choice the geometric concept of tangency offers a vivid image with which to picture economizing.

Observe, however, that represented in set notation, such models look oddly restricted. Their form would be as follows:

$$\{x_0\}$$
$$|$$
$$\{y_0, y_1, \ldots\}$$
$$|$$
$$\{z_0, z_1, \ldots\}$$

Let $\{y_0, y_1, \ldots\}$ be any indifference set representing an outer curve. One then notices the odd fact that in

FIGURE 6-5

The optimal choice
is the bundle, x_0

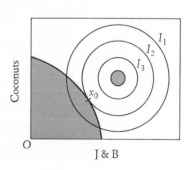

J & B

the resulting ordering, all indifference sets in the attainable set are transfinite, except for the most highly ordered, which contains only one member. This is of course simply a result of the tangency: If the innermost indifference curve, any of whose points are attainable, is just tangential at one point to the frontier of the attainable region, that point x_0 will be the only member of the highest attainable indifference set in the attainable set.

But as we have seen, it is a matter of common experience that our most highly ordered attainable indifference set may contain two members (Marina and Marie, for example) or more than two members.

The geometry, however, can be adapted to allow for this. It is all a matter of the *shape* of the frontier of the attainable region. As we have seen, this shape can take many forms. Consider Fig. 6-6. Here we have a representation of an optimal set with two members, $\{x_0, x_1\}$, since there are two tangencies. The rule for decision is as for all such situations: An arbitrary process can be allowed to select one of the two elements in the most highly ordered indifference set within the attainable set.

We can even represent the situation where the most highly ordered indifference set in the attainable set is transfinite, as in Fig. 6-7. This happens if we allow the innermost attainable indifference curve to "fit" the curve of part of the frontier of the attainable region.[7]

It remains to consider a situation in which there is a breakdown in the geometric representation of economizing as a movement to a point or points of tangency or, more generally, to a frontier, as in Fig. 6-8. Here the optimal region lies *within* the attainable region. To follow usual rules and go to x_0, where a curve is tangential to the frontier, is clearly to go *beyond* the target, pass the optimal region, and take up a position less preferred than any of those in the optimal region.

Notice that here a certain property of all geometric models we have previously considered has suddenly disappeared. Previously, the most preferred position or positions lay on the frontier of the attainable region. That is, they lay somewhere along the line defining *maximum possible* combinations of J & B and coconuts. But all the

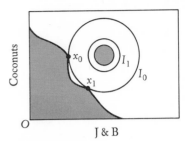

FIGURE 6-6
Optimal set with two tangencies

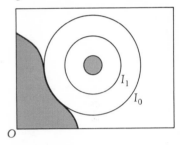

FIGURE 6-7
The innermost attainable indifference curve "fits" a section of the attainable region

OPTIMIZING VERSUS MAXIMIZING

FIGURE 6-8
Optimal region lies within the attainable region

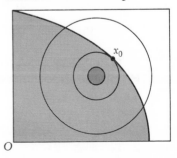

points within the optimal region in Fig. 6-8 have the property that they involve taking *less* of *both* J & B and coconuts than are attainable in the given situation, should the choosing agent simply wish to go to the frontier of possibility. Here the link between "physically greatest quantity" and "most preferred choice" has finally broken down even within the restrictions of the Edgeworth box. In such a situation we must distinguish between maximizing (going to the frontier) and optimizing (going to the optimal region).

The picture just presented is far from being without significance for our times, and above all for our future. In a poor society or in solving the problems of a poor section of any society, the concept of physical maximizing—of going to the frontier of physical possibility in simply turning out stuff—is not a bad model of economizing. But as our technology is transformed by the effects of scientific revolutions, we shall find more and more areas in which we have more than enough sheer hardware, in which systems will improve the quality of our life and take us to preferred positions only if they are instructed to optimize and not to maximize—to use the distinction to which one is led by the picture in Fig. 6-8.

Fortunately, however, this point needs to be stressed only for geometric models for choice theories (or more sophisticated models still dependent on concepts derived from such geometric representations). For a set-theoretic general choice theory, the maximal set is, as we know, simply the most preferred indifference set in the attainable set. It has nothing to do with physical quantities, simply with orderings. No one ever said Marina and Marie were the largest girls.

Thus we never need an optimizing-maximizing distinction, except for commenting *on models* for choice theory where "more preferred" is represented by spatial or quantitative concepts.

COMPARISON WITH THE HICKSIAN VERSION

We shall end this chapter with the promised comparison of an elementary contemporary use of geometry with that popularized by Hicks in *Value and Capital*.

Let me stress once more that most of the *geometric* concepts used in our contemporary discussion were available to Hicks. Closed curves had been described and used in an article in the early thirties[8] by Abba P. Lerner, who was at the London School of Economics at that time. They had been even more elaborately analyzed by R. G. D. Allen, Hicks' collaborator in journal articles.[9] Eccentrically shaped frontiers had also been discussed by Lerner.[10]

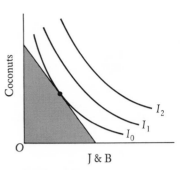

FIGURE 6-9

Open indifference curves

Hicks, however, chose to concentrate exclusively on the structure shown in Fig. 6-9. Indifference curves are presented as open without specified limit, thus "more preferred" is literally identified with "greater physical quantity." The only frontier considered is linear.

The overwhelming majority of undergraduate texts followed Hicks, presenting the theory of choice wholly in terms of indifference curves and the latter wholly in the form shown in Fig. 6-9. The one glowing exception I know of is Kenneth Boulding, who did present a system of closed curves in his massive work;[11] but I doubt that Boulding's book has ever been much used below at least the intermediate level, and his treatment of closed curves is brief.[12]

Why did this happen? Without claiming to read the minds of past writers or attempting profound historical analysis, two suggestions occur to me. One concerns the form of the frontier that they chose as typical, the other concerns their ignoring of closure in the curves.

First, as to the frontier: Remember that all the textbook writers of the fifties saw themselves essentially as

[8]Reprinted in Abba P. Lerner, *Essays in Economic Analysis*, Macmillan & Co., Ltd., London, 1953. (The relevant chapter, "The Diagrammatical Representation of Demand Conditions in International Trade," had originally appeared as an article in *Economica*, in August 1934.)

[9]As well as by Nicholas Georgescu-Roegen (in the *Quarterly Journal of Economics*, 1936) and others.

[10]Lerner, *Op. cit.*, pp. 92-100.

[11]Kenneth E. Boulding, *Economic Analysis*, 4th ed., Harper & Row, Publishers, Incorporated, New York, 1966.

[12]*Ibid.*, vol. I, *Micro-economics*, pp. 604-607. Boulding's diagrams do not show the closed curves as perfect circles. Realistically, their being exactly circular is highly unlikely. I have drawn them as circles only for simplicity. Significant use of closed indifference curves is made in a new text at a more advanced level: James Quirk and Rubin Saposnik, *Introduction to General Equilibrium Theory and Welfare Economics*, McGraw-Hill Book Company, New York, 1968.

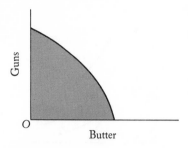

FIGURE 6-10

Concentrating on either specialty
shows decreasing returns

FIGURE 6-11

The effective region, *OABC*

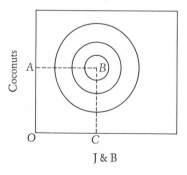

presenting a theory of *prices*. They were not intentionally
giving a general choice theory. Now, the theory of the
behavior of a consumer facing prices in a market that he
cannot affect can properly be presented in terms of a linear
frontier. Given that the prices of commodity *x* and commodity *y* are fixed, there is some fixed rate at which he
can give up *x* and acquire *y* by diverting his income from
one to the other. Hence Fig. 6-9 will correctly depict his
situation. Curiously enough, there was usually one place
in such books where a frontier of a different shape was
considered; that is, where the authors were describing the
possibilities of production facing a whole economy. The
books have flowed not with milk and honey but with guns
and butter, and the following inevitable example is always
used. So I reproduce it as Fig. 6-10 out of *gravitas*.

The shape of the frontier shows decreasing returns
as the economy concentrates on either specialty, which
is a way of saying that dairymaids are bad at engineering
and Krupps probably equally bad at milking a cow. What
was not usually pointed out, however, is that both Figs. 6-9
and 6-10 are simply special cases of the concept of an
attainable region with a frontier, of some form or other.
Matters were further confused by even introducing them
under different names: The frontier of the attainable region
in consumers' behavior theory was called a "price line" or
a "budget restraint," while that in the theory of production
was called the "production possibility curve" or "transformation curve"—among other things. As students moved to
more advanced work and to new areas of application of
economic theory, they often got the impression that they
were meeting new concepts, whereas in fact they were
only running into attainable regions with differently shaped
frontiers, each appropriate to the particular application
being considered.

Now, the point about the ignoring of closure. I think
it is very hard not to see here the influence of the times.
In the days when Hicks was giving indifference-curve
theory the form that was to become definitive in the textbooks, affluence was not yet pressing on people's minds.
In a very revealing phrase in one of his articles, R. G. D.
Allen even called the open segment of an indifference map
the "effective region" (Fig. 6-11). Probably no one expected
to be physically in a position to pass the optimal region for
significantly many things—it is taking a series of scientific

revolutions to make this a reality. Don't forget that for a poor society Allen's "effective region" is still the scene—*as it is for the poor in our society*—they still can construe economizing as physical maximizing.

Moreover, no one was thinking in terms of computer science, so the idea that an Edgeworth box containing closed curves around an optimal region offers a vivid picture of a target would not be in people's minds.

Thus mathematical style, like literary style, reflects in its idiosyncrasies the spirit of an intellectual age and even the brutal physical conditions of life.

1. Was there a Hicksian revolution? What was it about? How important are its results to us today?

2. Why was the spirit of the 1930s hostile to the neoclassical concept of utility?

3. If Hicks and Allen did not invent the indifference curve, what was original about their use of it?

4. What might have happened to the development of microtheory if Hicks had not converted the scientific world in the late thirties and in the forties?

5. Give a contemporary account of the representation of indifference in an Edgeworth box. Explain the concepts of attainable region, closed curve, and optimal region.

6. What restrictions if any does general choice theory place upon the shape of the frontier of the attainable region? Illustrate some interesting possible forms it might take. How may we use these to illustrate the problems of Irish playwrights?

7. Discuss the concept of tangency in relation to the geometric representation of optimizing.

7
CONTEMPORARY UTILITY THEORY

Pythagoras planned it. Why did the people stare?
His numbers, though they moved or seemed to move
In marble or in bronze, lacked character.
But boys and girls, pale from the imagined love
Of solitary beds, knew what they were,
That passion could bring character enough,
And pressed at midnight in some public place
Live lips upon a plummet-measured face.

W. B. Yeats

Numbers have always at once fascinated and repelled mankind. The ancient Greeks knew this, and later Plotinus passed the heady potion of neo-Platonist mathematical philosophy to St. Augustine and through him into the Christian centuries. "What *are* numbers?" was one of the great traditional questions of philosophy, and the answer remained shrouded in mystery right up to Gottlob Frege and, in our own day, Bertrand Russell.

Even the formalist mathematicians of this century did not altogether vanquish Plato's ghost. To say that numbers are just sets of sets will not stop in his tracks anyone determined upon mysticism, for he will immediately ask the same question about the ultimate meaning of the new concepts. The logical positivists and their successors discovered that there is no infallible therapy for anyone who is really hell-bent on being a metaphysician.

During the thirties, however, there was a very fashionable cure. If someone showed the tendency to fall mystically in love with a concept, you showed him how this supposedly mysterious and fascinating construct could be simply translated into notions each one of which was capable of scientific or mathematical explanation. The process was called "logical translation."

Long ago, during the glorious reign of Victoria, an English gentleman had given a new word, "bowdlerize," to the language by producing a version of the works of Shakespeare stripped of all words and ideas unfit for the ears of nineteenth-century young ladies. The logical translater of the 1930s hoped to preserve the young from temptations to metaphysical sins by translating the dangerous concepts of the past into harmless ones with none but scientific connotations.

Sir John Hicks was no exception to this prevailing fashion: He hoped to lay the ghost of utilitarianism precisely by translating economic theory into an ordinal-preference language in which no concepts of a quantitative nature were allowed to appear. But clearly it is not the use in choice theory of cardinal numbers as such that makes a man a utilitarian. One may use a notation involving cardinal concepts without in the least embracing utilitarian metaphysics.

Suppose we call the set M "3," and call the set K "2." Now, we know that M is preferred to K, which we may write as $M \, P \, K$. But suppose we taught a person or a computer that of a pair of sets represented by two numbers, the one called by the larger number was the preferred. Since three is greater than two (which we may write "$3 > 2$"), such a person or computer would pick the set called "3" over that called "2." Thus one can clearly use numbers like 3 and 2 and symbols like $>$ as a language for representing the preference relation.[1]

[1] I ignore the case of "lexicographic" orderings for this level of argument. Good informal discussions of the problems these orderings pose will be found in Peter Newman, *The Theory of Exchange*, Prentice-Hall, Inc., Englewood Cliffs, N.J., 1965, pp. 23-28; also James Quirk and Rubin Saposnik, *Introduction to General Equilibrium Theory and Welfare Economics*, McGraw-Hill Book Company, New York, 1968, pp. 17-18. For a formal proof that, if a choosing agent ranks choices lexicographically and the objects of choice are infinitely divisible, there is no real-valued representation, see Gerard Debreu, *Theory of Value: An Axiomatic Analysis of Economic Equilibrium*, Cowles Foundation Monograph 17, John Wiley & Sons, Inc., New York, 1959, pp. 72-73.

UTILITY SURFACES

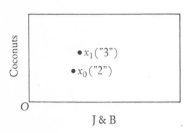

FIGURE 7-1

Edgeworth box
showing points named

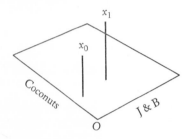

FIGURE 7-2

Edgeworth box
with perpendiculars

Let us carry this a little further. Consider an Edgeworth box, Fig. 7-1, and in it two points x_0 and x_1, such that x_1 is preferred to x_0. Following our rule we could name x_0 "2" and x_1 "3." Suppose we were to erect perpendiculars at right angles to the surface of the box at the points x_0 and x_1, making these 2 inches long and 3 inches long, respectively (Fig. 7-2). Clearly, the 3-inch length at point x_1 could be contrasted with the 2-inch length at x_0. The greater length would symbolize the preferred position.

If we assume continuity, all the points in the Edgeworth box could be considered as represented by such vertical lengths. Any two points would have different lengths if one was preferred and would have the same length if they were indifferent. We might get a curved surface, a dome, as shown in Fig. 7-3.

I have drawn a few rings round the dome through points of equal height—clearly these are closed indifference curves. The flat top of the dome is the optimal area—or it could come to a point: the optimal point.

We have thus used a curved surface to represent an ordering simply by picking suitable lengths for representing the relations involved in the ordering. Observe that we could have made the perpendicular length at x_0, the point we started with, any height whatever we chose, as long as we picked heights for x_1, and so on, which preserved the representation, in terms of height, of the ordering.

This tells us something very important about what we are doing. To clarify this importance, we shall contrast what is implied in the surfaces just described with the crucial properties of apparently similar surfaces constructed in terms of neoclassical utility theory.

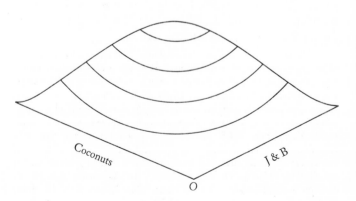

FIGURE 7-3

Connecting the points of the
perpendiculars forms a dome

In the neoclassical utility theory, you will remember, every increment obtained of any desired thing was associated with a definite increment of utility, a definite quantity of the latter, as shown in Fig. 4-1.

From the marginal utility curve, it was an elementary operation for the neoclassical economists to derive what were called "total utility" curves. These showed, not the utility added by the last blackberry, but the total utility derived from each possible total quantity of blackberries.

Very crudely, for one blackberry, the total utility and the marginal utility will be the same; for two blackberries, the marginal utility will be the utility of the second and the total utility will be that of both; and for the third, to the last total is added the new marginal utility of the third berry, and so on. On continuity assumptions, a smooth curve results, as shown in Fig. 7-4. The curve will be rising as long as marginal utility, though diminishing, is positive. It will turn downward for the same quantity which, in the marginal diagram, was the first to produce negative utility.

By x_1 in Fig. 7-5, a considerable amount of disutility is being subtracted, so the total curve is falling.

If one can draw total utility curves, one can certainly also draw total utility surfaces—by plotting the total utility for different quantities of some desired thing along one side of an Edgeworth box and erecting perpendiculars to indicate the amount of utility, then plotting the total utility of different amounts of the other thing along the other side, as in Fig. 7-6. And of course, there will be a total utility associated with any point within the space represented by the box indicating the utility derived from that *combination* of the two things (Fig. 7-7). Assuming continuity, we clearly get a dome, the exact shape of which depends on how much utility is derived from so much of one or the

NEOCLASSICAL VERSUS CONTEMPORARY UTILITY SURFACES

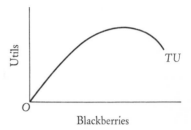

FIGURE 7-4

Total utility curve, *TU*

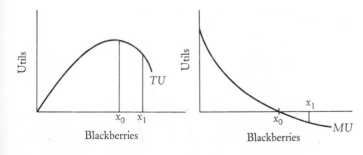

FIGURE 7-5

Negative marginal utility

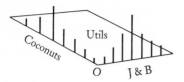

FIGURE 7-6

Plotting total utility surfaces

other or both of the two desired things. What makes this dome different from the one constructed on contemporary assumptions?

The difference is not necessarily determined by its shape: The neoclassical dome will show equal heights for equal utility and greater heights for greater total utility, which is just what we would have chosen to represent an ordering. However, each height in the neoclassical dome will be intended to represent something more than just an *ordering*: it will represent a *quantity* of utility. Remember that there is no limit to the number of different domes that would represent an *ordering*. There is, as a matter of fact, a transfinite set of such domes; but only one will represent a particular configuration of quantities of utility.

We can use the same sort of surfaces to represent orderings that the neoclassicists used to represent quantities of utility; we simply pick one at random where the shape reflects the ordering we are interested in. We are much freer than they were, because we are not trying to claim that the height and shape actually measure quantities of something called utility. They are just curved models of orderings.

It is important to see that we are absolutely free to use such models without in the least assuming

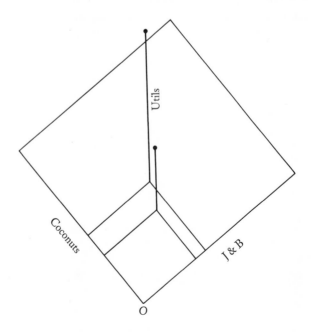

FIGURE 7-7

Total utility derived from combination of two things

that quantities of something called utility exist or are even meaningful.

Thus the use of cardinal numbers and perpendicular heights and whole curved surfaces to represent orderings in no way reinvolves us with the utilitarian concept of utility. So Hicks need not have worried—it was not necessary to banish all cardinal language in order to escape utilitarianism.

Many contemporary mathematical choice theorists even refer to these surfaces of ours today as "utility surfaces." Again, this does not mean that they have regained the faith in utilitarianism. It is simply a convenient name; and it recognizes the historical fact that these useful and harmless geometric constructions were first invented by men who called them this and who happened to believe as well that the domes and curves represented something called "utility," a belief that we have given up. The contemporary literature is full of references to utility surfaces, but it would be naïve to imagine that this widespread usage implies a massive return to utilitarianism. The term "utility surface" can mislead only somebody who doesn't know the gossip of the current literature. I suppose that, as a matter of exquisite linguistic carefulness, one could avoid misleading the naïve if one called the surfaces used today by some other name. One might speak of them as "cardinal representations of orderings," or something of the sort. It seems, however, unnecessarily pedantic to insist on this, because there is an established usage and because the established usage misleads nobody who understands what is going on.

JOHN VON NEUMANN, CARDINALITY, AND GAMES

The use of cardinal concepts in choice theory has a much more powerful and important form, however, and it is time we discussed it. It arose from the path-breaking work in this area of the late John von Neumann and of Oskar Morgenstern in their *The Theory of Games and Economic Behavior*.

The implications of their great work for the importance and feasibility of cardinal concepts in decision theory were at first widely misunderstood. Many older men seemed to accept their astounding discoveries in the theory of mathematical games as a restoration of the reputation of utilitarianism. To understand the issues and to see why this was not in the least so, we must digress for a moment on uncertainty and games.

So far in this book I have assumed that we always know enough to partition the choice set into its attainable and unattainable subsets. To use the language of geometric models, we know the *frontier* of the attainable region.

This assumption is entirely proper in laying the foundations of the most simple and fundamental pure choice theory; but obviously, it is often not borne out in life. We often do not know the exact frontiers of the attainable. We can only make better or worse estimates of the probability of attaining different positions. In order to provide rules for decision in such situations, von Neumann and Morgenstern developed the mathematical theory of games, the formal study of possible optimal strategies for handling decisions in uncertain situations. The decision situation becomes analogous to a game when outcomes are unknown: decision requires the selection of strategies.

A pure ordering does not give us enough information for rational decision in such situations. Suppose that we are *not* sure of the attainable set. Our ordering may tell us that Marina is preferred to Karen. But suppose that we only have the following estimate of availability: The probability of success with Marina is 0.001, whereas for Karen it is 0.5. Simply knowing that we rank Marina above Karen is no longer enough. Suppose we only slightly prefer Marina. To make her our goal is then clearly irrational, given the minute chances of success as contrasted with the very solid chances of success with Karen. On the other hand, suppose Marina is our Juliet, our Cressida, our Deirdre, our Katherine Earnshaw. And Karen is simply a nice ordinary girl. Then, like Heathcliff, we may feel that it is not merely romantic but in fact a matter of what one might in the highest sense call "rational necessity" to pursue her relentlessly—and damn the odds.

Manifestly, a strategy requires more than a mere ordering by the preference relation.

Suppose, to return to the example of Chapter 2, we know only that someone prefers Marina to Karen and Karen to Inge-Britt. We now ask the choosing agent his preference between the certainty of getting Karen and a gamble with Marina or Inge-Britt as the outcome. If the chance of getting Marina is sufficiently great, we may expect our friend to gamble. On the other hand, if the probability of Marina is very small, he will choose the certainty of Karen. As the probability of Marina changes continuously from 1 to 0 his preference for the gamble must at some point change into preference for the certainty of Karen. It is customary to assume that there is just one point of change, and that at this point the agent is indifferent between the gamble and the certainty. Suppose this happens at the point where the probability of Marina is ⅔. If we now attach the arbitrary cardinal number 3 to Marina, and 0 to Inge-Britt, Karen may be given the von Neumann utility index of 2.[2]

Notice that any triple of cardinal numbers would do equally well to symbolize what we have found out about our agent's tastes, *provided* the numerical *difference* between the utility assigned to Karen and Inge-Britt is twice that between Marina and Karen. Thus no meaning has been attached to the idea that anyone experiences "3 utils"— nothing has been proved about quantities of pleasure or satisfaction.

We cannot even say that for this agent the difference in satisfaction from being offered the certainty of Karen instead of the certainty of Inge-Britt is twice as great as the difference in satisfaction upon being offered the certainty of Marina instead of the certainty of Karen. The von Neumann utility indices reflect the choosing agent's like or dislike of *gambling*, not his evaluation of three certain outcomes. Consider someone who really hated uncertainty: Even if he liked Marina *much* more than Karen, he might prefer the *certainty* of Karen to even a very high probability of Marina, thus misleading anyone who took his resulting von Neumann utility numbers as reflecting his evaluation, in terms of satisfaction, simply of the three girls.

The von Neumann utility index *does* give one an ordering, not just over the certainty of Marina, Karen, and Inge-Britt, but over all possible *gambles* involving them. Obviously, this places severe restrictions on the sets of numbers used to express this ordering. Many triples of numbers that would have expressed the mere ordering among certain outcomes of Chapter 2 will not express the ordering in terms of von Neumann utility.

But what is offered to the decision theorist is still an *ordering*—despite the misleading sound of "cardinal utility": it is simply an ordering of gambles. As has been

[2]See R. Duncan Luce and Howard Raiffa, *Games and Decisions*, John Wiley & Sons, Inc., New York, 1957, pp. 21-22.

well expressed by Luce and Raiffa:[3] "In this theory it is extremely important to accept the fact that the subject's preferences among alternatives and lotteries came prior to our numerical characterization of them. We do not want to slip into saying that he preferred A to B because A has the higher utility; rather, because A is preferred to B, we assign A the higher utility."

Clearly, this has nothing to do with "utils" or "quantities of satisfaction."

QUESTIONS

1. Does the use of a system of cardinal numbers or of concepts of a quantitative kind in general commit one to a return to utilitarianism? If not, why not?

2. Starting with an Edgeworth box, how would one construct a three-dimensional representation of an ordering?

3. Is there only one surface that could be used to represent a particular ordering or are there many such surfaces, and if so, how many? What property of any such surface must remain constant for it to represent adequately a particular preference ordering?

4. How would closed indifference curves and an optimal region or point appear on a surface of the kind described in Question 3?

5. Show the relationship between marginal and total utility curves in neoclassical theory.

6. What does a utility surface stand for in neoclassical theory that is absent in contemporary uses of such surfaces?

7. What problem led John von Neumann to wish to introduce a concept of cardinality into choice theory?

8. If Heathcliff had read John von Neumann, would he have behaved any differently from the way he behaves in *Wuthering Heights*?

9. Were old-fashioned utilitarians justified in feeling that the *Theory of Games and Economic Behavior* does anything to revive their claims?

10. Do you think contemporary mathematical economists should give up using the word "utility"? Are terms like "utility surface" misleading when used of contemporary cardinal constructions?

[3]*Ibid.*, p. 22.

8
FORMAL LANGUAGES

Sets, if you will forgive me for parodying John
Stuart Mill, are permanent possibilities of selection.

Hilary Putnam

We have now completed our survey of implicit pieces of
decision theory to be found in neoclassical economics and
also have come nearly to the end of our brief introductory
sketch of the basic concepts and structure of the simplest
possible pure theory of choice. So far, this theory has been
described in a highly informal manner, as was necessary
and proper in an introductory sketch. It is characteristic
of this field, however, that as normally presented it is
highly formalized. It seems a shame to give no glimpse of
choice theory in, as it were, full dress. But to do this is no
easy task. It is easy to reproduce the notation, of course, if
that is all that is to be meant by formalism. But these notations may easily seem lacking in character and vigor: our
sense of formal beauty has been so badly blunted in our
childhood.

FORMAL VERSUS
NATURAL LANGUAGES

In the arts we are open to the idea of a dependence of beauty on form. In mathematical structures we have been so conditioned by the childhood misery of memorizing the petty pieces of calculation presented to us as mathematical, that we instinctively tend to identify formality with pettifogging technicality, thus missing entirely the fact that cultivation of form has given to the new ideas their scope and soaring power. Repeatedly in these pages we shall see old ideas revealed as merely half-carved parts of the structures seen today. Underlying every such insight is an issue of form, moving like a reflection over still water, guiding our eyes. To turn our full gaze upon the form itself is our most exacting and our most exciting task.

NATURAL VERSUS CONSTRUCTED LANGUAGES

Since we are concerned with form, we are concerned with expression—that is, with language. Certain confusions concerning formal languages demand immediate attention and avoidance. In old-fashioned books on mathematical economics, a contrast is drawn between "verbal" and "mathematical" statements of economic theories. "Literary" economics is said to be vague because of the imprecision of ordinary English, whereas "mathematical" economics is said to be exact and precise. Whatever may have been the germ of truth in these assertions, this way of putting the matter will not do.

The contrast is not between mathematics and language. A mathematical argument may need for its clear expression several different sorts of language: English (or some other natural language); symbolic logic, which is a highly general constructed language; and some specific constructed concepts needed to express the special mathematical ideas at issue. The mathematical argument does not become vague simply because parts of it are expressed in plain English. Indeed, the deliberate suppression of English where its use would make for clarity is regarded by stylish formalists as an *inelegance* in a proof!

Natural languages like English or French are not irredeemably vague by nature, and to suppose that they are simply reveals ignorance. They are vague where their circumstances of growth did not require precision. They can be extremely precise in contexts where their flexibility and genius fairly shows. If you doubt this, try making love in the notation of symbolic logic or try translating a lawyer's courtroom argument bearing on a fine point of law.

We turn to so-called "constructed languages," such as the notation of symbolic logic, not because English is hopelessly vague, but because we need precision in areas where the language did not develop it up to our requirements, or where the language did not develop at all. Much of the symbolism of pure mathematics was constructed to fill *complete gaps* in our linguistic apparatus.

The notations of symbolic logic and of special mathematical discussions do not escape the problems common to all languages, constructed or natural. However carefully defined it may be, a constructed concept may eventually reveal a fatal vagueness. Formalists have demonstrated such flaws in many cases in traditional mathematics during the past seventy years or so.

Symbolic languages do have certain advantages. For instance, if an argument can be symbolized in the notation of logic or set theory, its implications can be precisely investigated by mathematicians. On the other hand, a mistake concealed by the initial symbolization may remain hidden in the subsequent manipulations, whose apparent rigor will induce a false sense of scientific accuracy. Hence, as more and more matters vital to our lives are axiomatized, it becomes ever more essential to scrutinize critically the assumptions made in the initial symbolization of the axioms.

The essence of the axiomatic method is this: Since *some* things must be assumed without proof, let them be as simple and as intuitively obvious as possible, and let these primitive, unproved notions be built into *explicit* axioms so that they are trapped under a powerful logical microscope for all to see and criticize.

Clearly, the language used in formulating these primitive notions into axioms is of utmost importance. It must be as clear as possible and must not (as far as possible) import further, hidden assumptions. On the other hand, one cannot start from scratch. The issue has been well expressed by Patrick Suppes:[1]

A preliminary step in fixing on the primitive notions of a theory is to become clear about what other theories are to be assumed in developing the axiomatization. For most axiomatic work in mathematics the standard development of logic and general set theory is assumed without comment. If such an assumption is

[1]Patrick Suppes, *Introduction to Logic*, D. Van Nostrand Company, Inc., Princeton, N.J., 1957, pp. 247-248.

not made, then the complete apparatus must be built from the ground up; that is, the theory must be constructed with a completely and explicitly formalized language. In axiomatic work in the empirical sciences, such as physics, psychology, and economics, it is customary to assume not only logic and general set theory, but the standard portions of mathematics as well. This permits such concepts as those of number to be used in the axiomatizations of portions of physics or economics, say, and yet not be regarded as primitive.

Following this practice, we shall now introduce certain notations from elementary symbolic logic and from set theory, without any attempt to derive these notations from axioms. We begin with symbolic logic.

BASIC LOGICAL NOTATION   We shall borrow from logic certain pieces of notation that will enable us to write out axioms and theorems briefly and to give precise form to some elementary ideas.

For "it is not the case that" we write "−." For instance, we write "it is not the case that Marina likes José" as "− Marina likes José." Phrases like "it is not true that," "it is false that" are likewise rendered by the symbol "−." Denial of any assertion is expressed by writing "−" before the assertion. Let the assertion "Marina is prettier than Karen" be symbolized by the letter "p"; then we write "Marina is not prettier than Karen" as "$-p$."

The connective "and" will be abbreviated simply by using the printer's sign "&" (the ampersand). Thus, if we symbolize "Marina is prettier than Karen" by "p" and "Karen is prettier than Inge-Britt" as "q" the *conjunction* "Marina is prettier than Karen and Karen is prettier than Inge-Britt" becomes "p & q."

The word "or" is symbolized by "$\vee$," which is short for the Latin word "vel." "Vel" in Latin has the sense of the legal expression "and/or," and this is the force of "$\vee$" in logic. Thus, "Marina is pretty $\vee$ Karen is pretty" is true if *either or both* girls are pretty. It rules out only the case where *neither* is pretty. This usage was adopted for "$\vee$" because it proved highly convenient in symbolic argument.

The words "if . . . then" are written "$\Rightarrow$." We write "Marina is prettiest $\Rightarrow$ Marina is chosen" for "*if* Marina is prettiest *then* Marina is chosen." The *exact* force of "$\Rightarrow$" may be expressed in terms of our previous symbols: "−Marina is prettiest $\vee$ Marina is chosen." In words: "*either* it is false that Marina is prettiest, *or* it is true that Marina is chosen." For "Marina is prettiest" write "p"; for "Marina is chosen" write "q"; we may then define the force of "$\Rightarrow$" formally:

Definition 8-1: $p \Rightarrow q = -p \lor q$

For "if and only if" we write "$\Leftrightarrow$." Thus, "p if and only if q" is written "$p \Leftrightarrow q$." We write "a choice is optimal *if and only if* it is the most highly ordered" as "a choice is optimal $\Leftrightarrow$ it is the most highly ordered." In symbols: "$p \Leftrightarrow q$."

This may be formally defined in terms of previous symbols:

Definition 8-2: $p \Leftrightarrow q = p \Rightarrow q \,\&\, q \Rightarrow p$

Finally we need a most important and convenient device. For a set of things (or girls) we may want to say that some characteristic is true of all of them, or else that it is true of some of them—say *at least one* of them. Consider the assertion "Swedish girls are friendly." It does not specify *the range* of the property of being friendly. Does it apply to *all* Swedish girls or only to some?

Consider the assertion "every Swedish girl is either friendly or occupied with someone else." Suppose we use the lowercase letter "x" to stand for any Swedish girl. We may then write: "for every x, if x is a Swedish girl, then x is friendly or x is occupied."

Then we use capital letters to symbolize the properties of being a Swedish girl, being friendly, or being occupied: "S" for "is a Swedish girl," "F" for "is friendly," and "O" for "is occupied." We may then write: "for every x, $Sx \Rightarrow Fx \lor Ox$."

The phrase "for every x" is set out at the left of any symbolic expression thus:

For every x (. . .)

This makes it clear over what *range* of x's the properties that appeared throughout the expression hold. The phrase "for every x" acts as a quantifier, and the phrase "for every x" is called the "universal quantifier," since it is used to indicate that some property or properties are true of every single x. The phrase is shortened to (x) and is used thus:

$(x) [Sx \Rightarrow (Fx \lor Ox)]$

which is read "for every x, if x is a Swedish girl, then x is either friendly or occupied."

Suppose that we want to claim only that there is *at least one* thing that has a certain property. Suppose that you want to assert the hypothesis that there exists *at least one* Swedish girl who is unfriendly. We shorten "there is at least one x where x is a Swedish girl and x is unfriendly" to the following expression:

$$\exists\, x\, (Sx\, \&\, -Fx)$$

writing "$-F$" for the property "is unfriendly." The expression "$\exists\, x$," since it asserts the *existence* of at least one instance of something, is called the "*existential* quantifier."

The placing of quantifiers, in explicit brief notation at the left of long symbolic expressions, proves a vastly convenient way to specify exactly over what range of objects the properties hold. Suppose that you want to assert "all freshettes are young and pretty but none are discriminating." Writing "x" for any freshette, we express the statement thus:

$$(x)\, [Fx \Rightarrow (Yx\, \&\, Px\, \&\, -Dx)]$$

NAÏVE SET THEORY

We now turn to the other type of notation that we need to borrow: The notation of elementary set theory. Our development of set notation will be "naïve," in the sense that it will take for granted that any problems that arise within set theory have already been solved elsewhere. We shall simply borrow the notation of set theory without any attempt to justify this theory by axiomatizing it here. In this we follow the line of thought indicated by Patrick Suppes in the passage already quoted. There is, however, another argument that can be used to justify the naïve adoption of set theory in axiomatizing a science. For choice theory, the argument may be stated simply thus: The largest set with which we shall be concerned—our universal set—is the set of all conceivable choices or actions. Since we shall never be concerned with such notions as the "set of all sets," we need not explicitly consider the axiomatizations of set theory that have been aimed at avoiding certain paradoxes into which set theory is led if it has to consider the "set of all sets."

We thus accept intuitively the notion of a "set" "S," as being a collection of well-defined objects x, finite or infinite in number, such that for any x, x either is or is not a member of S.

As we have already seen in earlier chapters, a set may be referred to briefly by a capital letter, such as "C" for the choice set and "A" for the attainable set. An *element* or *member* of the set will be written "x_0," "x_1," and so on. For "x_0 is an element in the attainable set" we write "$x_0 \in A$."

We shall continue to use a couple of standard notations for referring to a set. First, one may write the names of its members between braces. Thus the attainable set from Chapter 2 may be written:

{Marina, Karen, Inge-Britt}

or one may write "$\{x_0, x_1, x_2\}$," where "x_0" stands for Marina, "x_1" for Karen, and "x_2" for Inge-Britt. If there are many elements, we may write "$\{x_0, x_1, \ldots, x_n\}$," and we may indicate that a set is infinite or transfinite thus:

$$\{x_0, x_1, x_2, \ldots\}$$

If it is not convenient to write out all the elements in a set, the set may be specified in terms of a property shared by all its members. The elements in the attainable set all have in common the property of attainability, so we may write "the set of all x in the choice set such that x is attainable" as follows:

$$\{x \in C \mid Ax\}$$

This may be shortened in the following way. As has already been said, we are solely concerned with *choices*, so for any x, x *will be* an element in the choice set. It is thus not necessary to repeat that "$x \in C$," since the phrase "$\in C$" can be understood. The property "is attainable" is being attributed to x, so we need not repeat "Ax." "The set of all x in C such that Ax" then becomes: [2]

$$\{x \mid A\}$$

The fact that the division of the choice set into attainable and unattainable subsets is a *partitioning* may be expressed by writing "$-A$" for the unattainable set.

[2] For this notation, see David Gale, *The Theory of Linear Economic Models*, McGraw-Hill Book Company, New York, 1960, p. 52.

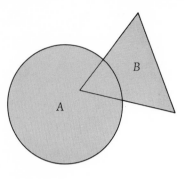

FIGURE 8-1

$A \cup B$

FIGURE 8-2

$A \cap B$

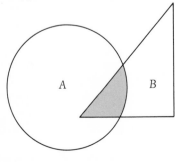

Trivially,

$$\{x \mid A \& -A\} = \varnothing$$

The empty set, $\varnothing$, plays a crucial role in the manipulations essential to set theory, in some ways resembling the role played by the number "0" in classical arithmetic. We could not get on without it.

If A and B are subsets of some given set X, then the *union* $A \cup B$ of A and B is the set containing all the members of A *and* all the members of B. In our notation:

$$A \cup B = \{x \mid x \in A \vee x \in B\}$$

This is illustrated in Fig. 8-1, where the union of A and B is the whole shaded area.

Notice that if the sets have an intersection—that is, if some members of A are also members of B, these are included in the union—indeed this is implied by the use of the inclusive sign "$\vee$." The *intersection* $A \cap B$ of A and B is the set of all x belonging to *both* A *and* B:

$$A \cap B = \{x \mid x \in A \& x \in B\}$$

which is illustrated in Fig. 8-2.

If A and B are sets, then "$A = B$" will mean that A and B have the same members—that for every x, if x is an element in A, then x is an element in B, expressed thus:

$$(x)\,(x \in A \Leftrightarrow x \in B)$$

If we want to say that A is *included* in B, that A is a subset of B, we write "$A \subseteq B$," that is:

$$(x)\,(x \in A \Rightarrow x \in B)$$

Thus, "the attainable set is a subset of the choice set" becomes "$A \subseteq C$." The inclusion sign "$\subseteq$" does not exclude the case where $A = B$. It simply asserts that everything which is in A is also in B, leaving open the question whether or not B has members, which are themselves not in A. If we want to assert the latter case, that A is only a *proper* subset of B, we write: "$A \subset B$." A is a proper subset of B, whenever $(A \subseteq B)$ and $(A \neq B)$.

The attainable set is normally a proper subset of the choice set, but it *might* not be—there might be no desired but unattainable choices. To leave this open we write "$A \subseteq C$."

The case where two sets are equal may then be

written:

$$(A = B) \Leftrightarrow (A \subseteq B \,\&\, B \subseteq A)$$

At the other extreme lies the case where two sets, A and B, have no members in common. They are then called *disjoint* sets. This is the case where their *intersection* is the empty set:

$$(A \cap B) = \varnothing$$

If $A \subset C$, the complement of A in C, written "$C - A$," is the set of all $x \in C$, such that x is *not* a member of A. A *partitioning*, you will recall, divides a set into two *disjoint*, or *exclusive*, subsets. The choice set is said to be *partitioned* into the attainable and unattainable sets. No choice is a member of both A and $-A$.

$$(A \cap -A) = \varnothing$$

We now have all the basic notation we need for axiomatizing choice theory. To this we shall immediately turn in Chapter 9.

QUESTIONS

1. If a mathematical argument about the theory of choice is expressed solely in English words, is this an instance of verbal economics?

2. In what sense can one say that natural languages (like English or French) are "vague"? Mention some sorts of use in which English words are notably less vague than the symbols of symbolic logic. Exactly why would you not want to make love in the notation of symbolic logic?

3. Briefly stated, what is the character and what are the advantages of the axiomatic method? What disadvantages of the method need watching?

4. Translate into the notation of symbolic logic the following: "Some Swedish girls like Spanish men"; "All Swedish girls like either Spaniards, Englishmen, or Frenchmen"; "All Irish sailors are either drunken or at sea"; "If Cordobes is fighting then Marina will go to the bullfight and if Marina goes to the bullfight José will not be in Pedro's."

5. Define "$p \Rightarrow q$" in terms of "$\vee$" and "$-$."

6. Define "$p \Leftrightarrow q$" in terms of "$\Rightarrow$" and "&."

7. Translate into symbolic notation with quantifiers: "Swedish girls are friendly or occupied"; "Nothing is a Swedish girl and unfriendly"; "Some freshettes are pretty and intelligent, but none are hardworking."

8. Justify the naïve adoption of set theory in axiomatizing a science.

9. Express in the notation of elementary set theory: "Marina is a member of the attainable set"; "The set of all numbers between 1 and 5"; "The set of all whole numbers greater than one."

10. What is the union of the attainable set and the unattainable set? What is the intersection of the attainable set and the unattainable set?

11. Express the union of any two sets A and B in terms of the notation for set membership.

12. Explain the notation "The set of Swedish girls $\subseteq$ the set of friendly girls."

9

AXIOMATIC
CHOICE
THEORY

Choice theory is concerned with whatever may be chosen.
We accordingly take the objects of the theory (the universe
of discourse of the theory) to be all objects x, such that x
may be chosen.

**THE PRIMITIVE NOTION
OF PREFERENCE**

Three notions will be taken as primitive, that is,
assumed to be intuitively understood, and will be left
undefined. The first of these is the notion "is preferred to."
We write "x_0 is preferred to x_1" as "$x_0 \, P \, x_1$." The relation
"P" is not assumed to be an exact translation of any English
phrase, and its character will be illuminated by the axiom
system.[1]

Obviously, the question arises: May any pair of

[1]On the failure of the relation "P" to express some of the
English usage of the verb "to prefer," see pp. 120-121.

choices, say x_0 and x_1, be ordered by the relation "P"? In Chapter 2 it was assumed that this was indeed so. It was assumed that any pair of girls might be compared and that one would be preferred to the other, so that this might be expressed "Marina P Karen" or by part of a chain. Subsequently, in Chapter 5, we introduced the notion that a choosing agent might be indifferent between two or more members of his attainable set.

It is intuitively obvious, after all, that two choices (say two girls) might have the same ranking in the eyes of the choosing agent—the romantic tradition notwithstanding. We now need a notation for expressing the fact that, from the point of view of the preference relation, the two choices are *equivalent*. This is sometimes done by adopting as a primitive idea the notion of indifference, so that if the choosing agent ranks two choices equally they are said to be indifferent; symbolically: "$x_0 \, I \, x_1$."

A notion of indifference, which is exactly what is required, can, however, be formally defined in terms of the "P" relation, and the introduction of another primitive concept is therefore redundant.

THE EQUIVALENCE SETS DEFINED IN TERMS OF THE "P" RELATION

We approach the definition of "indifference" in terms of the notion of an equivalence relation in any given set S.

Definition 9-1:   "R" is an equivalence relation in any set "S," if and only if, for all x_0, x_1, x_2 in S:
1. "R" is *reflexive*: $x_0 \, R \, x_0$
2. "R" is *symmetric*: $x_0 \, R \, x_1 \Rightarrow x_1 \, R \, x_0$
3. "R" is *transitive*: $x_0 \, R \, x_1 \, \& \, x_1 \, R \, x_2 \Rightarrow x_0 \, R \, x_2$

Equivalence relations of the form "R" thus defined are fundamental to mathematics and science.[2] The relation of identity, "$=$," in arithmetic is an equivalence relation, but the notion of equivalence is much wider than that of identity: Any set of objects that are equivalent in some respect form an equivalence set. Clearly, the sets of choices that have the same ranking in terms of the preference relation form equivalence sets. The relation "I" is an equivalence relation, and is now defined in terms of the preference relation as follows:

[2]See R. G. D. Allen, *Mathematical Economics*, 2d ed., The Macmillan Company, New York, 1965, p. 748; Patrick Suppes, *Introduction to Logic*, D. Van Nostrand Company, Inc., Princeton, N.J., 1957, pp. 218-220.

Definition 9-2:[3] $x_0 \, I \, x_1 \Leftrightarrow (x_2) \, [(x_2 \, P \, x_0 \Leftrightarrow x_2 \, P \, x_1) \, \&$
$(x_0 \, P \, x_2 \Leftrightarrow x_1 \, P \, x_2)]$

In words, Alice and Anastasia form an indifference set if and only if, for any other girl Beatrice, Beatrice is preferred to Alice if and only if Beatrice is preferred to Anastasia, and Alice is preferred to Beatrice if and only if Anastasia is preferred to Beatrice.

It will be recalled that indifference sets were introduced to answer the question, "May any pair of choices x_0 and x_1 be ordered by the relation 'P'?"

The answer, as we know, is that not all pairs of elements in the choice set can be ordered by "P." This is sometimes expressed by saying that "P" only partially orders the choice set.

If, as we know from Chapter 5, there is even one girl, "Marie," such that "Marina I Marie" the diagram illustrating the ordering in Chapter 2 (Fig. 2-2) becomes (writing "m_1" for Marie) that shown in Fig. 9-1.

To indicate that they have the same preference ranking and are not part of the chain of elements ordered by "P," "m_0" and "m_1" are shown linked horizontally.

The simplicity of the original chain diagram can, however, be restored—and the structure needed for decision theory carved out—by the following obvious move. The equivalence sets in terms of the "P" relation (the indifference sets) form a partitioning of the choice set—no object of choice can be in two different indifference sets. The indifference sets are disjoint subsets of the choice set. Hence we may begin by partitioning the choice set (or its attainable subset, if we do not want to waste effort ranking the unattainable choices) into the equivalence sets of the "P" relation. We may then rank the resulting *indifference sets* by the "P" relation, which gives us a simple, or complete, ordering, since every pair of indifference sets can be ordered by preference.

You will recall from Chapter 5 that it does not matter how many elements an indifference set contains.

You may have felt like questioning the indifference set "$\{k_0\}$." Mathematically, it is of course impeccable,

SIMPLE, OR COMPLETE, VERSUS PARTIAL, OR INCOMPLETE, ORDERINGS

FIGURE 9-1
A partial ordering by "P"

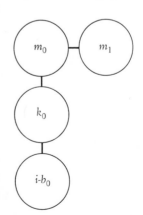

[3]This definition of "I" is discussed and justified in an unpublished paper by H. Putnam and the present author, "On the Necessity for a Change in the Axioms of Choice Theory."

since a unit set is a distinct mathematical object from the single element it contains; that is, "$\{x_0\}$" is not the same as "x_0." But you may perhaps doubt the scientific usefulness of the idea. Actually, its usefulness is considerable. The possibility of indifference sets that contain only one member is the price paid for the great simplicity of ordering the equivalence sets of the "P" relation and not the individual elements of the choice set. If you instruct a computer to partition a set of possible choices into the equivalence sets of the "P" relation and order them by preference, you must face the fact that the computer will smugly dish up an indifference set with only one member, just in case there is only one choice with a particular ranking.

THE AXIOMS OF CHOICE THEORY

We are now ready to state the axioms of the most general pure choice theory.

Axiom 1   *The Axiom of Comparability*:
$(x_0)(x_1)(x_0\,P\,x_1 \lor x_1\,P\,x_0 \lor x_0\,I\,x_1)$

At first sight this looks completely innocent, even trivial: All it is asserting, one may remark, is that, of any two things that are available to us, we must either prefer one of them or else be indifferent which we have. In fact, however, the implications of Axiom 1 are extremely sweeping. For it asserts nothing less than that *any* two states of affairs between which we could possibly have to choose can be *compared*. I think, if you examine your experience, you will find that you do not normally assume this, nor does ordinary language take it for granted. People assume that, within broad areas of experience, alternatives can be compared. But not necessarily outside these areas. You will hear people say: "If I became a musician, I would want to be a violinist." They are assuming that one can compare all *musical* alternatives. But if you ask someone, "Which would you rather do, race across the Atlantic or play concert violin?" he is likely to reply, "Why, I simply can't compare the two."

Implicit in our whole discussion, however, has been the assumption that takes formal shape as Axiom 1: One can partition the attainable set into indifference sets and can order these simply in terms of the "P" relation.

One cannot do this if two elements in the attainable set could ever prove to be incomparable in terms of P or I—

if one can say of them *neither* that one is preferred *nor* that they are members of the same indifference set.

Choice theorists have reacted to this situation by making the concept of comparability the explicit foundation of the system, that is by adopting Axiom 1. Let us look briefly at the consequences. Consider two extreme situations, with both of which a pure choice theory must be able to deal but which pose very different problems. They are both well known to us by now.

First, the kind of case that is well represented in an Edgeworth box (Fig. 9-2). Remember we are here, by the nature of the construction, dealing with choice solely between different combinations of amounts of two continuously divisible things. Axiom 1 now amounts to the claim that, no matter where we place two such points as x_0 and x_1, they will always be comparable. Although there are an infinity of such points, there will never be found two that we cannot compare.

The decision to allow areas of incomparability, would be in a sense the decision to study structures more complicated than can be obtained by any model that satisfies Axiom 1.

Consider a very different case, in which continuity does not even appear, an attainable set with just three elements: a chance to race across the Atlantic, a chance to stay with a particular girl, a chance to write and publish an article for a particular journal.

Clearly, the very freedom as to the kinds of things that can appear as elements in the attainable set in this sort of case allows the issue of incomparability to arise vividly and at once. The very properties of the model no longer, as with the Edgeworth box, keep the issue of possible incomparability at bay, so to speak. Neoclassical economists, doing more or less implicit choice theory without ever recognizing exactly what this implied, found the assumption of universal comparability natural because it followed so closely upon[4] the continuity assumptions that were a built-in part of their intellectual equipment.

A fully self-conscious choice theory, intended to be applicable to any kind of decision making, may need the development of an axiom set that allows for the possibility of incomparabilities and offers rules of decision for handling situations in which they arise.

[4]Though strictly independent of continuity.

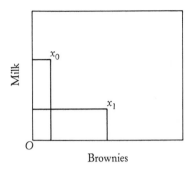

FIGURE 9-2
Different combinations of amounts of two continuously divisible things, say brownies (you can cut them as small as you please) and milk

Existing structures, however, have all been built on Axiom 1, and thus have the limitation that they cannot handle attainable sets whose members are not all comparable. Within these limitations, however, a highly elegant theory has been constructed, and Axiom 1 was certainly an appropriate choice for a first formalization of the subject, whatever complications may need to be introduced later.

Two axioms are needed to express the fact that P is a partial ordering. The first of these two axioms seems, at first sight at any rate, to be less sweeping and also less controversial than Axiom 1, although it has been criticized, and there has been suggestion that it is in certain ways linked to the first.[5]

Axiom 2   *Axiom of Transitivity*:
$$(x_0) (x_1) (x_2) (x_1 \, P \, x_0 \, \& \, x_2 \, P \, x_1 \Rightarrow x_2 \, P \, x_0)$$

We have already informally discussed transitivity. Axiom 2 formalized the notion that the relations of choice theory must be assumed to have the property of transitivity. Notice that, as stated above, Axiom 2 need be assumed only for the relation of preference.

This axiom is sometimes criticized in terms of a concept taken from experimental psychology: The notion of thresholds of distinction. If x_0, x_1, and x_2 are, say, three colors, among which we are to choose, we may be able to distinguish x_0 from x_2 and say that we prefer x_2, but the difference in shade between x_0 and x_1 and between x_1 and x_2 may be too small—it may be below the threshold of our perceptions.

There is no possible question that there are such thresholds: There are certainly minimum differences that must exist for us to *perceive* a difference in many areas of experience. The question, however, is whether this really affects the Axiom of Transitivity. We are well accustomed by now to the notion that the objects of choice may be discontinuous—indeed, they may not be even the same sort of physical thing. A hangover from the assumption of universal continuity accounts for the notion that be-

[5]This suggestion was made by Kenneth Arrow in private correspondence and discussion with the author and also in his contribution, "Public and Private Values," in Sidney Hook (ed.), *Human Values and Economic Policy, a Symposium,* New York University Press, New York, 1967, pp. 5-6.

tween any two objects, one of which is preferred, there must be an intermediate position. But Axiom 1 does not require continuity; it requires only *comparability*, which is not the same thing. In a model with continuity, we cannot allow the realistic notion of minimum perceivable differences—we must make the ruthless assumption that the whole choice space within, say, the Edgeworth box is an infinite set of points, each with a preference ranking. So the Axiom of Transitivity is assured by the implications of the continuity assumption. We have thus pointed up the limited reality of Edgeworth box models, of which we were already aware. If we abandon continuity and construct discrete choice models, as we have often done with girls and cars and ocean racers and other indivisible things and states of affairs as the objects of choice, then again the problem cannot arise. The choice set contains just those things that the choosing agent does distinguish and does rank by the preference and indifference relations. And if Marina P Karen and Karen P Inge-Britt, then it is obviously reasonable to infer that Marina P Inge-Britt, as the Axiom of Transitivity requires.

There is another objection often raised to Axiom 2 of choice theory. This concerns the effect of multiple criteria of ranking. To cite an example from an experiment of K. May:[6] Suppose we are ranking girls in terms of the three criteria, looks, intelligence, and wealth. Then we may find that one girl stands highest in terms of two of the criteria, another in terms of another combination of two. I think it could be argued that ranking in terms of several criteria is somewhat similar to ranking in terms of a single different criterion adopted by each of three people. It is like finding a majority decision for three people, one of whom ranks for looks, one for intelligence, and one for wealth. The problem, if this is the case, resembles that of finding satisfactory rules for majority voting. If so, the mathematical analysis of the question has a very ancient history: that bare majorities could yield inconsistent results was first noticed by the Marquis de Condorcet in the eighteenth century. It has been profoundly studied in our own times by Kenneth Arrow in

[6]Kenneth May, "Transitivity Utility and Aggregation in Preference Theory," *Econometrica*, vol. 22 (1954), pp. 1-13, cited by Peter Newman in *The Theory of Exchange*, Prentice-Hall, Inc., Englewood Cliffs, N.J., 1965, pp. 12-13.

Social Choice and Individual Values,[7] and subsequently by others.[8] All we can notice here is that the Axiom of Transitivity assumes either the solution of such problems or else their irrelevance to a basic pure choice theory. In either case, problems could clearly arise. Obviously, in a model that can yield inconsistent rankings, transitivity cannot be assumed as a universally valid axiom.

To express the fact that P is a partial ordering, the second of the group of two axioms needed is the following, which I give in a form developed by Hilary Putnam:

Axiom 3   *Axiom of Asymmetry:*
$$(x_0)(x_1)(-x_0 P x_1 \lor -x_1 P x_0)$$

In other words, there are no two things such that each is preferred to the other. From this it follows trivially that:

$$(x_0) -x_0 P x_0$$

substituting x_0 for x_1 in the preceding formula. Thus Axiom 3 incidentally guarantees that P is irreflexive—nothing bears P to itself.

The remaining few axioms that we need to consider are perhaps the least controversial. They may be thought of as Axioms of Rationality, and they are the equivalent in axiomatic choice theory of assumptions of rational behavior. "Rational" has, however, a specially restricted sense here. It means simply behavior in accordance with the axioms. In ordinary speech, people use the word "rational" in many different ways. For instance, it would be perfectly correct English to condemn as irrational a ranking of objectives that one felt was destructive of someone's true nature—we describe someone as behaving irrationally if we feel he is dissipating his energies in a way contrary to his best interests, or undertaking actions from something like a masochistic set of motives, or some other kind of motive that we feel to be an indication of mental disturbance or illness. Here "irrational" has tacit moral implications. In Axioms 4, 5, 6, and 7 of choice theory, however, nothing like this is implied. The purpose of these axioms is simply to guarantee *behavior in accordance*

[7]2d ed., John Wiley & Sons, Inc., New York, 1963.

[8]For a general discussion and history of the issue, see Duncan Black, *The Theory of Committees and Elections*, Cambridge University Press, New York, 1958.

with the axiom system. It is not the purpose of these axioms to see that what some people would call "sensible objectives" are ranked highest. It is simply their purpose to see that *whatever* objectives *are* ranked highest *are* in fact chosen.[9]

To state these axioms we need to introduce the two remaining primitive notions referred to at the beginning of this chapter. We shall accordingly introduce the notion of attainability as a primitive, written "A," also the predicate "chosen" written "C." We may now state the remaining axioms of pure choice theory, in a form due to Hilary Putnam (4, 5, and 6) and the present writer (7).

The first of these, Axiom 4, asserts that all choice implies that something is attainable.

Axiom 4 $(x)(Cx \Rightarrow Ax)$

We now add the assumption that, of two choices, the less preferred will never be chosen if the more preferred is attainable.

Axiom 5 $(x_0)(x_1)[(x_0 P x_1 \& Ax_0) \Rightarrow -Cx_1]$

Then, if something is attainable, *something* will be chosen:

Axiom 6 $\exists xAx \Rightarrow \exists xCx$

We have now ensured that, if something is attainable, the less preferred of two attainable things will never be chosen, and that *something* will be chosen. Taken together, these axioms suggest that there *exists* at least one most preferred choice. This has not, however, been explicitly guaranteed by the axiom set, and it is not as trivial as might appear. To see this, recall the representation of an attainable set in a two space. If the attainable region is unbounded, i.e., has no frontier but extends without limit, there will be no *most preferred* attainable position or set of positions. Again, even if the attainable set is bounded, there will be no *most preferred* set of attainable positions unless the attainable region includes its boundary points. Consider the set of points on a line *less than* 1 inch from its origin. There is no greatest point. Whereas there is a greatest point if you specify that the points are to be those less than *or equal to* 1 inch.

[9]See V. C. Walsh, "Axiomatic Choice Theory and Values," in Hook (ed.), *op. cit.*, pp. 196-198.

So I propose to guarantee the existence of a most desired attainable choice or choices by the following axiom:

Axiom 7 $\exists x_0 \, [Ax_0 \, \& \, (x_1) \, (Ax_1 \Rightarrow x_0 \, P \, x_1 \lor x_0 \, I \, x_1)]$

That is to say, there exists at least one x_0, such that x_0 is attainable, and for all x_1, if x_1 is attainable then x_0 is preferred or indifferent to x_1. This rules out, by implication, models for choice theory where the attainable set is an unbounded set, also the case where it is an open set (i.e., one that does not include its boundary points).

Many more special axioms are necessary if one is to apply pure choice theory to special sorts of decision situations and problems. But for the most fundamental general choice theory these are enough.[10]

General choice theory (and even some of its applications) can be formalized well within the logical notation of Chapter 8. The axioms of choice theory have therefore been expressed in logical notation.[11] Later axioms, specifying applications of choice theory that require notions such as "convexity" or topological notions, such as "open set" or "neighborhood," will be symbolized only when convenient.

In the remainder of this book we shall axiomatize as special models for choice theory, contemporary *received* accounts of consumption, exchange, and production. Thus presented, I believe the shortcomings of existing microtheory stand out. I stress that I shall *not*, in this introductory book, attempt to present a microtheory adequate to the insights obtainable from general choice theory. To do this would be nothing less than to rewrite microtheory, and

---

[10]It has been suggested that Axioms 5, 6, and 7 can be replaced by the following, forming an axiom set that is equivalent to that given in this chapter:

Axiom 5' $(x_0) \, [Cx_0 \Rightarrow \exists x_1$
$\qquad\qquad (x_0 \, I \, x_1 \, \& \, Ax_1 \, \& -\exists x_2 \, (Ax_2 \, \& \, x_2 \, P \, x_1))]$

This axiom was suggested by Oswaldo Chateaubriand. It is essentially a first-order version of what Peter Newman calls the "Axiom of Selection," *op. cit.*, p. 16-17. The axiom set in the text was chosen because it seemed to make the separate empirical assumptions needed for choice theory stand out more vividly.

[11]Choice theory is far from being unique: For an excellently varied discussion of axiomatizations of significant sections of mathematics and the sciences, the reader is referred to Patrick Suppes, *op. cit., passim.* Logicians will notice that the axiomatization of general choice theory offered in the present chapter is within first-order logic. Many significant models for choice theory clearly require the use of set-theoretic concepts.

this book is only an introduction to the most recent existing microtheory.

1. Mention some reasons why formalists should be interested in exact axiom systems.

2. Why is it not necessary to adopt the relation "I" as a primitive concept in axiomatizing choice theory? (*Hint*: Use the notion of equivalence sets.)

3. Which would you prefer: Miss Denmark of 1970 or a Nobel Prize in physics? If you do not know, why not? What does your answer imply about the Axiom of Comparability in cases of discontinuous choice sets?

4. For continuous choice sets represented in an Edgeworth box, if there is any point x_0 and any other point x_1 within the choice space, and between the two you pick any point x_n, what does the Axiom of Comparability imply about x_n?

5. Do the existence of thresholds of minimum distinguishable difference—in the discernment of sounds, colors, tastes, and the like—constitute an objection to the empirical realism of the Axiom of Transitivity? If not, why not?

6. Why does transitivity need to be assumed only for the "P" relation?

7. If somebody has decided to drink himself to death, what should stand most highly ranked in his ordering, if he is rational, in the sense of Axioms 4 to 7 of pure choice theory?

8. If someone picks an object that you think is best for him and that is not an element in his maximal set, is he rational in the sense of the axioms of choice theory?

9. Can one choose rationally if there is nothing one most prefers?

Part 2
2
Welfare
Theory

10
WELFARE ECONOMICS

Throughout Part 1 we have been concerned with the pure theory of choice as such. Now we begin to apply it. Of the historically important applications, one stands out as much the most general in scope, and may therefore reasonably be considered first. It has usually been called "economic welfare theory," or "welfare economics."

Now when I hear the word "welfare," I immediately think of unattractive women in social workers' hats, people standing in line for soup in stories of the great depression, and stern busybodies telling one that what one likes "isn't in one's own best interest." But none of this is what is meant by the word "welfare" in the present context. Pure choice theory studies the logic of the optimal attainment of objectives by individuals. Welfare theory which studies the optimal attainment of goals by groups (including whole

THE SCIENTIFIC CRITICISM OF POLICY

societies) is concerned with the discovery of social orderings and with their attainment, that is, with social policy.
You could say that mathematical welfare economics is
simply the most sophisticated form that can be taken by
the scientific criticism of policy decisions.

Of course, policy recommendations, more or less
backed by reasons, are made at all levels of sophistication
and have been made in all periods of history. When they
are made as the result of formal mathematical analysis of
the relevant structure, they are in effect "welfare economics"
—a scientifically informed critique of policy.

Prehistory of welfare analysis   For as long as there
have been economic theories with any pretense to scientific
status, there have, of course, been critiques of policy derived from these theories; indeed, early economic theory is
usually so written that the purely scientific model and the
welfare arguments based on it are not clearly separated
but are offered at the same time in the very same passage
and in, so to speak, the same logical tone of voice. In later
chapters, we will consider an instance of this that dates
from the early nineteenth century.[1]

A genuinely historical treatment should consider these
beginnings. For our purposes, however, it is enough to
begin with the 1920s, when fully *self-conscious* welfare
theory, recognized as a distinct application of pure economic theory, began to be written. This self-consciousness
about its distinct character, and even the name "welfare
economics," are due to a Cambridge economist of the
period, a follower of Alfred Marshall, Arthur Cecil Pigou.
His great book, *The Economics of Welfare*, may fairly be
taken as marking the beginnings of fully self-conscious
welfare analysis.

It is hardly surprising that one can distinguish three
stages in the development of welfare theory since its systematic beginnings with Pigou. The first stage, dominated
by Pigou himself and his followers, leaned heavily on the
concepts of Marshallian utility theory. The second depended upon Hicksian indifference-curve analysis. The
third arose out of contemporary choice theory. Each new
stage in the development of pure economic theory offered
a new set of concepts for the analysis of policy and was in
turn thus applied.

[1]The Torrens-Ricardo theory of non-supply-regulating incomes. See pp. 272-275.

We begin with Pigou and thus return once more to the neoclassical scene. I emphasize the dependence of Pigovian welfare theory on Marshall—not just on neoclassical utility theory in general, but upon the precise form that this took at Marshall's hands. Had Jevons' presentation become standard, Pigou could hardly have got a vital part of his argument off the ground.

The Economics of Welfare is a long, rich, tightly packed book. No attempt could possibly be made here to give an exhaustive account of its contents,[2] much less of the whole scope and range of Pigovian thinking as it developed and was applied by others. I shall concentrate on presenting one theorem that seems to me to typify the Pigovian point of view. It derives immediately from the Marshallian doctrine of diminishing marginal utility. It is no abstract toy, but a theorem of immediate, rich, practical import: It concerns the relation between the welfare of a society and the distribution of its incomes. Imagine two persons of identical capacity for experiencing utility but of widely differing incomes. It is then supposed that we draw one curve to represent the marginal utility to each of these persons of added increments of money income. They will, simply because of their different incomes, be able to consume different quantities of whatever gives them utility. To make this vivid and to point out Pigou's argument, consider Fig. 10-1, which shows the situations on a utility curve of the sort we are discussing of two persons of extremely different money incomes. The rich man can settle at *D*, where there is no point in further outlay. The poor man may well be at *A*. If the rich man's income is reduced, he may not have to shrink his current consumption—he may be rich enough to be at *E*—but in any case we may suppose him only to be forced to reduce to from *D* to *C*. This income, transferred to the poor man, enables him to move from *A* to *B*. On these assumptions, redistribution of income from the very rich to the very poor cannot help increasing total social welfare.

It is rather easy to attack the Pigovians today. Those who have read Chapter 4 of the present book already have all the ammunition necessary and might fairly be told to construct the attack for themselves. I shall, however, offer some criticism shortly. But there is something else I want

---

[2]When we come to production theory, we shall pay some tribute to Pigou's important concept of external economies and diseconomies.

FIGURE 10-1

The marginal utility of money to persons of widely different money incomes

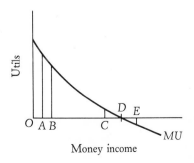

to do first. I want to try to make you see how powerful, how exciting, this was for those who were alive, especially for those who were young, in the twenties and thirties.

I wonder if you have any idea of the conditions in which the English working classes lived, even as late as the thirties of this century and even in a settled country like England. There was also a spirit abroad, young, idealistic, determined upon change. The young of the thirties resembled the young of today in certain respects more than those of any intervening generation—certainly more than they resembled the fat conformist young of the frightened, timid fifties. The young intellectuals of Cambridge and the London School of Economics in the thirties took Pigou's argument, used Marshall's diagram to bring it to vivid shape, and waved it as a banner, as James Connolly had waved the Plow and the Stars.

The role of the establishment was important and should be understood. Many of the young rebels of the day came from within the very core of the social and political establishment. They came from the top public schools and from the ancient universities, in particular from Eton and from King's College, Cambridge. And they found at Cambridge and in the intellectual circles of Bloomsbury that surrounded the London School of Economics a weapon of revolt that had itself been forged in the smithies of the establishment; for Pigou's concept depends utterly on Marshall, and Marshall's utility theory was the very core, the very holy of holies of the orthodox. Young revolt could rest fair and square on the very cornerstone of respectability—delicious irony, echoing laughter in the sacred halls, the very essence of palace revolution.

It is now a matter of history that, in a quiet, well-bred, and very British and Parliamentary way, there was in fact a social revolution in England. I am not going to claim that Pigou's argument won elections in Lancashire. But it is a matter of record that men who later became ministers of government had written books in which the curves that illustrate this argument held prominent place.[3]

Two things must clearly be admitted about the Pigovian welfare theorists. First, the social implications of their position are not trivial. Second, those who subscribed

[3]See, for example, Sir Hugh Dalton, *Some Aspects of the Inequality of Incomes in Modern Communities*, E. P. Dutton & Co., Inc., New York, 1920.

to the Marshallian position could not afford to ignore their argument.

In criticizing Pigou, we must carefully distinguish a number of different arguments. First, consider the position of someone who accepted neoclassical utility theory. Would such a person have to accept the Pigovian welfare theory? Remember that at that time most economists *did* accept neoclassical utility theory. The best answer was given by Lord Robbins, who pointed to Jevons. Jevons had stated the theory of utility in such a way that these uses could not be made of it. For one thing he had clearly shown his belief that drawing the whole curve was probably meaningless (Fig. 10-2).

According to Jevons, comparisons between extremely different situations were probably without significance. He was unwilling to attempt to answer the question how the curve would behave above and to the left of the point at which it stops in Fig. 10-2.

Moreover, Jevons explicitly stated that, as far as he could see, no meaning could be attached to comparisons between the utility experienced by one man and that experienced by another. These were states of mind and, in Jevons' opinion, forever inscrutable. This became the basis of Robbins' famous attack on what he called "interpersonal comparisons of utility."

Thus it was manifestly possible to accept the neoclassical notion of utility in its strict, carefully defined, Jevonian form, and yet not accept Pigovian welfare theory. The fact was, however, that utility theory had become influential principally in a less carefully stated Marshallian form, and this latter was of course defenseless against Pigovian interpretation. The final word must be left to the historians, but one can hazard the guess that the growing dissatisfaction with neoclassical utility theory, and the rapid success of the "Hicksian revolution," were not unconnected with the discovery that the whole notion of utility left the door dangerously open to embarrassing views. One can see the ranks of conservative opinion falling out of conceit with utility when this hitherto orthodox idea proved capable of such unexpectedly explosive consequences.

So far, we have considered criticism of Pigou by people who accepted the basic notion of neoclassical utility theory in some form. But what of a contemporary choice theorist? Obviously every difficulty with the notion of

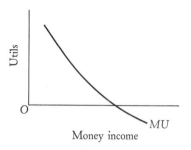

FIGURE 10-2

Marginal utility curve illustrating Jevon's argument

neoclassical utility considered in Chapter 3 applies with equal force to any attempt to use the theory to generate a welfare argument. I shall not bore you by repeating these objections here.

However, an additional objection to the use of the neoclassical concept of utility bears with peculiar force on any attempt to use this notion in welfare theory. This objection strikingly reveals the extent to which the neoclassical economists were using a concept still rich with utilitarian philosophical implications.

For a believer in utilitarian moral philosophy, knowledge that some action would maximize the utility experienced by a society (considered the sum of individual utilities) was a necessary *and sufficient* condition for regarding that action as his duty. Strictly, for such a person, to ask the question, "Is it always right to maximize social utility?" would be to ask a meaningless question.

However, if we are not utilitarians, if we do not believe that there is some one kind of experience—call it "utility," or whatever you will—that is the *sole* objective of all human desire, we may very well indeed ask this question. Adam Smith remarked long ago that defense is more than opulence. We may feel it our duty to sacrifice some sorts of satisfaction to other objectives. We may even judge that certain sorts of satisfactions are altogether bad and may not in the least approve of maximizing them: Who would have wanted to maximize the social utility of a society of Nazi Party members?

If we are not utilitarians, we must ask about any increase in something called "satisfaction" or "utility," what are the *concrete* satisfactions at issue, would we approve of them, what states of affairs are in fact being maximized?

As generally understood, Pigovian welfare theory depends upon the notion of quantities of utility. But for anyone who is not a utilitarian, it does not necessarily follow that, because something called "social utility" has increased, a better state of society exists. Expressed in terms of the technicalities of the Marshallian curve of diminishing marginal utility, the Pigovian argument sounds at first as if the policy conclusions it leads to follow simply from the properties of the scientific argument. In fact, they follow only if we are prepared to make the value judgments entailed in being a utilitarian. This objection was made by Lord Robbins, in his original attack on interpersonal comparisons of utility, and I think it must be admitted that it stands up. Built into the notion of utility, ever since its first use by the utilitarian philosophers, is the idea that we must approve of any increase in utility—for an individual or for society as a whole. But an economist obviously is not entitled to take any such ethical position for granted. Policies are undertaken for many purposes and have many effects. Some of these purposes are appropriately described as the gaining of satisfactions, and some equally obviously are not in the least appropriately so described. Clearly, the policies are to be approved of or not by those who agree to them for many different reasons based on many different considerations.

To beg this question by assuming that the sole and whole object of all policy is to maximize something called "utility," then to assume that if this supposed utility is being maximized no criticism of the policies undertaken can possibly be useful, is precisely to assume away all the important issues concerning which of the many possible policies the society should follow. It is also to give a pseudo-scientific look to what are in fact a set of implicit value recommendations and to pass off the concealed value judgments of the policy advocator as if they were pieces of pure science and were therefore of course (if sound pieces of science) beyond criticism by the uninformed.

The question must, however, be asked whether there were insights of truth and importance underlying the Pigovian position. If you consider the facts of life in the society about which Pigou wrote or the poor in our world today, it is hard to avoid sympathy with his aims, even if the technical arguments used to support them were blatantly unsound. What can be done to rescue his sound insights from the faulty arguments used to support them?

It seems to me that the answer is "much," but only if we are prepared to make some rather striking moves.

VALUE AXIOMS

To explain what I mean, I must raise here an issue that will bear on our treatment of all three stages of welfare economics. We can go no further without making it explicit.

I submit that a successful welfare theory would, in certain logical respects, resemble a sausage. To get sausages you must feed sausage meat into a sausage machine. Even if you have the most perfect, the most efficient, and the most elegant sausage machine in the world, you will not get sausages out of it unless you put sausage meat in.

In Pigovian theory, the meat was, so to speak, smuggled in—it went in under cover of the concept of utility. By the sausage meat, of course, I mean the value axioms. My point is just this: A system of welfare theory is based either explicitly or implicitly on an axiom system. If it is a contemporary welfare theory, it is likely to be based, like most recent economic theory, on an explicit axiom system. Earlier welfare theory, such as Pigou's, was based on an implicit axiom system. If this axiom system includes no value axioms, whether explicit or implicit, the so-called welfare theory will not generate results that contain any rich welfare recommendations. It will simply repeat the results of pure choice theory, refurbished and offered in a welfare theoretical language that makes them sound as if in fact they were rich policy recommendations, which, of course, they are not and cannot be.

The *meat* of a welfare theory consists of the information it gives about how some people could be made better off in some sense, which cannot be done unless some assumption is made initially as to what constitutes "better off."

This is not the time or the place to attempt a full-dress effort to axiomatize Pigou,[4] so I shall only offer a hint of how I believe it could be done. Let me put it very simply and inelegantly for our purposes. If a Madison Avenue executive's income goes from $50,000 a year to $60,000 a year, or from $50,000 a year to $40,000 a year, we may not feel very certain that we have any clear moral insights about the significance of this change. But suppose a family's income goes from $3,000 a year to $4,000 a year. At very low levels of money income like this, we might be willing to risk the assumption that the change was morally significant—that it meant, in fact, the possibility of things we would regard as morally significant, such as adequate food and medical care for children. For such levels of money income, we might be willing to risk making it axiomatic for the purposes of analysis that given changes in money income could be supposed to be associated with states of affairs of which we would approve.

[4]Though doing so would, I believe, be well worthwhile.

There are many places in the world where most of the children who are born simply die of malnutrition. It is not a daring moral hypothesis to suggest that it would be a better world if they lived.

A reformulated Pigovian theory need not be unscientific if it were so axiomatized that the moral assumptions necessary were explicitly built into the value axioms and the argument clearly based on them, so that it admittedly followed, *if and only if* one accepted the whole axiom set, including the value axioms.

As a matter of fact there are, if you read carefully, a number of passages in Pigou's *Economics of Welfare* that suggest strongly that had he lived in our day this would have been the logical route he himself would have followed in setting up his own theory. In a way, it is impossible to criticize fairly the work of an economist of an earlier generation on issues like this. The possibility is entirely open that could one put the issues to him (assuming him to be entirely acquainted with contemporary formalistic mathematics) he would simply say, "Why, of course this is how it should be done." Pigou was well aware, for example, that changing money income is only an indirect way at best to affect anything that you could meaningfully call "human welfare," and that at best the effects of such changes must be a trifle uncertain. The formalist is almost forced to feel that at this point in Pigou's work it was a great shame that the whole theory and apparatus of neoclassical utilitarianism lay so temptingly close to his hand. It offered a way in which things could be taken simply for granted that otherwise would have had to be built explicitly into value axioms. The neoclassical concept of utility was, for Pigou, a truly fatal crutch to lean upon: It provided his more stupid followers with a pat, easy formula, with which the subtler insights of his theory could be identified and which could be carried to absurd lengths, which in their caricature of his original position were bound to lead to its downfall; it provided his critics with a straw man that could very easily be knocked down—as indeed it was going to fall shortly anyway, as the whole of Marshallian utility theory collapsed before the onslaughts of the so-called Hicksian revolution.

To the men of the forties, caught up in the tide of that revolution, the possibility of saving valuable insights from the old welfare economics of Pigou by the use of axiomatic procedures was not in the least present as a possibility. It must be remembered that from our contemporary point of view the economists of the forties were mathematically and logically naïve: They thought that confining themselves to what could be said in terms of indifference curves was a necessary and sufficient condition for escaping from utilitarianism; and the logical positivists had terrified them into thinking that they would immediately cease to be scientists if they ever used in science any statement that was not either a report of a direct observation or an analysis of the consequences of such direct observations. They were particularly impressed by Lord Robbins' attack on interpersonal comparisons of utility.

For them, welfare theory, if it was to be acceptable, must avoid all language and all assumptions that did not run in terms of indifference curves, it must avoid all talk of utility, and most especially it must avoid all attempts to compare one person's utility with another's. Clinging tightly to these stern principles, they set out like the Pilgrim Fathers in search of a new land. What they produced has come to be known as the "new welfare economics." Like the New Look, it is not as new as it used to be.

QUESTIONS

1. How did Pigovian welfare theorists use the curve of diminishing marginal utility to generate a welfare theory?

2. Have you read *Sons and Lovers* or any other great novel of the English working class in Pigou's day? If so, comment on the relevance of his theory for the life around him. Do you think Pigou's concerns are just as relevant in contemporary America?

3. In what senses did Pigou depend on Marshall? In what senses was this a source of strength, and in what senses was it a source of weakness?

4. Could Pigou have rested his argument on William Stanley Jevons' version of utility theory?

5. Was it possible to accept neoclassical utility theory without accepting Pigou?

6. From a contemporary point of view, in precisely what sense was the Pigovian use of the concept of utility in a welfare theory unscientific? What was taken for granted?

7. Do you think that there were important valid insights embedded in Pigou's argument?

8. What sorts of axioms would we need in order to restate Pigou's welfare argument for the redistribution of incomes?

9. Can you suggest any reasons why the men of the 1940s were not likely to attempt any such operation?

11
THE
"NEW WELFARE
ECONOMICS"

Whereof one cannot speak,
Thereof one must be silent.

Ludwig Wittgenstein

THE FLIGHT FROM
INTERPERSONAL
COMPARISONS The new welfare economics began life with a denial, which
is perhaps not the most auspicious sort of beginning one
can have. Do not be under the impression, however, that
this stunted its growth: Literally hundreds of articles and
many, many books appeared which were written within
the conventions of new welfare theory. A certain question
arises as to why this luxuriant growth took place.

Remember that the new welfare theorists were dedi-
cated to the belief that value judgments must not appear
anywhere in their theory, not even as axioms—although of
course they were not consciously considering the possibility
of explicit value axioms; furthermore there must be no use
of any concept that did not result from direct observation;
and finally, no policy could ever be advocated that caused
the slightest damage to any one member of a society, since

to advocate such a policy would imply the interpersonal comparison that the damage caused to those who were injured was less important than the gain to those who were not. The project for the new welfare theorists may be parodied a trifle unkindly, as that of constructing a sausage machine so superlative that it would deliver sausages without the vulgar necessity of having any sausage meat fed into it at any point.

I think that anyone who does research in this area and therefore has to read extensively in the numbers of articles and volumes involved could hardly avoid the conclusion that after vast and intricate argument and great symbolic complexity this mountainous activity generates at the end a very tame policy mouse, if indeed even a mouse of substantial existence is to be found. It is not even that there are grandiose claims which are not met; that, after all, could be exciting. It is that even what is claimed is, when you look at it fair and square, of the very greatest triviality. One might question why these people thought it worth indulging in the intensely arduous activity necessary to bring forth this questionable mouse. There is a hypothesis for which I cannot claim to have done the necessary empirical research but which I find very tempting. It is this. Most of those who wrote the initial articles and the earliest books in the new welfare period had probably come into welfare theory earlier in their lives during a period when the grandiose metaphysical clouds of the old welfare theories of Pigou had not yet been dispelled in the cold operational dawn of the Hicksian revolution. Whatever the logical status of the various elements in the Pigovian welfare economics from our point of view today, I hope I have made it clear to you that there can be no doubts at all about its emotional power as an intellectual edifice. It touched upon the most acute issues of its day—perhaps even of ours. It offered revolutionary remedies apparently backed up by arguments whose cogency depended only upon the very structure of economic orthodoxy, upon the Marshallian marginal utility curve, which was then universally accepted. It offered to the young upper-class radicals of Eton and King's and the London School a technique of revolt and reform that seemed to carry the backing of absolute mathematical certainty. They could wave a banner whose device, though strange, apparently had the backing of mathematical science. No one who is both young and enthusiastic could fairly find this dull. Is it unreasonable to suggest that many who joined the ranks of the welfare theorists in their romantic youth stayed on from sheer immobility or from a lack of realization of how little remained that could possibly excite them after the cavalier period was over? What remained for them was the analysis of doctrines of an austere puritanism, whose consequences, in any event, offered little joy.

Of all the arguments of this arid period I shall offer you only two, making no claim that their presentation constitutes an adequate coverage in any sense of new welfare theory, but simply that they are typical of the tone and style of the whole enterprise. They are respectively the compensation principle and what was called "Pareto optimality."

THE COMPENSATION PRINCIPLE

Many versions of this doctrine appeared in the literature, and Sir John Hicks was the author of several of them. The doctrine can be stated wholly in indifference-curve terms, having no dependence at all upon the notion of quantities of utility; and it is thoroughly Hicksian in spirit. I shall not attempt to trace its development and its many versions here; the version I offer will be the simplest that can be constructed and I hope to show that the defects of this simple version would hold for any possible reformulation. They are, that is to say, defects in principle of any such doctrine.

In its boldest form, the idea can be presented as follows. Consider the effects of any economic policy on a society. One can divide the society into those who would gain, those who would lose, and those who would remain indifferent, which are construed in Hicksian terms as those who would move to a higher indifference curve, those who would move to a lower indifference curve, and those who would remain on the same indifference curve. Nothing is assumed about quantities of satisfaction or anything of that sort. It is argued that those who remain on the same indifference curve are unconcerned about the change. We are left with the gainers and the losers. Suppose the gainers can compensate the losers, that is, can offer them something regarded by the losers as moving them back to their previous indifference curve. If this can be done only at the cost of moving the gainers in turn back to their original indifference curve, of course the whole performance of, as it were, musical indifference curves has left everyone entirely where they stood at the beginning. On the other hand, if the gainers can restore the losers to their original position and themselves move to an indifference curve lower than the one they were on after the initial change but not so low as the indifference curve they were on initially, then it can be argued that the gainers are still gaining. Something has taken place that can be described as an increase in welfare on the part of the society: for the proponent of this doctrine an economic change could be described as an "increase in welfare" if some members of the society had gained while none had lost. Manifestly the situation we have been considering meets these requirements and would therefore have been thus described by the new welfare theorist.

Note that this argument carefully skirts the two reefs on which the new welfare theorists were terrified of shipwreck: Nothing has had to be said about quantities of satisfaction, and on the other hand, no interpersonal comparisons have been explicitly made. The change is described as an increase in welfare only because some people have gained and nobody has lost. It has not been necessary to judge anyone's gain, to whatever extent, however great or small, more important than anyone else's loss.

In criticizing this concept, we note first that it manifestly works only if the compensation is actually made.[1] If the compensation is not in fact made, some members of the society have in fact lost. Whether or not they could have been compensated in principle is beside the point. If someone has in fact lost, the society's situation after the policy has been carried out can be described as an increase in welfare only if we are willing to make interpersonal comparisons; and the new welfare theorists were never willing to do this. Actually compensating the losers, however, may prove quite a tall order. To begin with, we have to find out who they are, and this raises the question as to what evidence bears on who is a gainer and who is a loser. Are we to take their word for it? And if not, how do we know whether someone is a gainer or a loser without making an interpersonal comparison? If somebody claims to have lost, and we strongly suspect that he has

[1]This point and a number that follow are well argued by I. M. D. Little in his book *A Critique of Welfare Economics*, 2d ed., Oxford University Press, Fair Lawn, N.J., 1957.

not, how do we prove that he has not in fact lost? Then there is the question of how *much* compensation will compensate a particular loser.

Suppose there is a little old lady sitting in a cottage with roses around the door smack in the path of a state freeway. The highway authorities come to see the little old lady and to offer to compensate her for razing her cottage to the ground and building the freeway where it stood. They point out that society as a whole will gain enormously. They offer her generous compensation—suppose it to be as generous as you please. The little old lady smiles gently, and one can just detect a copy of Lionel Robbins' *Essay on the Nature and Significance of Economic Science* skulking behind the glass cover of one of her bookcases. She says: "Oh, but you see I've lived here all my life. I brought up my children here. They are now all scattered. Everything of life that mattered to me took place here. Nothing would compensate me." She might even add: "Show me if you dare, how I can be compensated. Show me how you can claim that I am compensated without making an interpersonal comparison."

The fact, of course, is that highway authorities and other public and quasi-public bodies make interpersonal comparisons like crazy. They do it all the time. They could never have used the new welfare economics for a moment. Not a single policy necessary to carry out any public project could ever have been based on the compensation principle, unless nobody in any way involved in the carrying out of the policy was in any way damaged: if they were damaged, however slightly, and if interpersonal comparisons were not allowed, obviously those who were damaged could insist that nothing would compensate them.

A further problem arises about the manner in which compensation is to be made. Typically, it was assumed that compensation would take the form of money payments. This may work if someone has been damaged in a very obvious way, such as losing $5,000 or $10,000 a year in money income. But in a society where the exciting and interesting changes profoundly alter the whole character and manner of life, the damage that occurs as a consequence—as an inevitable consequence—of social change very often is likely to take a form that cannot possibly be remedied simply by offering somebody hard cash. Anyone who is close to older people and to their reactions to the radical changes that scientific revolutions are bringing about in our society knows that one continually meets with this kind of remark: "It's that everything is so different, I just don't know how to cope with this new world. I don't feel comfortable in it. It isn't like the world I grew up in." How do you make such a person happy in an automated world simply by offering him an increase in money income?

Then there is the problem of so-called "external effects."[2] The new welfare theorists tended to assume that a person's welfare depended solely on his own economic state and was not affected one way or another by the states of those around him. Of course, as we know, this is not true. If an economic change has left you where you were before, able to buy about the same things, but has made other people much better off, you will not feel as well off as you did originally. Living at a level that puts you in the middle ranges of a rather poor society is an experience quite different from consuming exactly the same set of commodities as one of the poorest members of a rich society. Yet you will observe the second state of the society fully meets the compensation theory's criteria for being an increase in social welfare: some people have gained and the other people have remained in the same state. The gain by the gainers has simply had an unfavorable external effect on the situation of the other group, without the other group's own actual economic situation having changed in any direct or observable way.

PARETO OPTIMALITY

We commonly think that some arrangements of society must be more efficient than others. There must be ways of doing things that are more efficient from everyone's point of view. One accepts intuitively the notion that sheer waste and malfunctioning must damage everyone and can be to nobody's advantage. In ordinary speech, the notion of efficiency carries in it the germ of the idea of Pareto optimality. To examine this notion, let us consider it in the notation in which it has typically been expressed by new welfare theorists. This has consisted of a representation of the indifference curves of two individuals—say a boy called Axel and a girl called Bodil—in an Edgeworth

[2]These had been analyzed by Pigou long before the new welfare economics appeared. We shall return to externalities again in Chapter 20.

box (Fig. 11-1). Starting from the conventional origin O, Axel's indifference curves for bread and wine are shown moving outward through the box. To put in Bodil's indifference curves, we start again, this time from the opposite corner of the box, O_B, which will be treated as Bodil's origin. Moving downward from O_B in the opposite direction from Axel's are a family of Bodil's indifference curves.

Since this construction is a little different from any use that we have so far made of the Edgeworth box, a word or two might be in order as to its peculiar properties. Notice that for both A and B the indifference curves throughout are open. If they were continued throughout the box they would remain sections of open curve, because this diagram is simply based on the assumption that neither A nor B would reach satiation with respect to either bread or wine or both throughout the whole space in the box—in other words, both A and B have an interest in being as far toward the opposite corner from the one that is their own origin as they can get. This construction is designed, in a manner which will become evident as we proceed, to show to the maximum both the possibilities of conflict and the possibilities of agreement between A and B. Observe that within the box any movement in a vertical direction upward is a gain of bread for A and a loss of bread for B and vice versa and that any movement in a horizontal direction from left to right is a gain of wine to A and a loss of wine to B. This follows simply from the placing of their respective origins. We thus have a convenient representation of a choice space in which at first sight one would

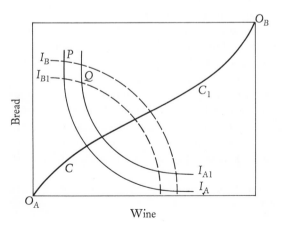

FIGURE 11-1

Pareto optimality
in an Edgeworth box

assume that A's gain must necessarily be B's loss, and
A's loss necessarily B's gain. This provides the backdrop
against which the conventional proof of Pareto optimality
can be seen most dramatically.

Consider a pair of A and B indifference curves such
as the A indifference curve I_A and the B indifference curve
I_B in Fig. 11-1. They intersect at P. Within the space
enclosed by I_A and I_B there must lie some other pair of
A and B indifference curves such as I_{A1} and I_{B1} whose intersection is inside the space enclosed by the previous two
indifference curves—say at point Q. But Q must be preferred to P in both A's and B's ordering, since Q is the
intersection of an A curve I_{A1}, which is higher than A's
previous curve I_A, and a B curve I_{B1}, which is higher than
B's previous curve I_B. The process can clearly be continued.
A point might be found within the space enclosed by I_{A1}
and I_{B1} and, indeed, an infinite set of such points can be
found on higher and higher indifference curves for A and
for B within the successively smaller spaces enclosed by
intersections between successive pairs of their curves. At
the limit we obviously reach a point of tangency between
an A curve and a B curve.

Let us compare this point of tangency with the suc-
cession of intersecting points that led to it. If one contrasts
the point of tangency with any of the previous points of
intersection, one can enunciate the following theorem,
which in effect is the core of Pareto optimality: For any
point that is an intersection between two curves, an A
curve and a B curve, there must be some point of tangency
that is a preferred position for both A and B. In other
words, neither A nor B would ever have an incentive to
stay at a point in the space that is a point of intersection
between their respective indifference curves. The set of
Pareto optimal points is thus the set of joint tangencies,
that is to say, of tangencies between an A curve and a B
curve, and the non-Pareto optimal set is the set of all points
that are points of intersection between A curves and B
curves respectively. The choice space has thus been partitioned into two proper and exclusive subsets, the set of
all Pareto optimal points and the set of all non-Pareto
optimal points. Note that, since continuity assumptions
have been made, both are infinite sets.

There is thus a set of points that both A and B can
agree is to be preferred to another set of points within the

choice space, and for their activities to be at one of the
latter points is clearly to be what we ordinarily describe
as "inefficient."

The locus of all tangencies between an A curve and
a B curve would be a line such as that shown in Fig. 11-1
and labeled CC_1. It is usually called the "contract curve"
for the following reason: No two contracting parties would
ever settle at any point in the choice space other than a
point on the line C. On the other hand, Kenneth Boulding
(who has made great use of these constructions in his
work) has aptly called it the "conflict curve," since it has
the property that any two points on it must be a matter of
disagreement. Between any point on the conflict curve and
any other point on the conflict curve there must be disagreement between A and B. Since both these points are
equally points of efficiency, the only issue is that at one
of them A gains more bread and more wine whereas at
the other B does. A point off the conflict curve may be
judged inferior to a point on it for both parties, but two
points on the conflict curve, being equally Pareto optimal
points, can differ only with respect to whether they favor
A or favor B. Welfare policies based on Pareto optimality
concepts and restricted by avoidance of interpersonal comparisons therefore had to be confined to recommendations
that a system move from a point off the conflict curve to
an agreed point on it. Such a point on the conflict curve
could always be found, since, starting from any point of
intersection and moving inward in the space enclosed between the two curves, one could progress to successively
higher and higher pairs of A and B curves until one finally
reached tangency, which was itself a tangency between a
higher A curve and a higher B curve than was involved in
any of the intersections whose path led one to the tangency.
This move shows the formal properties of policy decision
aimed at Pareto optimality. Observe that the conflict curve
need by no means be a straight line: its actual shape will
depend on the configuration of the A indifference curves
and the B indifference curves respectively, upon which
the placing of their tangencies will in turn depend; and the
shapes of these curves depend of course upon A's taste for
wine in relation to bread and upon B's similar taste.[3]

---

[3]Theorists will notice that I have ignored, for simplicity, the
case where tangencies lie along a side of the box.

We must now offer some appraisal of this concept of Pareto optimality in an Edgeworth box. It must, I feel, be immediately admitted that the concept has a power and formal beauty wholly lacking in the concept of the compensation principle. Pareto optimality, at least, offers one the picture of a formal concept of efficiency and of a path of movement toward this from successive approximations. The notion, unquestionably, is not without its charm for a computer age. However, one seriously questions whether this notion, no matter how valid and no matter how usable in other areas, will do much of the job the new welfare theorists wanted it to do. Remember that the job was very specific: It consisted in nothing less than generating significant policy recommendations without having to make interpersonal comparisons or to assume any other value judgments. The question arises whether the Pareto optimality construction, taken alone, really enables one to do without interpersonal comparisons or other such value judgments, in judging two rival social policies. Pareto optimality, although it states a necessary condition that must be met in any state of a society if that state is to be considered optimal, offers one no criterion for judging among an infinite set of different distributions of goods among the members of the society. Remember that all points on the contract curve are Pareto optimal, irrespective of the extent to which they favor Axel or Bodil.

The Pareto criterion, despite its force and validity, is therefore useful in generating policy recommendations only if it can be combined with devices that radically *cut down the relevant stretch of the contract curve.*

Certain very recent theorems in the theory of the core[4] of an economy appear to have this needed property, and Pareto optimality will be discussed again when we have this apparatus at our disposal. For the moment we have said enough to see that in the days of the "new" welfare economics, these theorists could not live by Pareto optimality alone.

In the light of what has already been said, it may seem curious that there should have been totally unexpected positive benefits from this analysis. One is in an area of pure science; and the other is at the very opposite

CRITICAL EVALUATION OF THE CONCEPT

STRANGE FRUITS OF NEW WELFARE ECONOMICS

[4]See Chapter 16, "Theory of Exchange," pp. 167-177.

pole, in an area of the strictest and most practical engineering. What makes the whole thing strange is that neither the area of pure science nor the area of engineering has had anything to do with what the new welfare theorists themselves wanted to achieve. The area of pure science is in fact axiomatic choice theory. The area of engineering is in fact operations research and its allied techniques and methods. The new welfare theorists, of course, had neither of these in mind when they wrote their work—it would, as a matter of fact, have been hard for them to have considered these consequences, since both the areas at issue have developed on the whole since new welfare theory. The new welfare theorists wanted to do something quite definite: They wanted to generate welfare theorems about an economy without making interpersonal comparisons of utility and without, therefore, falling victim to the attack that Lord Robbins had launched against the old welfare theory. We have seen that their efforts to generate social sausages from an elegant sausage machine without putting in any sausage meat were doomed to the kind of failure that one might expect of such ventures if one looked at them clearly in the abstract. However, they did something else, which was not without value even if it was not intentional. They were led, as Adam Smith once remarked in another context, by an invisible hand to promote an end that was no part of their intention.

For pure science, they provided detailed and searching analyses of optimizing activity under a whole series of special circumstances. They intended these analyses to have immediate bearing on issues of welfare policy. The fact that the analyses could not have such bearing is at the moment irrelevant. However, at a time when pure choice theory was not yet being constructed in and for itself by people explicitly concerned with it and nothing else, much work that now provides the foundations of the mathematical theory of choice was done by men whose avowed intention was to produce welfare theorems.

You can see this quite well if you look at the study of Pareto optimality that we have just made, considered simply as an analysis of certain special conditions under which agreement and disagreement are possible about particular optimizing moves. Pareto optimality is obviously an interesting addition to choice theory. The fact that one cannot immediately apply it to solving problems of welfare in an economy without having certain value judgments at hand to feed the sausage machine does not in the least affect its elegance as a piece of pure science. The welfare theorists, of course, would not have been very cheered to be told this. From our point of view, however, the reasons why some parts of the new welfare theory are still worth reading mainly have to do with the part they played in the development of mathematical choice theory and not at all to do with their immediate usability in the area of political decision.

Let us turn our attention to their contribution to engineering. As William Baumol[5] has remarked, a number of the theorems of the new welfare economics have been found useful and interesting by operations research engineers for the following reason. The operations research people were concerned with studying conditions of optimality on certain special assumptions. Since they were working for particular private organizations or for the government, they were always in a position to know how different goals and different parts of an organization were respectively valued. The possibility of total disagreement about objectives, which we have seen in the case of welfare analyses of the interests of different people, would therefore not arise. The O.R. engineers could be sure that such problems would not prove fatal, because before a situation reached this point, they could simply go to their superiors and demand a ruling. Given this situation, detailed and sometimes quite mathematically subtle analyses of possible paths to optimality were of course extremely interesting to them, and they were able to make use of these analyses, where a policy maker in the ordinary sense had not been able to, precisely because they could always solve just those value issues that the policy maker in the area, strictly speaking, of welfare theory is not in a position always to solve.

QUESTIONS

1. What precisely was the issue over interpersonal comparisons of utility? Was Lord Robbins' argument sound from our point of view today?

2. What policy did the new welfare economists adopt in the face of Lord Robbins' argument? What did this policy entail in regard to value judgments and welfare economics?

[5]See in *Econometrica*, vol. 27 (1959), pp. 317-318, his review of *Theoretical Welfare Economics*, by J. DeGraaf.

3. What was the compensation principle?

4. Can a little old lady who has read Lord Robbins criticize the compensation principle effectively?

5. If after an economic change that has made my friends better off I am consuming the same physical commodities that I consumed before the change, am I in the same economic position? Could I need to be compensated, and if so, for what?

6. Is there any relation between the limitations of the compensation principle and the limitations of the Hicksian indifference curve as a representation of choice-theoretic situations?

7. How is the concept of Pareto optimality related to the intuitive notion of efficiency?

8. In an Edgeworth box representation of the Pareto optimality theorem, why are certain movements in the choice space movements away from Pareto optimality and other movements toward it?

9. Why is the contract curve sometimes also called a "conflict curve"?

10. What possible unintended uses can the studies of optimality undertaken by the new welfare economists have for contemporary scientists and engineers?

12
AXIOMATIC
WELFARE
ECONOMICS

Some people have denied that any distinguishable and significant new movement in welfare analysis has come about since the days of the now somewhat old "new" welfare theorists of the thirties and forties. Ian Little, for example, in the preface to the second edition of his book *A Critique of Welfare Economics*, argues that Kenneth Arrow's great work, *Social Choice and Individual Values*, is not, strictly speaking, welfare analysis. He is honest enough to admit that he makes this contention on the highly reasonable ground that were he to regard it as welfare analysis he would have to rewrite his own book. There is, therefore, no widely acknowledged and accepted term for writings on policy at the scientific level that have happened since the analyses we considered in Chapter 11. I have adopted the term "axiomatic" for these writings simply

to give them a name. I hope to show that the distinct tone
and the distinct method common to these writings are
significantly different from anything that went before and
thus justify our treating them as a separate category.

The writings I have in mind as characteristic of this
somewhat embryonic new movement have in common at
least one of two characteristics: either technique of analysis
or, on the other hand, an assumption about value judgments. The technique of analysis is that of contemporary
axiomatic choice theory, which obviously makes these
writings look strikingly different from either of their prede-
cessors. The assumption about value judgments amounts
to a rejection of the logical positivist position of the thirties
and forties that made possible the unchallenged acceptance
of Lord Robbins. From this follows a willingness to consider the possibility of explicitly stated value axioms—
since value judgments are no longer regarded as nonsense
sentences—and the acceptance as perfectly scientific of the
analysis of the implications for a theory of a particular axiom
set, including axiom sets some of whose axioms are value
axioms.

As regards the first of these characteristics, a matter
of technique, the outstanding contribution to the whole
area is the famous work of Kenneth Arrow, both in *Social
Choice and Individual Values* and elsewhere since the
book was published. No account of the new stream of
thought in welfare analysis can possibly avoid some consideration of Arrow's work, however superficial this may
have to be for our present purposes. I therefore begin with
a sketch of the argument of *Social Choice and Individual
Values*.

SOCIAL ORDERINGS   For each individual in the society whose welfare he
is discussing, Arrow adopts a theory of choice which uses
now familiar general axioms: the Axiom of Comparability
and the Axiom of Transitivity, which we have already
discussed.[1] Each individual then has an ordering of a sort
familiar to us since Chapter 9. Because he is concerned
with welfare economics, however, the elements in this
ordering are not, as they have been with us, individual
actions or choices: they are total states of a whole society.

[1]See above, pp. 80-84.

In other words, if an individual ranks X above Y—prefers X to Y—in Arrow's theory, this is not to be considered a preference for some one object or state of affairs X over some other one object or state of affairs Y but rather to be thought of as a preference for a whole intricate social arrangement symbolized as possible social state X over another whole intricate social state symbolized by Y. The core problem of Arrow's book now becomes the attempt to prove a general theorem about the possibility of constructing an ordering for society as a whole—a social ordering—which will in some way *reflect* all the individual orderings of the members who make up the society.

Clearly, if some such way of passing from individual orderings to such a social ordering could be found, this would describe the essence of a rational welfare theory. Arrow is well aware, however, of the pitfalls into which earlier welfare theories had fallen, and he sets up a series of conditions that such a social ordering must fulfill if it is to be regarded as satisfactory. These conditions rule out social orderings that do not *reflect* the individual orderings of the members of society, that give more weight to the orderings of one member than another—and thus involve interpersonal comparisons—or that are imposed upon the society by fiat. The latter principle is regarded by Arrow as particularly important and is even given a special name —"condition of nondictatorship." Drawing on the usual axioms of choice theory and in particular on the Axiom of Transitivity, Arrow now proves his fundamental theorem. It is beyond the scope of this book to reproduce this proof in full, and therefore it is impossible to detail all the points in it that have been attacked. I shall attempt, however, to give some hint of Arrow's position and of that of his critics.

Consider a society of only two people, Adam and Eve, ranking three possible states of that society which we may write as x, y, and z. Let "x is preferred by Adam to y" be written "$x P_A y$." Let "x is preferred by Eve to y" be written "$x P_E y$." And let "x is preferred to y by the society composed of Adam and Eve" be written "$x P_S y$." Let "indifference" between x and y on the part of Adam, Eve, or the society be indicated by "I," with the same subscripts, A, E, and S, respectively.

A SKETCH OF THE IMPOSSIBILITY THEOREM

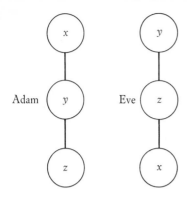

FIGURE 12-1

Individual orderings

By the condition of nondictatorship, it follows that if Adam and Eve disagree about x and y, the society cannot be said to prefer either:

1. $x P_A y \,\&\, y P_E x \Rightarrow -(x P_S y \lor y P_S x)$

since otherwise Adam's preference would dominate Eve's, or vice versa. Now, Arrow assumes that the social ordering must obey the Axiom of Comparability of pure choice theory,[2] so by Axiom 1:

2. $(x)\,(y)\,(x P_S y \lor y P_S x \lor x I_S y)$

Hence by (1) and (2),

3. $x P_A y \,\&\, y P_E x \Rightarrow x I_S y$

That is to say, if Adam and Eve have opposite preferences about x and y, we are obliged to say that the society of which they are the members is indifferent between x and y. Now consider the orderings as shown in Fig. 12-1. Obviously,

4. $y P_A z \,\&\, y P_E z \Rightarrow y P_S z$

That is, if both prefer y to z, then the society must prefer y to z. Now, we know from (3) above that $x I_S y$. But, by the Axiom of Transitivity (Axiom 2 of pure choice theory, which Arrow adopts for social orderings), it follows that:

5. $y P_S z \,\&\, x I_S y \Rightarrow x P_S z$

But, since Adam prefers x to z and Eve prefers z to x it follows that for the society x and z are indifferent:

6. $x P_A z \,\&\, z P_E x \Rightarrow x I_S z$

which contradicts (5) above. Hence even in this simple case a social ordering cannot be constructed out of individual orderings (upon the axioms accepted by Arrow) without contradiction.[3]

It has been pointed out that this contradiction directly follows from the necessity, on Arrow's axioms, of treating the opposition between two individual orderings as a case

[2] Recall the axiomatic discussion of Chapter 9, especially pp. 80-82.

[3] The simple case of two individuals and three alternatives is analyzed by Kenneth Arrow in *Social Choice and Individual Values*, 2d ed., John Wiley & Sons, Inc., New York, 1963, pp. 48-51.

of *indifference* in the social ordering, and then treating this social indifference as having the transitivity property of the indifference relation in individual choice theory.[4] To say that Adam and Eve have opposite preferences with respect to x and y does not seem to be happily translated into the system of a social ordering by the expression that the society composed of Adam and Eve is indifferent as between x and y, certainly not if the indifference relation is to mean what it ordinarily means in choice theory, to have, for example, the property of transitivity. As long as Axiom 1 of conventional choice theory is accepted, however, there does not seem to be any alternative. If one relaxes Axiom 1 of choice theory, of course, and allows that for some x and y, x might be simply not comparable to y, the problem may be somewhat different. Simply in terms of common intuition, it seems reasonable to argue that, in the case of a society composed simply of Adam and Eve, if Adam prefers x over y and Eve prefers y over x the only reasonable statement to make about the status of x and y from the point of view of the little group as a whole is that they can't be evaluated—that, in short, they are not comparable. As has already been mentioned earlier,[5] there are reasons within pure choice theory for admitting an incomparability relation into the axiom set. Clearly, this problem in welfare theory is a possible further field in which this change in the axiom structure might prove fruitful.

A number of attempts have been made by Kenneth Arrow and by others to adapt this system in such a way as to allow for the possibility of the formation of a social ordering. Various requirements of Arrow's original theory have been altered with this end in view. C. Hildreth, for example, has suggested the introduction of a cardinality concept as a way out of the impasse.[6] The idea, crudely, is that if Adam only barely prefers x to y whereas Eve desperately prefers y to x, the social system might rank y over x. Unfortunately, this involves the reintroduction of interpersonal comparisons: and whatever grounds one

[4]See E. J. Mishan, *Welfare Economics: Five Introductory Essays*, Random House, Inc., New York, 1964, p. 65.

[5]See pp. 33-35 and 80-82.

[6]C. Hildreth, "Alternative Conclusions for Social Orderings," *Econometrica*, vol. 21 (1953), pp. 81-94.

might put forward for reintroducing interpersonal comparisons, to do so is to render unnecessary the whole apparatus of social choice and individual values, since precisely the point of Arrow's analysis was to derive a social ordering simply from individual orderings without recourse to this expedient.

A possible line of escape depends on the structure of axiomatic choice theory itself. Possibly, this structure, as it exists, has a built-in tendency to make disagreements look more inevitable than they really are. Consider the P relation[7]—by now our very old friend. For any x and y, we are prepared to write $x\,P\,y$ if on any given occasion we are told that a choosing agent will choose x over y in an ordering of this kind. We habitually translate this state of affairs into English by speaking of his preferring x to y. But the English word "prefer" has a much more subtle and varied family of uses than we have been giving to the P relation in formal choice theory. To mention only one point, in English we use the word "prefer" normally to refer to a long-term disposition, not to an isolated act of choice. We say of someone that he made ten clear choices this morning but not that he made ten preferences. We describe someone as having a preference for something over something else only if during a long period of time we observe a tendency, a *disposition*, to order it more highly than the other thing. Fundamental axiomatic choice theory, because of its timelessness, is in no position to take account of this property of the English word "prefer" symbolically. The trouble is that this introduces into human conflict, when analyzed in terms of formal choice theory, a much wider area of apparent disagreement than probably exists in human life, spread out as we all know it is in time. Even two ideal lovers might not always make the same particular choices on particular occasions, but this does not mean that in ordinary life we are not aware that their long-term preferences may be the same. Axiomatic choice theory, constructed in terms of the P relation, will not be able to reflect the contrast between these isolated disagreements on particular occasions on the one hand, and the long-term agreement on the other. Even Juliet asks,

---

[7]Recall the discussion of the relations "P" and "I" in Chapter 9. "P" was adopted as an undefined primitive concept. The relation "P" was not assumed to be an exact translation of any English phrase.

"Wherefore art thou Romeo?" But we are quite sure nonetheless of her long-term preferences. In the formal language of fundamental axiomatic choice theory this would not, however, be revealed. A fully dynamic choice theory might be constructed in terms of a relation (let's call it P_1) that exhibited many more of the dispositional properties of our English word "prefer." A social ordering in terms of P_1 might exist in many instances in which a social ordering did not exist in terms of P.[8]

A more fundamental question concerns the bearing of Arrow's theorem upon the attempt to carry on welfare economics. Arrow's result is sometimes interpreted as a cry of despair—if we cannot derive a social ordering, we had better give up the whole idea of welfare theory.

But a radically different interpretation of the Impossibility Theorem is possible, and it makes the theorem highly nontrivial for policy making in today's world. This interpretation[9] is in two parts.

First, a society in a state of anarchy is a model for the Arrow theory. Recall that Arrow's individuals rank *total states of the society*—not just each individual's own state of affairs. Further, Arrow's theory specifies zero coercion of individuals' orderings. Thus the Arrow theorem can be interpreted as a proof of the impossibility of anarchy.

The second point concerns further work in welfare economics. Arrow proves that any attempt to construct an innocuous (i.e., value-free) social ordering must fail. So the welfare theorist *must adopt nontrivial value axioms*.

I now turn to what I have been claiming is the second characteristic of the tone of recent welfare economics, namely, its attitude toward value judgments.

[8]These remarks grew originally out of some comments made in private correspondence with James Buchannan. Professor Buchannan was commenting on an old article of mine, "On Descriptions of Consumer's Behaviour," *Economica*, NS, vol. XXI (1954), pp. 244-251. The notion expressed above is further discussed in my contribution to the New York University Seminar on the Philosophy of Science for 1966: "Axiomatic Choice Theory and Values," in Sidney Hook (ed.), *Human Values and Economic Policy, a Symposium*, New York University Press, New York, 1967, pp. 198-200.

[9]Which is due to conversation with G. C. Archibald. See also his paper, "The Qualitative Content of Maximizing Models," *Journal of Political Economy*, vol. LXXIII (1964), pp. 27-36.

VALUE AXIOMS

It will be clear from what has already been said that even as early as the first edition of *Social Choice and Individual Values*, which came out in 1951, Arrow was very far from regarding value judgments as pseudopropositions—as meaningless jumbles of sound that cannot have any valid place in a scientific argument.[10] The condition of nondictatorship, to mention only one important part of the structure of his book, which requires that a social ordering give equal weight to the preferences of each member of the society, is clearly a value axiom in essence. There is, however, an ambivalence about the role played by value axioms in the system constructed in *Social Choice and Individual Values*. Insofar as value axioms appear at all in that system, they appear only to set what are regarded as reasonable conditions for the formation of social orderings—to eliminate the imposition of a dictator's ordering, for instance. Value axioms do *not* appear in the following sense, which is the sense in which I have been speaking of them so far in this book.

Consider a welfare theory that takes as axiomatic that the level of real income of the poor must be radically changed and investigates the economic implications of carrying out this policy. Such a welfare theory would involve value axioms in the sense in which I have been using the term (when writing, for instance, of Pigou).

You will observe that in this theory the sausage machine of mathematical economics would be set to grind out policy sausages upon being fed the rich sausage meat of the value axioms. Nothing like this is happening in *Social Choice and Individual Values*. In the latter work the individual orderings are taken as the sole and ultimate source of the valuation, and the only value axioms that appear are concerned (as in the principle of nondictatorship) with policing, as it were, the way in which these individual values are fitted together in the hope of forming a social ordering. The idea of presenting to individuals or to society as a whole a suggested set of value axioms and the formally derived economic consequences of each of these axioms, is never considered as a possible move for a welfare theorist. The implication of all this is clear: If one accepts the posi-

[10]Recent discussion shows Professor Arrow if anything more willing to acknowledge the importance and status of value judgments. See his contribution, "Public and Private Values," in Hook (ed.), *op. cit.*, pp. 3-21.

tion of *Social Choice and Individual Values*, the welfare theorist is in no position to move at all unless he can get universal agreement—that is to say, a social ordering.

But if the welfare theorist cannot operate *at all* without *some* value axioms, he might as well be hanged for a sheep as for a lamb. He might as well start investigating (before it is too late) the economic consequences of some interesting value axioms. Pigou, the founder of self-conscious welfare economics, had a powerful influence and a devoted following among the young scientists of his day. As a matter of history, welfare economics has not always been morally timorous nor have its policy conclusions always been trivial or nonexistent. The development by contemporary axiomatic techniques of a structure of welfare theory at least as rich in policy conclusions as was Pigou's for his day is clearly a prerequisite if welfare theory is to be regarded with anything but ridicule by today's young scientific revolutionaries.

QUESTIONS

1. Can you describe any new directions in the stream of writings on welfare theory since the 1940s?

2. What is meant by a social ordering?

3. What is proved by Arrow's Impossibility Theorem?

4. What problems does the concept of social indifference in Arrow generate for his theory?

5. How does the Axiom of Transitivity bear upon Arrow's Impossibility Theorem?

6. What problems arise for Arrow over the interpretation of the "P" relation?

7. If I live half the year in Cambridge, Massachusetts, and half the year on a Swedish island and when I am in Massachusetts always wear swimming trunks when I swim, what do you make of my assertion "I prefer to swim in the nude"?

8. In what sense does the system in *Social Choice and Individual Values* contain value axioms?

9. Why are young people today likely to have more respect for an axiomatization of Pigou's welfare economics than for the new welfare economics of the forties and fifties?

Part
3
Consumption Theory

13

THE CONSUMPTION SET

We are now ready to apply the pure theory of choice developed in Part 1 to the task of generating theories of consumption, exchange, and production. As has been stressed in this book, the theory of choice, throughout most of its early development, grew up embedded in these theories, particularly in the theory of consumption, or consumers' behavior. Occasionally, choice theory could be glimpsed in a pure form—clearly in Edgeworth's *Mathematical Psychics*, again in the work of John von Neumann, and particularly in Kenneth Arrow's *Social Choice and Individual Values*. Most of its development, until very recently, must be sought in works explicitly devoted to the analysis of consumption and exchange. It follows that a study of contemporary theories on the latter topics can hardly help adding to our knowledge of the character and

APPLYING CHOICE THEORY TO THE ANALYSIS OF CONSUMPTION AND PRODUCTION background even of pure choice theory. There is, however, a further point that must be stressed here. I have been at pains in this book to give some glimpse of the foundations of pure decision theory as such, to separate the pure science from its applications—from the "engineering" based on it— and to show that the pure theory can be applied equally to any and all problems of optimizing, whatever their concrete content. But one must not infer that the conventional applications—to the explanation of consumption, exchange, and production—have become trivial or are no longer a major field for the application of the science.

There is an emotional problem here, which I think should be stated openly and faced. Try telling a freshman or sophomore who knows no economic theory, "It's exciting—one can explain the optimizing behavior of automated systems." You will probably get a fresh, interested reaction. Even if people think systems are sinister, they seldom think they are dull. Now try on some other friends of the same age the statement "Economic theory is exciting— it explains the activities of producers and consumers." Don't risk this with any girls you are interested in.

Yet producers in the next few years are more and more likely to be in fact thoroughly automated systems. A future-oriented analysis of production *must be* an analysis of the behavior of highly sophisticated optimizing systems. How did a theory of production come to be thought dull? I am not a social historian, but I cannot resist the following suggestions.

To begin with, as I have moved about the world, I have been struck by an important distinction between the reactions of young Americans as they encounter economics for the first time and the reactions I learned to expect from European, Indian, and African students. I think there are two points at issue: one concerns the social implications expected of economic theory, and the other concerns the stage of development of the economy in which people grow up.

We have seen in the discussion of Pigovian welfare theory in Chapter 10 that Pigou's *Economics of Welfare*, whatever its limitations, had a powerful social message. It may be heavy reading, but no one could have found it *dull* when it appeared. Of course, not all economists took Pigou's side—consider, for example, Lord Robbins. The point, however, is that they all *spoke out*: they lived in an atmosphere in which they could speak their minds without fear on major issues and habitually did so. And then— to consider England alone—a major social transformation was taking place that was being explained (rightly or wrongly) in terms taken from economic theory. To be reading economics at a university was to be an intellectual —possibly a radical intellectual—and did not at all suggest the image of a student at an American business school. If you were in a flat in Bloomsbury in those days, looking over a girl's bookshelves for some information about her attitudes, you might have looked for some of these: Russell: *Why I am Not a Christian, Marriage and Morals*; Ayer: *Language Truth and Logic*; Keynes: *The General Theory of Employment, Interest and Money*; Pigou: *The Economics of Welfare*; Lawrence: *Sons and Lovers, The Rainbow, Women in Love*.

If one found significant work by any three of these authors, one might well have considered that all systems were go.

Textbooks written and widely used in the forties and fifties in America managed to make the late Lord Keynes, one of the most brilliantly iconoclastic, devilishly witty, and controversial men who ever lived, sound tame and harmless. There was an enormous demand from both faculty *and students* in the America of those days for introductory texts that were intellectually undemanding, emotionally undisturbing, and, above all, uncontroversial. The highly spirited American youth of today will surely hardly be surprised, on reflection, that they should find these texts (which are still in use) extremely dull—after all, the texts were written for their parents.

The other reason for differences in attitude has to do with stages of development in an economy. Students from underdeveloped countries are likely to find exciting the idea of an analysis of ways to increase sheer physical output. The more affluent segment of our so-called affluent society notably fails to find the prospect of production of more and more physical things any cause for elation. Their elders, who knew insecurity and want and therefore are consciously grateful for the new abundance, cannot understand this. But the youth of today rightly rejects an ideal that construes a better life simply as one in which larger and larger quantities of material things are consumed by the affluent segment of a population and a view of production that judges the latter simply by size. They are seeing what we have illustrated by the use of indifference curves closing round a satiated area in an Edgeworth box, but they have not been exposed to an economic theory in which these considerations are built into the conceptual structure, so they dismiss theories of consumption and production as containing nothing of value for the future.

Let us look then at these old familiar topics with the somewhat new eyes of people coming to them with the point of view derived from pure choice theory. To begin with, we shall need a few new definitions and axioms designed to specialize the general theory of choice to the particular kinds of situation that are now relevant. The seven axioms of general choice theory continue to apply, since choices to consume are a proper subset of all choices. Upon this basis we construct the received theory of consumption decisions, as a model for choice theory, by the addition of further axioms.

COMMODITY SETS

The universe of discourse for general choice theory is delimited by the choice set,[1] but choices, as we have seen, may be among alternatives of any kind. In this chapter, we are concerned only with choice among *commodities*. The word "commodity" is not used in mathematical economics exactly as it is in ordinary English. To begin with, for simplicity, economists lump physical goods and services of all kinds together, and call them all simply "commodities." Durable goods like a truck or a house are considered in terms of the set of services derived from them—as truck-hours or house-months—and thus as groups of commodities. Note that the problem of indivisibilities is not therefore solved; it is only removed from the notation by which we refer to a commodity.

A "consumer" may be an individual, a household, a ménage à trois, the crew of an ocean racer, or any group that acts in unison to acquire commodities. Of the choice set conceivably open to a consumer, a proper subset is made up of choices among *commodities*. It will be assumed that there are only a finite number of distinguishable commodities. (If we care to use geometry for illustration, we

---

[1]Recall the argument of Chapters 2 and 9.

can only exhibit the case of two commodities if we are to use a two space and only three in a three-dimensional construction.)

A consumer, i, chooses from the attainable subset of X_i, his commodity set. The concept of "commodity set" must now be made as precise as possible. We begin by considering some concepts needed to axiomatize received consumption theory. In the first part of this book, we made use of naïve geometrical notions without any explicit explanation. We shall now adopt and use certain elementary concepts of logic and mathematics, without feeling obliged to regard these as extra primitives, on the grounds indicated in Chapter 8.[2]

We begin with the notion of the "product" (or "Cartesian product") of two sets, which may be written "$A \times B$." The Cartesian product of two sets is the set of all ordered couples (x, y), such that $x \in A$ and $y \in B$. Two sets A and B are defined as equal if and only if they have the same members, but two "ordered couples" are equal if and only if the member x_0 of the first is equal to x_1 in the second, and y_0 in the first ordered couple to y_1 in the second:

Definition 13-1: $(x_0, y_0) = (x_1, y_1) \Leftrightarrow (x_0 = x_1 \,\&\, y_0 = y_1)$

We may therefore define the Cartesian product set $X \times Y$ in terms of the notion of a set of ordered couples:

Definition 13-2: $X \times Y = \{(x, y) \mid x \in X \,\&\, y \in Y\}$

Strictly speaking, from the point of view of formal logic, a "two-place relation" (or "binary relation") "$x \, R \, y$" is simply a set of ordered couples. In ordinary language, when we speak of two things—or even more of two people —as being in some relation, we think of them as being bound together in some way. But in formal logic a binary relation simply specifies a set of ordered couples. Thus, as Patrick Suppes remarks, the relation of "loving" is the set of ordered couples,[3] such that x loves y. Thus if Marina loves José we may write "L" for the relation and say that (Marina,

[2]See the passage in justification of the adoption into the axioms of a science of standard parts of mathematics, pp. 69-70.

[3]Or ordered triples, and so on. I am confining the argument to couples reluctantly in an effort to keep things simple. We shall presently generalize it.

José) $\in$ L. If X and Y are two sets, any relation R between members of X and members of Y is a set of ordered couples (x, y), such that we may write:

Definition 13-3: $R = \{(x, y) | x \in X \& y \in Y \& x R y\}$

A relation between members of X and members of Y is thus a subset of the Cartesian product set $X \times Y$.

Suppose a villa contains three boys, b_1, b_2, b_3, and three girls, g_1, g_2, g_3. Suppose $b_1 L g_1$ and $b_2 L g_2$, but b_3 couldn't care less about g_3. Then the set $\{(b_1, g_1), (b_2, g_2)\}$ is the relation L for that villa. Notice that this relation is a proper subset of the Cartesian product set $B \times G$.[4] A relation is not *necessarily* a *proper* subset of the Cartesian product set: suppose every boy in the villa loved every girl. In general, a relation is simply *any* subset of the Cartesian product set.

This is an austere view of relations—you may feel that there is a lot to loving that gets left out. But it is completely precise, and it can be formalized within the notation of logic and set theory. And I have already warned you against *making* love in the notation of symbolic logic. Everything said about relations up to here in this book is consistent with this view, and we shall from now on regard it as explicitly adopted.

Now a commodity set is going to be a set of *bundles*, each of which contains so much ale and so much bread, in case there are just two commodities, ale and bread. A bundle is clearly an ordered couple, containing "a_0" of commodity a and "b_0" of commodity b. Then the commodity *set* must be the set of all ordered couples (a, b), that is to say, the Cartesian product set $A \times B$.

But to axiomatize received consumption theory we must depart from the generality of choice theory and assume that the consumer is always dealing with continuously divisible commodities,[5] that is to say, commodities that can be had in any nonnegative amount within some budget constraint. To do this, we must generate a commodity set adequate to the purpose. This may be done

---

[4]$B \times G = \{(b_1, g_1), (b_1, g_2), (b_1, g_3), (b_2, g_1), (b_2, g_2), (b_2, g_3), (b_3, g_1), (b_3, g_2), (b_3, g_3)\}$

What a lot of possibilities for one small villa!

[5]Clearly, an exciting task would be to develop a consumption theory that did not rely on this assumption of continuous divisibility.

by associating the quantities of one commodity with all the points on an ordinary geometric straight line, whose points are in turn identified with the set "R," of all real numbers. Such a line is called "the real line," and "R," is used to designate this line as well as the set of all real numbers, indifferently.

The continuously divisible commodity "*a*" will now be represented by all points on the real line within some closed interval, from a point "0," chosen to represent zero quantity of the commodity, to a point "*I*," chosen to represent the total quantity of *a* in existence. The segment from 0 to *I* is called a "*closed* interval" because it includes its limit points. It may be written "$[0, I]$." It can be shown that a segment of the real line is uncountably infinite.

To represent all of commodity *b*, we now take another replica of the real line and place it on a plane at right angles to the former so that they cross at the zero point for each commodity. The set of all points in the closed interval of the real line chosen to represent ale may be written "A," and those in the closed interval representing bread may be written "B." The set of all commodity bundles, composed of some nonnegative amount of bread and some nonnegative amount of ale is then the set of all ordered couples (a, b), that is to say, the Cartesian product set $A \times B$. As the product of uncountably infinite sets, this is clearly an uncountably infinite set, and it may be represented by all the points of the familiar Edgeworth box, including its boundary points.

Where there are *n* commodities, for some finite number *n*, a bundle is an ordered *n-tuple* written:

$(a_1, a_2, \ldots, a_n)$

An ordered triple may be identified with a point in three-dimensional space, and an ordered *n*-tuple may be identified with a point in *n*-dimensional space. An *n*-dimensional space of this kind is known as an "*n*-dimensional Euclidean space." The real line is written "R_1," and the "*real plane*"—the Cartesian product set $R_1 \times R_1$—is written "R_2." So the "*Euclidean n space*" may be written "R_n."

If there are "L" commodities, we may write the L-dimensional commodity space "X_L." The needed property of continuous divisibility of X_L can then be assured by

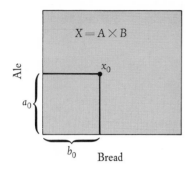

$$X = A \times B$$

Ale

a_0

x_0

b_0　　Bread

FIGURE 13-1

X showing a commodity bundle x_0 being the ordered couple (a_0, b_0)

identifying X_L with a coordinate subspace of R_n (that is to say, a space of fewer dimensions contained within the Euclidean space of n dimensions). Our Axiom of Continuous Divisibility of the commodity set may then be expressed:

Axiom 8　X_L *is a subspace of* R_n.

Any individual consumer, say the ith consumer, will typically not consume a *positive* quantity of *every* commodity in X_L, so his activities may be described within a subspace of X_L of fewer dimensions. We shall often consider the case where he consumes only two commodities so that his commodity space is the plane X_2, doing this not because it is at all realistic but because it is easy to visualize in a diagram. What we say, however, will always apply to a commodity space of more dimensions, and diagrams are to be considered only as aids to the imagination. When considering the situation of any consumer i and his commodity set in the two-commodity case, we shall write "X_{2i}" simply as "X" in order to lighten notation.

The two-dimensional case of X appears in Fig. 13-1 as the familiar Edgeworth box, where the vertical dimension represents a closed segment of the real line depicting all nonnegative quantities of ale in existence, and the horizontal dimension represents a closed interval depicting all nonnegative quantities of bread.

A particular point $x_0 \in X$ is an ordered couple made up of a_0 amount of ale and b_0 amount of bread, (a_0, b_0). Visibly, $X = A \times B$.

ECONOMIC IMPLICATIONS OF CONTINUOUS DIVISIBILITY

This first axiom of consumption theory, Axiom 8, may strike the reader as giving up a very great deal of the freedom and generality of pure choice theory. We have seen at length in Part 1 of this book how much of life does not present us with continuous divisibility. If we are unwilling to accept continuity in the choice set of general choice theory, it may be asked why we should be willing to accept this property as holding universally of commodity sets in consumption theory. I answer that I do not think that this assumption should be maintained in future work, even in the theory of consumers' behavior. In this book, however, I am attempting only an axiomatic account of *existing* consumption theory. And existing mathematical theories of consumption do in fact rest on this assumption —even the highly sophisticated work of writers like Debreu and Arrow.

In line with this policy of showing how one has to give up part of the generality of choice theory in order to construct received consumption theory as a model for choice theory, we shall now make explicit our acceptance of an assumption upon consumption sets, which for Debreu is a separate axiom, which he expresses:[6]

X_L is connected.

The implications of attributing connectedness to a set will come up again later in this book when we consider the connectedness of preferences.[7] For the moment, it is enough to remark that connectedness implies that the set at issue is all of one piece, that it is not, so to speak, made up of subsets that are separate and not joined to one another. Evidently our Axiom 8, by identifying the commodity space X_L with a subspace of Euclidean space, already implies its connectedness.

Notice that, if the consumer is to optimize, the *attainable* subset of his commodity set, which we shall write "A_c," must be bounded and closed.[8] Otherwise there will be no best point or best set of points, unless, of course, he reaches a satiated point or area within the attainable set.

No new axiom, however, is needed to guarantee this. Axiom 7 postulates that there is at least one x_0 in the attainable set (of choice theory) to which no point is preferred. But the attainable consumption set A_c is a *proper* subset of the attainable set of general choice theory. (Some attainable choices are attainable consumption choices.) So we assume that the consumption set is a model for the axioms of choice theory. Then Axiom 7 will apply to the attainable consumption set—there will be some consumption choice to which no attainable choice is preferred.

The axioms so far adopted ensure us smooth, sleek, and well-behaved commodity sets. Notice, however, that

[6]Gerard Debreu, *Theory of Value, An Axiomatic Analysis of Economic Equilibrium*, Cowles Foundation Monograph 17, John Wiley & Sons, Inc., New York, 1959, p. 53.

[7]See below, pp. 145-146.

[8]Recall the discussion of Axiom 7 in Chapter 9.

they tell us absolutely nothing about the structure of preferences. For a commodity set to be continuously divisible and connected does not tell us that preferences have the same properties. Continuity of divisibility in a physical object may, of course, make it likely that we have continuous patterns of preference about it. This is not, however, by any means entailed: remember the drug example. On the whole, the *chemicals used in* prescriptions approximate to being continuously divisible, but this does not mean that they give rise to continuous preference patterns. We are interested in the *right* prescription, not in an infinite set of slightly stronger and slightly weaker ones. More will be said of this when we discuss continuity assumptions upon preference.[9]

In this chapter, we began on very familiar ground. This is hardly surprising, since choices among bundles of commodities are simply a subset of choices in general. However, the further development of the received theory of consumers' behavior depends, as we are beginning to see, precisely on introducing special restrictions on our general theory, restrictions designed to delineate the theory of consumption and the theory of exchange as such. These restrictions necessarily take us further and further from general choice theory. Throughout the rest of this book, the special axioms needed for different special models for choice theory and the theorems derived from them will be more directly before our attention than the seven basic axioms of Part 1. Do not forget, however, that the seven fundamental axioms underlie everything we ever say in this book and that a change in any one of them would have consequences running through the *entire body* of mathematical economics.

There are clearly two sides to a theory of consumption: on the one hand, there are consumption sets, and on the other hand, there are the preferences of the consumers. We have, therefore, in this chapter placed assumptions first upon the character of commodity sets. In the chapters that follow we shall consider the assumptions that have to be placed upon the preferences of consumers in order to generate the received theory which explains their behavior in consumption situations. The first few necessary axioms, which are among the most powerful and controversial, will take our attention immediately in Chapter 14.

[9]See below, pp. 142-147.

1. Why should young intellectuals in Europe in the 1950s have found economic theory a natural field of interest and excitement, while American students did not?

2. Consider the following facts: (1) a large section of the population of the continental United States has probably reached an economic level at which physical satiation exists with respect to many conventional commodities; (2) a large section of the population of the United States still lives notoriously in conditions of the direst poverty; (3) a large part of the population of the world still lives in conditions of dire poverty. In the light of these facts comment on the following statements: (1) "The increasing of physical output is no longer an intellectually exciting possibility." (2) "The great challenge of our age is an overwhelming increase in physical output." (3) "A fully contemporary economic theory needs to be able to cope with showing the relations between sheer physical maximizing and many more sophisticated optimizing activities."

3. What are commodity sets and how are they related to choice sets?

4. Is the ordered couple (a bullfight ticket, Marina) equal to the ordered couple (Karen, a bullfight ticket)?

5. Is the assumption of continuous divisibility of commodity sets any less disastrous to the construction of consumption theory than a similar assumption would be in general choice theory?

6. If it is true that you can hire a Rolls Royce in New York for $5.00 an hour, how does this affect your attitude toward the realism of Axiom 8?

7. Given the following three facts in an imaginary economy, (1) Rolls Royces may be hired at varying rates for any period from five minutes up; (2) inhabitants of this economy are interested in Rolls Royces only for the prestige derived from its being universally known that they own a car of this make; (3) hired Rolls Royces can be distinguished from owned Rolls Royces at sight; comment on the following: (1) the relations between an assumption of continuity on commodity spaces and an assumption of continuity on preferences, and (2) the prospects of investing in the Rolls Royce hiring industry in the said economy.

14

AXIOMS
OF
INSATIABILITY
AND
CONVEXITY

THE AXIOM OF INSATIABILITY

The assumption embodied in the next axiom that we shall consider has a long history in microtheory as an informal, even as an implicit, assumption, although it has only recently been formalized.

It will be recalled from our discussion of the Hicksian revolution[1] that when Sir John Hicks popularized the indifference-curve account of choice at the end of the 1930s, he used a geometric construction that showed only the bottom left-hand corner of a complete system of curves with closure round a satiated area, as in Fig. 14-1.

Hicks concentrated on what Allen had called the "effective region," where the curves show no satiation for *either* or for *both* commodities. It will be recalled that Hicks and Allen were fully aware of the whole structure,

[1]See Chapter 6, pp. 45-57.

so that their decision to confine analysis to the effective region clearly was quite deliberate.

We have already remarked that the world of those days was not such as to make the prospects of widespread satiation seem pressing. It may surprise the reader, however, to learn that not only introductory texts but also intermediate and advanced ones still habitually present consumption theory within the straitjacket of the Hicks-Allen effective region, so that no recognition of satiation appears anywhere in the picture.

Contemporary formalists adopt an explicit axiom, which is sometimes called the Axiom of "Nonsatiation," but this axiom is much less restrictive in its effects and exists to serve one simple purpose.

You will recall from the discussion of open Hicksian indifference[2] that in the effective region of an indifference map there is a single clear criterion for optimizing, namely, tangency between an indifference curve and the frontier of the attainable region. This simplicity disappears the moment curves close and the frontier of attainability passes beyond the satiated area.

The question now arises: Can we combine the tempting formal simplicity of the Hicksian theory with a recognition of the important fact of satiation? The answer, happily, is Yes, and the most economical way to achieve this result is to adopt an axiom introduced by Gerard Debreu:[3] "*No satiation consumption exists for the ith consumer.*" The effect of this axiom, which he calls the "Insatiability Assumption on Preferences," is simply to rule out one's being satiated with *all* commodities.

Consider first the case of a two-commodity world. In such a world, Debreu's assumption would make the indifference curves look like those in Fig. 14-2. In such a world, we may be satiated, beyond certain points, with milk alone and also with brownies alone, but there are combinations of the two things in which we would still prefer to have more of them both. Given the right combination, the whole existing stock of both would not satiate us.

Notice that, in this two-commodity world, the effect of Debreu's axiom is to allow the curves to become horse-

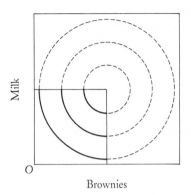

Milk

O   Brownies

FIGURE 14-1

The Hicks-Allen effective region

[2]See Chapter 6, pp. 55-57.

[3]Gerard Debreu, *Theory of Value: An Axiomatic Analysis of Economic Equilibrium*, Cowles Foundation Monograph 17, John Wiley & Sons, Inc., 1959, p. 55. Italics are in the original.

shoe shaped, exhibiting satiation for either commodity in excessive amounts. But the familiar section of curve showing satiation with *both*, the section that closes the curves, does not appear. Nor does the satiated area, or point.

The tangency rule for optimizing clearly holds—as the frontier[4] of the attainable region moves from F_0 to F_3, the consumer moves to more and more preferred positions from x_0 to x_3.

Debreu's axiom, however, is even less restrictive the moment we move to a space of a higher number of dimensions. Consider a three-commodity world. Here the axiom allows closure and satiation in the plane representing two of the commodities. Let the surface of a tray represent the familiar Edgeworth box. On the tray stand a set of nested cups. Now, if you look down from above, the cups can be

[4]The frontier has been drawn linear, thus embodying the usual assumption of consumption theory that an individual cannot change relative prices by his consumption decisions; and successive positions of the frontier are drawn parallel, showing rising income (in terms of the two commodities) at fixed relative prices. This frontier, which is the Hicksian price line, or budget restraint, or wealth constraint (Debreu), thus takes for granted the explanation of pricing in a market and thus borrows from the theory of exchange. I ask the reader's indulgence for the anticipation of the next part of the book, but the actual *issue* over the Axiom of Nonsatiation does not in fact depend on *what* exact shape the frontier of the attainable region has. The character of the wealth constraint will be further discussed in Chapter 15, and the nature of prices will be explored when we come to the theory of exchange.

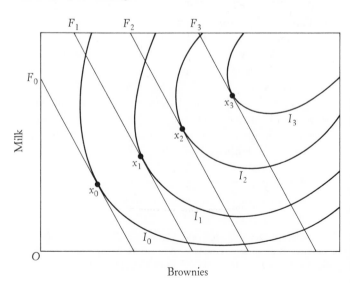

FIGURE 14-2

A two-commodity world with Debreu's Assumption of Insatiability

seen as closed curves within a two space. But looked at from the side, they can be seen as higher and higher horse-shoe curves, showing the existence of preferred positions, in the plane at right angles to the surface of the tray.

Thus even in a model with as few as three commodities, the axiom allows complete satiation with two of these. And the tangency rule still holds: The frontier of the attainable region becomes a three-dimensional plane; and optimizing consists in picking the indifference surface, the "cup," which is tangent to the agent's given attainability plane.

Generalizing, if the commodity space X is a space of L dimensions, then the axiom allows the consumer to be satiated in X_{L-1} dimensions, or in any proper subspace of X_L.

Clearly this axiom gives adequate recognition to the facts of satiation, since the only case ruled out is a world wherein one cannot improve his position by having more of *anything*. We simply postulate that, for any point x_0 in the commodity space, there exists a point x_1 that would be preferred. This may be formalized as our Axiom of Insatiability on Consumption Preferences:

Axiom 9 $(x_0) \exists x_1 (x_1 \, P \, x_0)$

We thus allow for the important consideration of building into the structure of our theory of consumers' behavior our informal insights about the need for improving the style and quality of things and not just for consuming ever-greater quantities of the same old things.

To give the simplest picture of the theory of consumption, we can go back to a two space, regarding this as simply a slice, if you like, of a commodity space of more dimensions. You could suppose that the consumer is already satiated in the other dimensions.

We are moving toward a society in which most material things will be available in redundant quantities,[5] and the things about which people will remain not satiated will consist mainly of experiences, a situation that most people over twenty today find it hard even to imagine.

[5]You may ask "what about the poor?" But if you picture the kind and degree of affluence made possible by the sort of technology I am speaking of, you will see that its existence entails either the abolition of poverty through social reform, or revolution. And the increasing satiation of the affluent youth with material things is far from irrelevant.

To emphasize this and to stress the radical nature of the sort of commodity about which we may not be satiated in days to come, I shall label the axes of our two space rather abstractly, simply as "sounds," written "S," and "textures," written "T." In the two space consisting of all nonnegative quantities of S and T, we shall now get indifference curves that may be horseshoe-shaped but that will not close or contain segments for which both S and T are redundant or have a satiated area.

THE AXIOM OF CONTINUITY OF PREFERENCE

So far, however, we have no axiom that ensures the existence of continuous indifference *curves* at all. We have assumed their existence informally in Part 1 as a special case of indifference sets, and have used them in this chapter to illustrate the force of the Axiom of Insatiability. This axiom, however, does not *entail* their existence: it simply asserts that for any x_0, some x_1 exists such that x_1 is *preferred* to x_0. Nor, you will recall, do the assumptions of continuity and connectedness of the commodity space, made in Chapter 13, entail the continuity of preferences. Existing consumption theories, however, habitually depend on indifference curves, so the time has come to consider an axiom that guarantees their existence.

You will remember that I have objected strongly to the assumption of indifference curves (except in special cases) in pure general choice theory. Is it all right to assume their existence in the special theories of consumption and exchange?

Obviously, we consume many things for which there are not even a large *finite* set of combinations of two commodities that would leave us indifferent. Consumers' behavior theory from Edgeworth right down to Debreu has assumed the continuity of preference and indifference. To give any picture of received consumption theory, this assumption must be made.

But it is with great misgivings that I shall follow tradition here. When many or most commodities were very commonplace physical things that could be bought by weight or quantity, like flour or sugar, the assumption was probably not too bad (although physical divisibility in a commodity does not entail continuity of preference— remember the doctor's prescription). But one can foresee that in our future more and more of the things with which we are not satiated are likely to be rather esoteric commodities, which very possibly will come in only one minimal form. If the nature of consumption changes in this way, the axiom we are about to adopt will have to be dropped even from consumers' behavior theory. Pending this, since we are axiomatizing existing consumption theory, we shall go ahead.

The axiom guaranteeing the existence of indifference curves can be introduced by considering the structure of a pair of sets that will be important to us for a number of reasons. Consider any point x_0 in the two space in Fig. 14-3, which represents all nonnegative combinations of T and S.

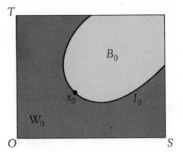

FIGURE 14-3
The sets B_0 and W_0

What is the set of bundles that are at *least as good* as x_0? What is the set of bundles such that x_0 is *no worse than any bundle in the set?* We shall use the term "better set[6] associated with x_0," written "B_0" for the set of all bundles x such that x is preferred to x_0, or is indifferent to x_0. Symbolically,

Definition 14-1: $(x_0)(x_1)(x_1 \in B_0 \Leftrightarrow x_1 P x_0 \vee x_1 I x_0)$

We shall use the term "worse set associated with x_0" for the set of all bundles x such that x_0 is preferred to x or is indifferent to x. Symbolically,

Definition 14-2: $(x_0)(x_1)(x_1 \in W_0 \Leftrightarrow x_0 P x_1 \vee x_0 I x_1)$

These two sets B_0 and W_0 do not form a partition of the commodity set, since they have at least one element in common, namely, x_0. Whether their intersection $B_0 \cap W_0$ is more than the unit set $\{x_0\}$ depends upon what we assume about the indifference sets. Notice that by Axiom 1, $B_0 \cup W_0 = X$, their union exhausts the commodity set.

The axioms needed to guarantee the existence of indifference curves may now be illustrated as in Fig. 14-4, in which circles stand for points to which x_0 is preferred. Asterisks indicate the positions of x_0 itself and of all points indifferent to it. Finally, triangles mark points preferred to x_0. B_0 is therefore the set of triangles plus the set of asterisks, and W_0 is the set of circles plus the set of asterisks. The boundary of the better and worse sets associated with x_0 is not a continuous curve but simply a finite set of points at some distance from one another. If we are to

FIGURE 14-4
B_0 and W_0 as finite sets

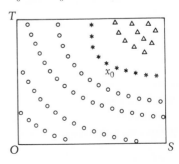

[6]Peter Newman's term (see *The Theory of Exchange,* Prentice-Hall, Inc., Englewood Cliffs, N.J., 1965, *passim*).

get indifference *curves* we need assumptions that will fill in the gaps. If we are to state these assumptions we must pause to devote a little time to extending our formal apparatus slightly in order to include certain elementary properties of sets of points.

A set of points S is said to be *bounded* if there is some square (or cube of the relevant number of dimensions), however large, that contains all its points. A set is *unbounded* if it has points that are arbitrarily far from its origin, as in the case of a straight line, indefinitely extended.

Now consider the sets B_0 and W_0, which are proper subsets of X in Fig. 14-5. Choosing any point x, draw a circle around x, making the radius of the circle as small as you please. The set of points contained in this arbitrarily small circle is called a "neighborhood" of x. A point x is a "boundary point" of the set B_0 if and only if an arbitrarily small neighborhood of x contains at least one point of W_0 as well as a point of B_0. In Fig. 14-5, x_0 is such a boundary point. A point such as x_1 is said to be an "interior point" of B_0.

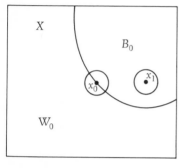

FIGURE 14-5

Neighborhoods of a boundary point and an interior point

A set is said to be "closed" if it contains all its boundary points. We may add that if a set is both bounded and closed it is called "compact." ("Compactness," however, is defined in terms of other notions.)

A set is said to be "open" if each of its points is an interior point; that is, if it does not contain its boundary points.

[7]I use the word "topology" to refer to that branch of contemporary mathematics which takes the concept of open set as primitive. The notions of topology will be adopted here without regarding them as new primitive concepts, just as the concepts of formal logic and set theory have been used. Once more recall the discussion of this practice in Chapter 8, pp. 69-70.

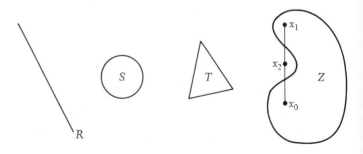

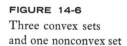

FIGURE 14-6

Three convex sets and one nonconvex set

A point set S is said to be "convex" if and only if, for all x_0, x_1 in S, any point x_2 of the straight line joining x_0 and x_1 is also in S.

In Fig. 14-6, R, S, and T are convex sets, but Z is not, since x_2 is not in Z despite being on the straight line joining x_0 and x_1.

The more restrictive concept of "strict" convexity may be defined in terms of the concepts of neighborhood, boundary point, and interior point. Let x_0 and x_1 be elements in a set S. Then S is strictly convex if and only if every point x_2 on the straight line joining x_0 and x_1 is an interior point of S. That is to say, for any such point x_2 on the straight line, x_2 has a neighborhood which lies wholly in S. In Fig. 14-6, only the set S is strictly convex.

We may speak of strict convexity, not of an entire set, but of part of its boundary. A convex set S may be said to be *strictly convex in a boundary point*[8] x_0. This condition is fulfilled when all points on the line joining x_0 to some other point of S, say x_1, except x_0 and x_1 themselves, are interior points of S.

The set S in Fig. 14-7 is strictly convex in x_0 but not in x_1 or x_2. Notice that it follows from the definition of a convex set that it is an infinite set. Starting with any set, finite or infinite, one may construct a convex set in the following way. Simply fill in all the points lying between any two elements in the original set. This can be carried on until the resultant set is a convex set: "The extended set so obtained is called the 'convex hull' of the original set."[9]

Every convex set is "connected." A line segment is, so to speak, all of a piece. Since any two points in a convex set S may be joined by a line such that every point on the line is a member of S, it follows that the set S is all of a piece. Such sets are said to be connected.

Some spaces divide naturally into two or more parts, like all Gaul; for example, the space composed simply of the two lines A and B in Fig. 14-8.

On the other hand, we can readily think of sets that

[8]See Tjalling C. Koopmans, *Three Essays on the State of Economic Science*, McGraw-Hill Book Company, New York, 1957, p. 24.

[9]R. G. D. Allen, *Mathematical Economics*, 2d ed., The Macmillan Company, New York, 1965, p. 386.

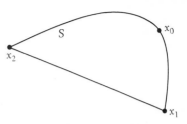

FIGURE 14-7

A convex set strictly convex in x_0

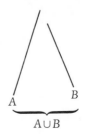

FIGURE 14-8

$A \cup B$, a set that is not connected

cannot be divided in any natural way, such as a single line, a triangle, a disc, a continuous curve.[10]

We are now ready to impose upon the set B_0 associated with any point x_0 the assumptions that guarantee the existence of indifference curves.

THE CONVEXITY AND CONNECTEDNESS OF B_0

We first assume that the better set associated with any point x_0 is a convex set.

Axiom 10 B_0 *is convex.*

As we know, this axiom entails that B_0 is also connected and ensures that B_0 is filled out and has a continuous boundary. The boundary can, however, take the form shown in Fig. 14-9*b*. That is to say, the boundary of B_0 can have linear segments. This follows from our not having assumed *strict* convexity in our Axiom 10. Consider the set of boundary points of B_0 that make up the set I_0. This infinite set, composed of points all indifferent to x_0, would be exactly the indifference curve we have been looking for. We can ensure that *just this* set of points is indifferent to x_0 by adopting the following:

Axiom 11   *There are no interior points of* $B_0 \cap W_0$.

The better and worse sets associated with x_0 can have as intersection only the set of points indifferent to x_0. If they intersect just in the set of boundary points, I_0, we get exactly the indifference curve we need for consumption theory.

Notice that a result of assuming that $B_0 \cap W_0$ is a set of *boundary points* is to rule out thick indifference sets, such as that shown in Fig. 14-10. As drawn, the indifference set I_0 has elements, such as x_1, that are *interior points* of B_0; x_1 has a neighborhood all of whose points are in B_0. Such an indifference set is said to be "thick."

FIGURE 14-9

Forms of B_0 allowable under Axiom 10

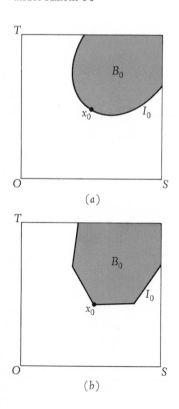

(a)

(b)

[10]A good introductory treatment of the concepts hinted at in this section is George F. Simmons, *Introduction to Topology and Modern Analysis*, McGraw-Hill Book Company, New York, 1963, Part I. An advanced treatment, written with the interests of choice theory in mind, is Claude Berge, *Espaces Topologiques et Fonctions Multivoques*, Dunod, Paris, 1959 (English translation: *Topological Spaces*, The Macmillan Company, New York, 1963.)

What is here described as a "thick indifference set" may well exist in life: there probably are many commodities for which small increases in the quantity of one (the other remaining constant), or in both, do not move us to a preferred position. Perhaps only larger changes matter to us. Essentially, however, this argument in favor of thick indifference sets is an appeal to the unreality of assumptions of continuous divisibility. We have already noted the unreality of these assumptions, when we made the transition from general choice theory to consumption theory. Having embraced assumptions of continuity in order to axiomatize received consumption theory, we might as well be hanged for a sheep as a lamb, so I have ruled out thick indifference sets as being a half-baked return to the discontinuity of the real world. In general choice theory, we habitually used one thick indifference set, the satiated area, but this is already ruled out for consumption theory by the Axiom of Insatiability, Axiom 9.

Having thus made sure that we shall have indifference curves throughout the theory of consumers' behavior based on our axiom set, we turn to the statement of this theory.

1. What is the effect of Debreu's Axiom of Insatiability upon the indifference curves in a two-commodity world?

QUESTIONS

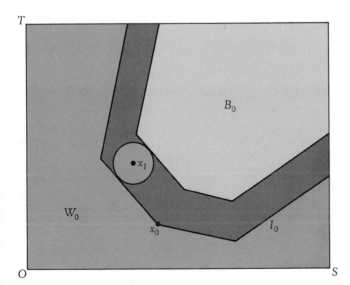

FIGURE 14-10

A thick indifference set

2. In a three-commodity world, with how many commodities does this axiom allow the consumer to be satiated?

3. Is the Axiom of Insatiability inconsistent with Axiom 7 of choice theory? If not, why not?

4. Under what circumstances might $B_0 \cap W_0$ be $\{x_0\}$? On what assumptions could $B_0 \cap W_0$ be $\{x_0, x_1, x_2\}$?

5. Restate Axiom 7 in terms of the concepts of boundedness and closedness.

6. Is the set composed of the single point x_0 a convex set? Can a finite set be convex? Is $\{x\}$ connected?

7. What is the convex hull of the set composed of all the asterisks and all the triangles in Fig. 14-4?

8. Does Axiom 10, "B_0 is convex," guarantee the existence of indifference curves? Describe exactly what this axiom allows.

9. If there exists a point, x_1, which has a neighborhood all of whose points are in $B_0 \cap W_0$, what is implied about the character of indifference curves?

10. In what way is the assumption that I_0 is a set of boundary points a departure from realism?

15

THEORY
OF
CONSUMPTION

The axioms so far adopted provide the consumer with a consumption set that is continuously divisible and connected, and they guarantee that his ordering of the points in this set will be representable by an indifference map. They thus exhibit the character of received consumption theory, as a model for the theory of choice. To exhibit his optimizing behavior we need now only to specify the frontier of the attainable subset of his commodity set. In received consumption theory this frontier is called the "wealth constraint" or "price line." Given the wealth constraint, the consumer chooses a consumption (a bundle of commodities) x_0, which is optimal according to the axioms of general choice theory and of consumption theory. In particular, the Axiom of Insatiability, Axiom 9, guarantees that x will lie on the *frontier* of his attainable region, and

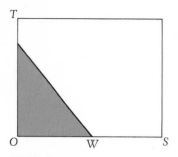

FIGURE 15-1

The wealth constraint, W

not within it. This is called an "equilibrium consumption for the consumer."

We now turn to the task of characterizing the limits of the consumer's attainable set, that is to say, his wealth constraint. For the moment, we do not investigate how commodities come to have prices in the market (this must wait for the theory of exchange, which will be developed in Part 4). Saying that the commodities available to the consumer have fixed prices amounts to no more than saying that, like Crusoe, he can have so many coconuts *or* so much J & B or any combination of the two, except that we now add the condition: *at some fixed rate*. From the many cases that might exist for Crusoe, we pick the one in which the frontier of the attainable region is linear. This linear frontier, shown in Fig. 15-1, is the wealth constraint.

The wealth constraint must now be characterized in terms of notions derived from the theory of point sets. This will make precise the concept of an optimal point and thus the notion of a consumer's equilibrium.

BOUNDING HYPERPLANES

In any two-dimensional space, let H be any straight line. Then H divides the space into three subsets: points to one side of the line, points on the line H, and points on the other side. In a three-dimensional space, the same is true of any plane H, within the space (Fig. 15-2).

A similar set of points H may be considered as dividing a space of any number of dimensions into three proper and nonempty subsets. In this case, the set H is called a "hyperplane." In a two space, the set H takes the form of a one-dimensional line; in a three space it is a two-dimensional plane; in the commodity space, X_L, the set H is therefore an $(L - 1)$-dimensional hyperplane.

FIGURE 15-2

Division of a three-dimensional space by a plane H

We shall continue to conduct our argument in terms of our familiar proper subspace of the commodity space X_L, consisting of only the two commodities T and S. So "H" will appear as a straight line. Nevertheless, we shall always refer to "H" as a hyperplane, since our argument applies to the whole commodity space X_L and the two-dimensional pictures of the point sets at issue have merely the status of illustrations.

The set of all points x, to one specified side of H, taken together with the set of all points $x \in H$, is known as a "closed half-space." It follows that any hyperplane H

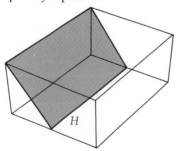

divides any space into two half-spaces, which have H as their intersection.

A hyperplane H is said to be "bounding" for a given point set K, if and only if all points of K are contained in one of the two half-spaces determined by H (Fig. 15-3). A bounding hyperplane of a set K is said to be a "supporting" hyperplane of K if and only if it contains at least one point of the boundary of K (Fig. 15-3b). H is said to be a "separating" hyperplane of two sets, K and S, if and only if it is a bounding hyperplane to both S and K, and K lies in one of the half-spaces defined by H while S lies in the other (Fig. 15-4). Furthermore, if two sets K and S have in common a boundary point or points, any separating hyperplane they have must be a supporting hyperplane to both K and S (Fig. 15-4b).

The wealth constraint is a hyperplane in the commodity space X_L, and optimizing manifestly consists in finding in the commodity space a point x_0 such that the wealth hyperplane, written "WH," is a supporting hyperplane to the better set associated with x_0 (Fig. 15-5).

The traditional concept of *tangency* between the wealth constraint and the indifference curve is simply a special case of the above and is shown in Fig. 15-5c. Notice that the situation in Fig. 15-5a, where x_0 is a corner point, offers no problem for the notion of a supporting hyperplane, nor does that in Fig. 15-5b, in which x_0 is not unique and WH and B_0 have as intersection a line segment of the boundary of B_0.

This seems to be the moment to draw attention to the difference between the uses of "convex" in two formal languages. Contemporary mathematical economists use the word "convex" to refer to properties of point sets, which are said to be "weakly" or "strictly" convex or "strictly convex in a boundary point" in the manner briefly indicated

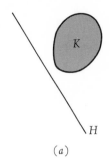

(a)

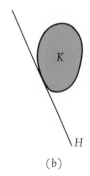

(b)

FIGURE 15-3

Two bounding hyperplanes, one of which (b) is also supporting

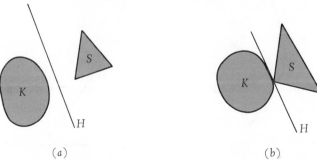

(a) (b)

FIGURE 15-4

A separating hyperplane, (a), and a separating hyperplane that is also a supporting hyperplane to both K and S, (b)

in the last chapter. Writers from Edgeworth to Hicks, concerned with indifference curves, used the word "convex" to refer to properties of a *curve*, adapting for this purpose the concepts of classical mathematics. The traditional position may be expressed by saying that "each indifference curve is *convex* to each axis of reference, implying that ever larger and larger increases in the purchase of one good are required to compensate (i.e., to preserve a given level of indifference) for a steadily decreasing purchase of the other good."[1]

For Hicks, the convexity of indifference curves and the assumption of a linear wealth constraint guaranteed the existence of an optimal point x_0, which was also unique. This point was the equilibrium of the consumer.

On our axioms, there will exist at least one optimal point x_0, lying on some indifference curve I_0, whose points are boundary points of a convex set B_0, such that there is a wealth hyperplane through x_0.

The point x_0 need not, however, be unique, since the wealth hyperplane may go through a line segment of the boundary of B_0. In that case, the most preferred available indifference set is a transfinite set, and the consumer is optimizing if he picks any point at random from this set.

RATES OF SUBSTITUTION

Our axiom of convexity allows the boundary of the better set associated with any point x_0 to have linear segments. The two limiting cases of Fig. 15-6 may be contrasted to introduce some concepts important in the theory of consumers' behavior.

FIGURE 15-5

The wealth hyperplane, WH, supporting B_0 in three cases, case (c) being covered by traditional theory

[1]R. G. D. Allen, *Mathematical Analysis for Economists*, 2d ed., The Macmillan Company, New York, 1966, p. 126. Italics are in the original.

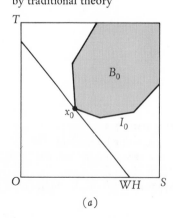

(a)

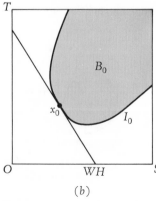

(b)

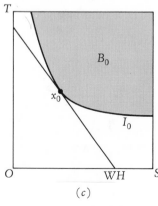

(c)

For an indifference curve to be simply one straight line, as is I_0 in Fig. 15-6a, would imply that the rate at which the consumer was willing to substitute one commodity for the other did not change, no matter how much or how little he had of one of them. He is indifferent whether he has all T, all S, or any combination, at a given fixed rate. Any two such goods are said to be "perfect substitutes," and from the point of view of economic theory they may be treated as one good.

Contrast the indifference curve I_0 in Fig. 15-6b. This is the opposite extreme: the case in which two things are of interest to the consumer only in some exact combination—like bolts that need exactly one nut each. Starting from x_0, if S is held at a constant quantity, no increase in the amount of T moves the consumer to a preferred position. Again in this case, there is something to be said for treating the unit "one nut plus one bolt" as a single commodity. Indifference curves will be somewhere between these limiting cases.

As you move along an indifference curve, such as I_0 in Fig. 15-7, the slope of the curve indicates how much of one commodity must be offered to the consumer to compensate him for losing units of the other. Where either commodity set or preferences are not bound by continuity assumptions, there may be *no* alternative bundle that

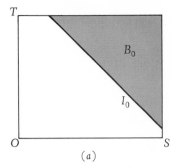

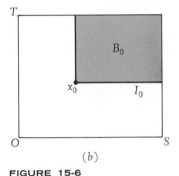

(b)

FIGURE 15-6

Indifference curve, I_0, for (a) perfect substitutes and (b) case of zero substitution

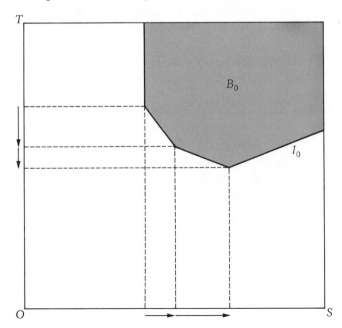

FIGURE 15-7

Changing rate of substitution of T for S

exactly compensates the consumer for the loss of another—
which is another way of saying that the set B_0 may not be
convex (and therefore may not be connected). In general
choice theory, there may be members of the choice set for
whose loss *nothing* would compensate: Karen, for instance,
does not compensate me for losing Marina. In general, if
a set of individual objects of choice (as distinct from a set
of indifference sets) is linearly ordered, no one member
compensates for the loss of another, since, by definition,
no two members are indifferent.

As you move along I_0 in Fig. 15-7, the rate of
substitution changes but not continuously—it remains the
same along linear segments of the curve. In real life, a
person's rate of substitution between two commodities
might not register a change until his holdings of them were
substantially different, and the assumption of weak convexity of B_0 that we have built into consumers' behavior
theory expresses this fact. Hicksian indifference curves,
which were assumed to be (strictly) convex to the axes,
were given a character that ensured that they would show
continuously changing marginal rates of substitution of one
good for the other. This concept was a consequence of
using the techniques of classical mathematics. It is not
needed in the consumption theory of, for instance, Debreu.

CONCLUSION   Our sketch of the structure of the received contemporary theory of consumption is now complete. In
Chapter 16 we leave the study of optimizing by an individual agent and turn to the simplest possible model for
the theory of an *economy*: The analysis of exchange in a
society composed of only two people, who are assumed
to own stocks of goods but not to engage in production.

QUESTIONS   1. Is the attainable set of consumption theory a closed
set? Of what two significant sets of points is the
attainable consumption set the intersection? Is it a
closed half-space?

2. If a wealth hyperplane WH is bounding for a better
set B_0, is the consumer optimizing at some boundary
point of B_0?

3. If WH is supporting to B_0 in some point $x_0 \in B_0$,
does x_0 represent the equilibrium of the consumer?

4. If WH_0 is supporting to B_0 in x_0, and WH_1 represents a different set of relative prices, can WH_1 be supporting to B_0 in x_0?

5. How would you answer question 4 if the boundary of B_0, I_0, were supposed to be strictly convex?

6. Explain the concept of rates of substitution. How is the form of this concept changed as we go from Hicksian to contemporary assumptions in consumption theory?

7. If the rate of substitution of a commodity "S" for a commodity "T" remains unchanged throughout an indifference curve, what does this imply?

8. If the rate of substitution of S for T changes continuously throughout an indifference curve what axiomatic structure is being assumed?

9. In what sense does the Hicksian assumption about the convexity of indifference curves represent a departure from reality?

10. If the better set associated with any bundle x_0 be supposed not to be a connected set, what would this imply about the existence of bundles x_1, x_2, which exactly compensate the consumer for the loss of x_0?

Part
4
Economic Systems

16

THEORY
OF
EXCHANGE

Viola: "What country, friends, is this?"
Captain: "This is Illyria, lady."

William Shakespeare

We are now ready to introduce a concept which, in conventional textbooks, would assuredly have been discussed in the first chapter—if not on the first page: The concept of an *economy*, or economic *system*.

We have at our disposal now an axiom set adequate to the explanation of the optimizing behavior of individual consumers in such a system. We have not yet discussed producers, but a theory of pure exchange need not involve production (as we shall see). We are thus ready to construct the simplest model for the theory of an economic system, namely, one based on pure exchange.

It will be shown in this chapter that the core of the theory of a private ownership economy is provided by the theory of exchange. This was known intuitively to Adam Smith, was given brilliant mathematical expression by Edgeworth, and then lay fallow until certain highly sophisticated developments in the past few years.

There is, however, a striking and fascinating paradox about this theory. It will be discussed at length in Chapter 17, but its existence should be noted from the very beginning. It is this: Those who think that a book on economics should be about how a market economy works cannot but regard the theory of exchange as of the essence of economics *on their terms* (particularly in the light of the powerful results of a number of recent writers[1]). On the other hand, the pure theory of exchange illustrates one of the central themes of this book: it explains many relationships that have nothing to do with the conventional market economy. *Whenever* two or more optimizing agents are faced with possibilities of mutual advantage and conflict, Edgeworth's theory applies. The states of affairs about which they agree or disagree need not be bundles of conventional commodities; they can be policies, strategies—anything, in fact, that can be a matter of sharing or conflict.

The present chapter will develop the theory of exchange in terms of its classical role, the explanation of prices in a market economy. In Chapter 17 it will be shown that the same structure underlies systems that might be thought to have nothing in common with a pricing system.

BILATERAL EXCHANGE

The simplest possible model for the theory of an exchange system is one involving only two parties and only two commodities—a system of bilateral exchange. This situation can be handled with perfect convenience in a

[1]The sources include Martin Shubick, "Edgeworth Market Games," in R. D. Luce and A. W. Tucker (eds.), *Contributions to the Theory of Games*, Princeton University Press, Princeton, N.J., 1958, vol. IV, pp. 267-278; Herbert Scarf, *An Analysis of Markets with a Large Number of Participants*, The Princeton University Conference, Ivy Curtis Press, Philadelphia, 1962; Herbert Scarf and Gerard Debreu, "A Limit Theorem on the Core of an Economy," *International Economic Review*, vol. 4 (1963), pp. 235-247; Gerard Debreu, "On a Theorem of Scarf," *Review of Economic Studies*, vol. 30 (1962-1963), pp. 177-180; R. J. Aumann, "Markets with a Continuum of Traders," *Econometrica*, vol. 32 (1964), pp. 39-50; Karl Vind, "Edgeworth Allocations in an Exchange Economy with Many Traders," *International Economic Review*, vol. 5, no. 2 (1964), pp. 165-177; Peter Newman, *The Theory of Exchange*, Prentice-Hall, Inc., Englewood Cliffs, N.J., 1965.

two space; and as it happens, many of its properties are characteristic of exchange in general, irrespective of the number of participants.

Each of our two parties is thought of as possessing a commodity bundle, his object being to exchange this for a more preferred bundle. The total stock of commodities held by the two traders collectively is assumed to be fixed throughout the analysis. This is often said to rule out production in the model, but it only does so in a very special sense, which has to do with the set of decisions to be analyzed.

The two stocks of commodities may have been *physically* produced; they need not be supposed to have fallen from heaven. The theory of pure exchange does not include an analysis of the making of production *decisions* in *response* to the exchange situation. The goods are *there* (however they got there), and the concern of the theory is to explain how they will be exchanged.

Peter Newman in his recent book[2] laid stress on the unworldliness of models of exchange between two people by writing about Adam and Eve. I do not know about the reader, but—granting Newman the distinction of having improved upon Milton—I am a bit fed up with Adam and Eve. Newman is right, however, that we should pick characters with a certain aura of unreality, since we want to bear in mind that a model of bilateral exchange is very far from being a full picture of the many-dimensional world we live in. To maintain an appropriate gravity and yet introduce variety, I suggest we pick the late Queen Victoria and, naturally, her famous prime minister, Benjamin Disraeli. We must suppose them transplanted in Lewis Carrollian fashion to an elysian world where they are the only inhabitants and are endowed with fixed stocks of two commodities, both of which they each desire. We could assume them each to hold, before trade, any combination of the two commodities, but it is most convenient to take the case where each holds the little society's *entire stock* of one good. Thus we may write the commodity that is initially wholly held by Victoria as "V" goods and those held by Disraeli as "D" goods.

We now construct an Edgeworth box, whose horizontal boundaries represent the quantity of "V" goods in

[2]Newman, *op. cit.* My treatment of exchange owes much to Newman's book.

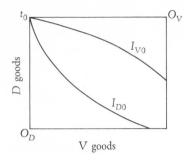

FIGURE 16-1

Victoria and Disraeli
in Edgeworth-land

existence, with O_V as Victoria's origin, and whose vertical
sides measure Disraeli's stock of "D" goods, O_D being his
origin (Fig. 16-1).

In our discussion of Pareto optimality, we have
already made use of some of the concepts of Edgeworth's
theory of exchange, without going into the analysis of
trade as such.[3] This we must now take up.

If we assume that the total stock of each commodity
is in the hands of one person intially, then the initial
position of the system is at the corner point "t_0," which
may be read "the point of zero trade" (positions of the
system will be written $t_0, t_1, t_2, \ldots$).

The two indifference curves that appear in Fig. 16-1
have a special significance: both end in t_0. Since these
indifference curves can be attained without trade, Victoria
will not be interested in any curve of hers below I_{V0}, nor
will Disraeli be interested in any curve below his curve I_{D0}.
They will trade only by moving to points in the better
set associated with their indifference curves through t_0
(Fig. 16-2).

Observe that part of Victoria's better set is included
in Disraeli's worse set and that part of his better set is
included in her worse set. The two better sets, however,
do overlap, as is shown in Fig. 16-3. They have an
intersection.

As we saw in Chapter 8, one of the most fundamental operations upon sets is to find the set that includes
all the elements common to both of two sets, such as B_{D0}
and B_{V0}. This operation, of finding their *intersection*,[4] is

[3]See pp. 107-111.

[4]See pp. 74-75.

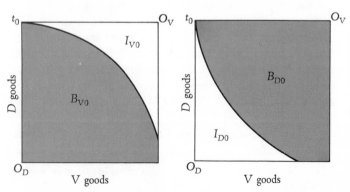

FIGURE 16-2

The better sets
associated with t_0
for Victoria and Disraeli

crucial to our present argument, since the trading set—or set of points t such that both parties gain by trade—is precisely the intersection, $B_{D0} \cap B_{V0}$. Notice that the *union* of the two sets, $B_{D0} \cup B_{V0}$ (the set of all points t such that t is a member of *either B_{V0} or B_{D0}*) is identical with the commodity space within the entire Edgeworth box. Notice that B_{D0}, B_{V0} and $B_{D0} \cap B_{V0}$ are all closed convex sets.

You will have noticed that I have drawn the better sets B_{D0} and B_{V0} in Figs. 1 to 3 of this chapter so that no satiation occurs with respect to either D goods or V goods, either for Victoria or Disraeli. The indifference curves I_{D0} and I_{V0} are *strictly* convex to their respective origins O_D and O_V, in the classical sense of Edgeworth and Hicks. To restrict the theory to these limits, two axioms must be imposed: An Axiom of Dominance that is powerful enough to rule out all occurrence of satiation within the Edgeworth box, and an axiom that ensures strict convexity of the indifference curves of both traders.

I have resisted such axioms in the theory of consumption. Should one give in to them in the theory of exchange? Ideally, the answer is obviously "No"—we have seen often enough how unrealistic they are. In an introduction to the theory of exchange, however, the case for their adoption is strong. First of all, enough has already been said in this chapter for you to have seen clearly how unrealistic an elementary model for the theory of exchange *must* be: If we are to picture it in a two space, we must confine ourselves to two traders, and only two commodities being exchanged. Most or all of one commodity must be somehow in the hands of one trader and most or all of the other commodity in the hands of the other. No account is offered of how they are produced. If we simplify things to this extent, we may as well adopt axioms that make the diagrams simple and clear and the proofs easy and intuitive; and it so happens that these axioms *do* vastly simplify things. Then again, it happens that most of the essential structure of the pure theory of exchange is preserved—and clearly visible—in the simple case. Finally, there is a historical point. Edgeworth largely created the pure theory of exchange, and it remained much as he left it until the very recent work of Scarf, Debreu, Aumann, and others in the sixties. Edgeworth assumes complete nonsatiation and classical, strict convexity of all indifference curves, so these

AXIOMS OF DOMINANCE AND STRICT CONVEXITY

FIGURE 16-3

The intersection of the better sets

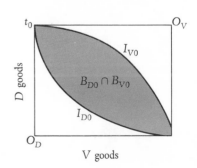

assumptions exhibit precisely the original Edgeworthian theory.

We shall accordingly begin by adopting an Axiom of Dominance. If there is no satiation, larger quantities of a commodity will dominate—will be preferred to—smaller quantities. If we rule out all satiation, a commodity bundle x_0 will be preferred to another bundle x_1 if x_0 *contains more of at least one commodity than x_1 and no less of any other*. We shall say that such a bundle x_0 is "greater than" x_1, and write this "$x_0 > x_1$." We may then symbolize our Axiom of Dominance[5] as:

Axiom 12[6] $(x_0)\,(x_1)\,(x_0 > x_1 \Rightarrow x_0\,P\,x_1)$

The effect of Axiom 12 shows in Fig. 16-4. It is clear that a point such as x_1 is greater than x_0; so also are x_2 and x_3. Each of these points represents a commodity bundle offering Disraeli more of at least one commodity and less of none. Two important sets may be distinguished. The upper shaded area, in which lie x_1, x_2 and x_3 is $\{x\,|\,x \geqq x_0\}$, the set of all x such that x is greater than or equal to x_0, which is called the "upper wedge" associated with x_0. The lower shaded area represents the "lower wedge" associated with x_0, consisting of the set of all points less than or equal to x_0, $\{x\,|\,x \leqq x_0\}$.

[5]Often called an Axiom of Monotonicity.

[6]It is perfectly correct to write out an axiom in full as we have been doing so far, and it seemed like good practice in symbolizing axioms and definitions in formal notation. It is, however, an accepted practice (which we shall now adopt) to drop a universal quantifier whose scope runs over the whole formula (see Patrick Suppes, *Introduction to Logic*, D. Van Nostrand Company, Inc., Princeton, N.J., 1957, pp. 58-62). By the *scope* of a quantifier one means the quantifier itself together with the smallest formula immediately following the quantifier, indicated by brackets, as, for instance, $|(x)\,()|$. The scope of the initial quantifiers in Axiom 12 is clearly the whole formula:

$$|(x_0)\,(x_1)\,(x_0 > x_1 \Rightarrow x_0\,P\,x_1)|$$

So we may drop the initial quantifiers and write the axiom more briefly as:

Axiom 12 $x_0 > x_1 \Rightarrow x_0\,P\,x_1$

An example of quantifiers that cannot be dropped in writing out a formula are, for instance, the existential quantifiers in Axiom 6:

$$\exists\,xAx \Rightarrow \exists\,xCx$$

The upper wedge, written "U_0," and the lower wedge, written "L_0," associated with x_0, intersect in a boundary point, namely x_0 itself. They are bounded and closed (and therefore compact), convex (and therefore connected) sets.

Notice that Axiom 12 is powerful enough to tell us the preference ranking of any point in two important proper subsets of the commodity space. By itself, however, it does not enable us to tell how the choosing agent would rank a point like x_4 or x_5. For this we need his indifference curves. Of course, if we knew that some one bundle, say x_4, was preferred to x_0, this would take another slice out of the area of ignorance.

If we put in the indifference curve through x_0 (Fig. 16-5), we see that the upper and lower wedges must be proper subsets of the sets B_0 and W_0, respectively.[7] U_0 must be a *proper* subset of B_0. Suppose boundary points

[7] While discussing the Axioms of Dominance and Strict Convexity, we shall for simplicity confine ourselves to Disraeli's situation, drawing only his better set, and so forth, and regarding his origin, O_D as *the* origin of the diagrams. Needless to say, everything said holds equally when seen from Victoria's point of view. To lighten notation, we shall drop the subscript "D," writing "B_{D0}" as "B_0" and "I_{D0}" as "I_0" throughout this section, where this should not cause confusion. The axes represent the same pair of commodities.

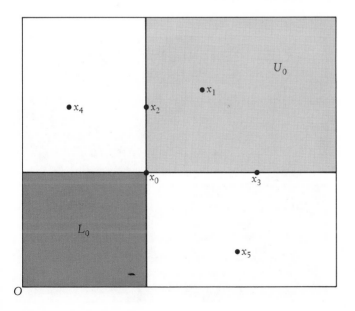

FIGURE 16-4

The upper and lower wedges, U_0 and L_0, associated with x_0

of U_0, such as x_1 and x_2, were boundary points of B_0; that is, were points on the indifference curve I_0. Then $x_1 I x_2$. But $x_2 > x_1$ (since at x_2 there is more of one commodity in the bundle and no less of the other). Therefore, $x_2 P x_1$ by Axiom 12. So points like x_1 and x_2 cannot be boundary points of B_0, and must therefore be interior points of B_0. So $U_0 \subset B_0$.

We are now ready for the second necessary axiom, the assumption of strict convexity. The indifference curve in Fig. 16-5 has in fact the right form. To begin with, only the open segment appears in the Edgeworth box, as a result of the Axiom of Dominance, which in effect cuts the commodity space within the box down to the effective region. Furthermore, the curve has been drawn convex to the origin 0. The indifference curve I_0, made up of boundary points of the set B_0, can be characterized, within the notation of the theory of point sets, in such a way that I_0 has the properties of an Edgeworthian indifference curve, convex to the origin.

Recall that a set is called "strictly convex" if, for any two distinct points of the set x_0 and x_1, every point of the straight line segment joining them, other than x_0 and x_1 themselves, is an interior point of the set, that is to say, a point with a neighborhood wholly in the set.

We may then say:

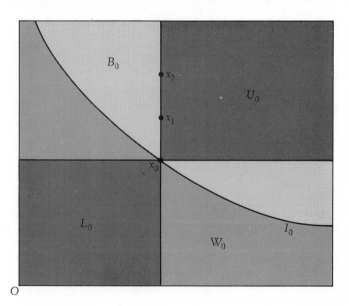

FIGURE 16-5

$U_0 \subset B_0$ and $L_0 \subset W_0$

Axiom 13 *Where x_0, x_1 are points on I_0 and x_2 is on the line joining them, x_2 is an interior point of B_0.*

This is to say that any point like x_2 in Fig. 16-6 is an interior point of B_0. Therefore x_2 is preferred to x_0—since only boundary points of B_0 are indifferent to x_0 (by Axiom 11).

This essential consequence of assuming strict convexity—that a consumer will prefer any average of two bundles between which he is indifferent to either of the bundles themselves, was fully understood and discussed at length by Edgeworth,[8] and it is fundamentally important to his theory of exchange.

Given the Axioms of Dominance and Strict Convexity, we may return to the trading set, assured that we shall see it through Edgeworthian eyes.

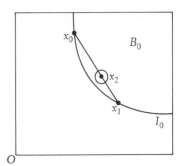

FIGURE 16-6

Axiom of Strict Convexity

It is obvious that exchange will take place if and only if the trading set contains more than just the point t_0—the point of zero trade. Notice that wherever we had chosen to place t_0—even if we were to relax our assumption that each party has initially only one kind of good to exchange—if their respective indifference curves through t_0 *cut* inside the box, then a nontrivial trading set must exist (Fig. 16-7).

We now use the Edgeworthian argument, familiar from our discussion of Pareto optimality, to point out that (this time in regard to trades) any point such as t_1 that involves an exchange of some V goods for some D goods will be preferable to t_0 if it lies within the trading set; further, that there is an infinite set of points t preferable to t_1, being the intersection of I_D curves and I_V curves closer and closer to tangency[9] (Fig. 16-8).

THE TRADING SET

$(B_{D0} \cap B_{V0})$

[8]Francis Y. Edgeworth, *Mathematical Psychics*, Kegan Paul, Trench, Trubner & Co., Ltd., London, 1881 (reprinted by Kelley & Milman, New York 1954) p. 130.

[9]"Tangency" was the concept Edgeworth used, and since his methods were those of classical mathematics it was always appropriate. Even after Axioms 12 and 13, our theory is not exactly equivalent to his. However, since the situations that arise within Edgeworthian exchange theory were motivated by classical mathematics, the concept of tangency rather than the more general set-theoretic concept of supporting hyperplane is perhaps the less misleading to use in this chapter.

FIGURE 16-7

The set $B_{D0} \cap B_{V0}$ for any point t_0 where the curves I_{D0} and I_{V0} cut

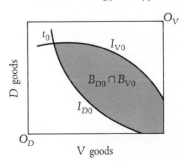

THE SET OF EFFICIENT
TRADES

Finally, a point of tangency is an efficient trade, there being no further exchange that will benefit both parties or even benefit one party and leave the other indifferent. Notice that at t_n the trading set has shrunk to the unit set $\{t_n\}$. We may thus define the set of efficient trades as:

Definition 16-1: The set of efficient trades is the set of all t, such that the trading set associated with t is $\{t\}$.

Notice that in the pure theory of exchange, unlike the theory of Pareto optimality, we are interested only in efficient points lying *between* I_{D0} and I_{V0}—the indifference curves that Vicky and Dizzy can reach without trading, given their initial stocks. As Newman remarks, Edgeworth sometimes used the term "contract curve" for the whole curve we considered in the discussion of welfare theory and sometimes for the section lying between I_{D0} and I_{V0} in Fig. 16-8, and labeled CC_1. In the theory of exchange we shall use the term "contract curve," for the set of efficient trades, lying within the trading set determined by the initial position of the two parties. As Newman puts it, the contract curve consists of the set of all efficient trades that are acceptable to both parties.[10]

Let us contemplate this result briefly. Notice that exchange between two people, each the sole source of one of the only two commodities, is in fact the case of a bi-

[10]See Newman, *op. cit.*, p. 60.

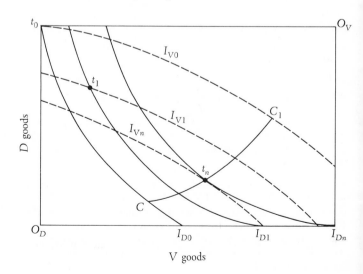

FIGURE 16-8
The set of efficient trades

lateral monopoly. Aside altogether from particular personality disagreements on the part of Vicky and Dizzy, one might have expected this case to be one in which everything was so hopelessly random that nothing could be said about it in theory. It is therefore all the more striking that Edgeworth managed to define clearly the set of efficient trades.

So far, however, the model tells us only that Vicky and Dizzy will have motives to change their respective trades unless or until they are at a point on the contract curve. It does not offer us any criteria for saying at precisely *what* point they will settle. In order to take up this question we need a new concept, that of an *exchange rate*.

In Fig. 16-9, the slope of the straight line $t_0 t_z$ can be used to indicate a possible rate of exchange between D goods and V goods. Because it indicates the rate at which Dizzy can exchange his goods for V goods, such a line delimits Dizzy's attainable region. But by the same token, seen from Vicky's point of view, it also delimits her attainable region. In fact, it divides the commodity space into two half-spaces, Dizzy's attainable region and Vicky's attainable region, which have the points on the line as their intersection. By the Axioms of Dominance and Strict Convexity, Dizzy will optimize by moving to whichever of his indifference curves has exactly one point that is a point on the ruling exchange line. This is his optimum point.

Viewed from her corner, Vicky's optimum will also be a point on the exchange line, which is also a point on the furthest I_V curve from her origin O_V that she can reach.

The exchange line has other features which must now be noted. Imagine the exchange line to be attached at the corner t_0 but free to swing to and fro like a windshield wiper, and consider what happens when it swings. Start with it lying along the vertical side of the box, $t_0 O_D$, then begin to swing it outward; consider this from Dizzy's point of view.

Consider Dizzy's attitude toward the rate of exchange of his goods for V goods represented by $t_0 t_1$ (Fig. 16-10). Here his whole stock of D goods would, at the rate indicated by the slope $t_0 t_1$, bring him only the tiny amount $O_D t_1$ of Vicky's goods. Clearly the no-trade indifference curve I_{D0}, which he can reach by staying at the corner t_0

THE EXCHANGE RATE AND THE CONCEPT OF PRICE

FIGURE 16-9

The exchange line $t_0 t_z$

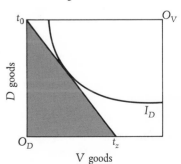

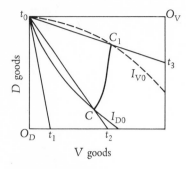

FIGURE 16-10
Rates of exchange, or
relative prices, within which
trade will benefit both parties

and not trading, is higher than any he can reach by trade. He will begin to trade only when the rate of exchange has swung so that he can reach curves within his trading set. Likewise, Vicky will not trade when the rate of exchange is such that she can be on a higher indifference curve by staying at t_0 and retaining all her own stock. The contract curve CC_1 measures the swing of the exchange line within which efficient trades are possible. There is thus *a range of relative prices* within which it will benefit both to trade. Showing at *which* relative price trade will settle is thus demonstrating the equilibrium of relative prices.

I admit that we do not habitually think of prices simply as rates of exchange—we think of so many dollars and cents. So the fact that we have in fact generated, with the aid of our axiom set, a formal model of an exchange economy with a pricing system may not be clearly apparent to us.

Let us do something about this. It is hard enough on her late Majesty to ask her to engage in *trade* without further requiring that she or Dizzy actually *handle* filthy lucre. There is, however, a dignified and very British solution to the problem. In England, professional people, such as doctors and lawyers, do not send bills asking one for anything so crude as pounds or shillings. They ask for a sum expressed in "guineas." Now, there is no coin or note minted or printed which is in fact a physical "guinea." One knows, however, that a guinea is worth £1.1.0, or twenty-one shillings. In our system, let us adopt the convention of expressing prices in guineas.

If the slope of the exchange line indicated that a unit of V goods could be acquired only at the cost of offering three units of D goods, we might express this by saying that the price of a unit of D goods was one guinea and that of a unit of V goods was three guineas. No new information has in fact been conveyed, but prices have been *expressed* in a way we recognized.[11] Any slope of the exchange line can be expressed as a pair of guinea prices, one for V goods and one for D goods. The contract curve, by tracing out the trading arc of the exchange line, thus shows the set of pairs of prices for V goods and D goods, respectively, within which both parties will gain from trade.

[11]On guineas and prices, see Don Patinkin, *Money, Interest and Prices*, Harper & Row, Publishers, Incorporated, New York, 1956.

We must still show that there is an equilibrium pair of prices, and exhibit the paths of convergence toward the equilibrium. This is done by the use of a concept introduced by Edgeworth.

What we need for a "trading curve"[12] is the path traced out by the set of optimal trades for Dizzy as the prices of the two goods change. This path is in fact the locus of the points of tangency of the swinging exchange line and Dizzy's successive indifference curves. A similar curve can be found for Victoria.

When the exchange line is at t_1 in Fig. 16-11, Dizzy will not trade at all but will remain in his corner position. When the exchange line swings to t_2 he will find it worth trading—he is now inside his trading set—and will take up the position where his indifference curve I_{D1} is tangent to the exchange line. At the rate of exchange represented by $t_0 t_3$ he is at the point of tangency with his indifference curve I_{D2}. The trading curve must be wholly within

---

[12]The term "trading curve" is Newman's. The usual terms are "offer curve" and "reciprocal demand curve." Newman rightly observes that the former is misleading, since a point on a trading curve is both an offer and a demand, and the latter term is clumsy.

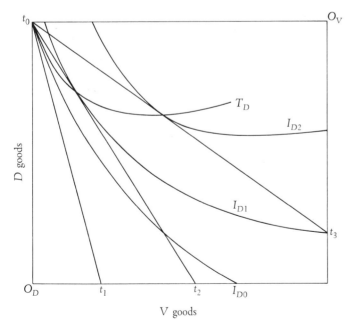

FIGURE 16-11

The trading curve

Disraeli's better set, associated with t_0, since below the indifference curve I_{D0} he has no incentive to trade.

In Fig. 16-12, where the curves T_D and T_V cut, both persons' indifference curves must be tangential to the exchange line, so this point must be a member of the set of efficient trades. This is therefore the equilibrium point, and the prices determined by the slope of $t_0 t_*$ are the equilibrium prices of the system.[13]

THE INDETERMINACY OF BILATERAL EXCHANGE

One ought not to be hypnotized, by these trading curves and their nice neat point of intersection on the contract curve, into thinking that he has now proved that bilateral exchange is in every sense determinate. It is "determinate" in the sense that one can show the paths toward equilibrium and that the equilibrium must be somewhere on the contract curve. It is "indeterminate" in the sense that the shape of each trader's indifference curves reflects the strength of each party's need for the other's goods: So *bargaining strength* is built into the *shape* of the trading curves, which are derived from these indifference curves, and therefore, this determines at what point on the contract curve they cut.

The indeterminacy (in this sense) of bilateral exchange was not a discovery of Edgeworth's. It had been debated at length by John Stuart Mill[14] and was known to the classical English political economy.

At the opposite extreme from bilateral monopoly would be a situation in which prices were beyond the power of the individual trader to affect. This situation is the essence of the concept of *perfect competition*, as this idea was evolved by the neoclassical economists. It is intuitively a reasonable notion that, starting with the extreme

FIGURE 16-12

The equilibrium rate of exchange t_*

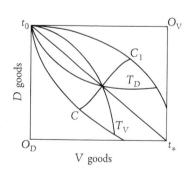

V goods

[13]There are special cases in which the trading curves can intersect at more than one point. See Newman, *op. cit.*, pp. 93-99. Notice, by the way, that we need not concern ourselves with the shape of any tail end of either T_D or T_V *outside* the trading set, since no trade can take place outside the set.

[14]*Principles of Political Economy* (first published in 1848), 5th ed., D. Appleton, New York, 1862, vol. I, pp. 545-546. See further John Chipman, "The Nature and Meaning of Equilibrium in Economic Theory," in *Functionalism in the Social Sciences*, American Academy of Political and Social Science, Monograph 5, Philadelphia, 1965, pp. 54-57.

of bilateral monopoly, as more traders are added the area of indeterminacy of relative prices might be gradually reduced and might ultimately vanish.

A systematic analysis of a manner in which, as more traders are added, an exchange system converges to a system of perfect competition was given by Edgeworth in 1881.[15] Recognized today as one of his most brilliant accomplishments,[16] this analysis lay virtually ignored until the work of Martin Shubick (1958) and the elegant developments of Scarf (1962) and of Scarf and Debreu (1963) and of Aumann (1964).[17]

These papers have defined and characterized what they call the *"core* of an economy." Karl Vind wrote:[18]

THE CORE OF AN ECONOMY

The economy is a pure trade economy, i.e., an economy where a set of consumers possess initially certain quantities of commodities. The trade is simply a reallocation of the commodities. We assume that the consumers have preferences relations. A final allocation is by definition in the core, or an *Edgeworth-allocation*, if no group of consumers can combine and reallocate their initial allocation in such a way that all consumers in the group prefer the new allocation to the final allocation.

When an allocation is an Edgeworth allocation it means in particular that none of the individual consumers prefers his initial allocation. At the other extreme it means that the set of all consumers cannot reallocate in such a way that everybody is made better off. An Edgeworth-allocation is thus a special case of a Pareto-optimal allocation. Given an Edgeworth-allocation it is not only impossible for the individual consumer or the set of all consumers to get a better allocation, it is also impossible for any subset of consumers to combine and get a better allocation by re-allocating this subset's initial allocation.

A group of consumers who combined to *block* an allocation is called a *"blocking coalition,"* about which Vind has said,[19] "If an allocation is such that no coalitions are

[15]Edgeworth, *op. cit.*, pp. 29-50.

[16]See, for instance, Chipman, *op. cit.*, p. 54.

[17]See Footnote 1 of this chapter.

[18]Vind, *op. cit.*, p. 165. Italics are in the original.

[19]Karl Vind, "A Theorem on the Core of an Economy," *Review of Economic Studies*, vol. 32 (1965), pp. 47-48. Italics are in the original. I owe these references to a pleasant meeting with Karl Vind in Copenhagen during the summer of 1966.

blocking we say that the allocation is in the core or that it is an *Edgeworth-allocation.*"

We shall follow Edgeworth by increasing the number of people in the economy in a rather special way—by adding, as it were, a second Vicky and a second Dizzy with identical preference structures and identical stocks of commodities to trade. This makes it possible to continue to use two-dimensional box constructions for some purposes and vastly simplifies the proofs. (Contemporary mathematical treatments do not require these restrictions.) We shall keep a distinction of sex between our participants, as a convenient way to distinguish between the two subsets of traders, with both members of each subset having identical tastes and endowments. But the late Queen and her Prime Minister must, I think, depart. We need more sprightly couples, as may be seen from Edgeworth's own account of the scene:[20] "The particles of an economic system neither cohere as a solid, nor collide with the independence of a gas. Their liquid movements are comparable to a dance in which youths and maidens move in unison; harmoniously, but subject to a change of partner."

We can begin with two youths, whom we shall name Stanley and Harry, and two maidens named Sheila and Beth.[21] Our Edgeworth box now contains a pastoral scene: Enter at the bottom left-hand corner the two youths and at the top right-hand corner the two maidens. There is a small but vital technical point: Notice that, for reasons that will become evident, the horizontal sides of the box represent only *one* maiden's supply of m goods and the vertical sides only *one* youth's supply of y goods. This stipulation will permit us to show within the box possible relations between *two bilateral* trades.

Two theorems, both introduced by Edgeworth and powerfully generalized by recent writers, lead us to the

[20]"The Differential Calculus Applied to Economics," in Francis Y. Edgeworth, *Papers Relating to Political Economy*, Macmillan & Co., Ltd., London, 1925, vol II, p. 369.

[21]The names come from a recent work that seems to fit Edgeworth's requirements, Robert H. Rimmer, *The Harrad Experiment*, Sherbourne Press, Los Angeles, 1966. I choose this work, not for any literary merits, but simply because it offers a detailed account of one aspect of idealistic young American life that emerged in the mid-sixties.

competitive core of the economy. They may be called the "Parity Theorem"[22] and the "Limit Theorem."

THE PARITY THEOREM

According to the Parity Theorem, in our pastoral situation no allocation is a final allocation (that is, in the core) unless all the youths and all the maidens are exchanging on the same terms. Intuitively, this may easily be seen. Suppose one couple (say Harry and Beth) have ended at a different point on the contract curve from another couple (say Stanley and Sheila). It will then be to Sheila and Harry's advantage to forsake Stanley and Beth, and *recontract* with each other, settling at any point on the contract curve between the two original contracts (see Fig. 16-13).

THE LIMIT THEOREM

The Limit Theorem is much more difficult to state, and I shall follow Chipman[23] and Newman[24] in attempting to give here only a sketch of the line of argument originally used by Edgeworth.

Edgeworth's approach was to show that as more and more couples identical with the original couple are added to the economy, segments are lost from the ends of the contract curve—the indeterminateness represented by the existence of a stretch of contract curve is progressively lessened. In the limit, only one point is left (or perhaps in special cases a few points are left). Such a final point describes an allocation that is referred to as "competitive" because it is beyond the power of any trader or coalition of traders to block it—to prevent its coming about or to change its terms.

Suppose that Stanley and Sheila are at the end of the contract curve most unfavorable to Stanley. From the Parity Theorem, we know that if another couple, Harry and Beth, are on the scene, they must be exchanging at the same rate if this allocation is to be final. Edgeworth argues that this extreme end of the old contract curve cannot be a final allocation for two couples. The argument rests on the fact that a coalition of three can advantageously form, in the following way.

[22]See Chipman, *op. cit.*, p. 56.

[23]Chipman, *op. cit.*, p. 57.

[24]Newman, *op. cit.*, pp. 112-114.

FIGURE 16-13
Parity

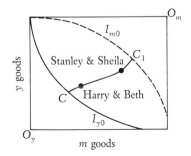

It will benefit either Sheila or Beth to enter into a coalition with the two youths. Sheila (let us say) offers the youths FG of her goods in return for an amount $t_0 F$ of theirs *to be supplied in equal shares* by each youth. Let us inspect the situation that results in Fig. 16-14.

Each youth supplies $t_0 D$ and gains DE. But since E is on the straight line from t_0 to C, then by the Axiom of Strict Convexity[25] E must be an interior point of the better set associated with each youth's indifference curve I_{y0}. The youths, therefore, gain from the coalition. It remains to show that Sheila will also gain. Sheila trades FG of her good for $t_0 F$ of y goods (half supplied by each youth), so she ends up at point G. Now the straight line $t_0 G$ cuts the youth's indifference curve I_{y0} at C. But at C this curve is tangent to Sheila's indifference curve I_{m1} (because C is a point on the contract curve and therefore a point of tangency between a youth indifference curve and a maiden indifference curve). Therefore $t_0 G$ also cuts Sheila's curve I_{m1} at C. Therefore, the point G lies in Sheila's better set associated with I_{m1}. So Sheila also will prefer G to C.

Meanwhile, what has Beth been up to? She "has been left out in the cold"[26] by the blocking coalition composed of Stanley, Harry, and Sheila. As Edgeworth says,

[25]The exact form of the Axiom of Convexity is crucial to the Edgeworthian version of the proof. See the discussion of this axiom, pp. 166-167. Our version of this axiom stipulates *strict* convexity, and this property is needed in the proof of the Limit Theorem sketched above.

[26]Edgeworth, *Mathematical Psychics, op. cit.*, p. 37.

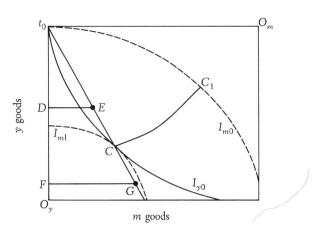

FIGURE 16-14

A coalition of one maiden and two youths

she "will now strike in, with the result the system will be worked down to the contract curve again; to a point at least as favorable"[27] for the youths as E. Thus, to paraphrase the Master, the maidens will have lost some of their initial advantage by competition. By a similar argument, it can be shown that the allocation represented by C_1 at the northeast end of the old contract curve is no longer viable once there is a second couple. Thus both ends of the original contract curve drop off when a second couple join the scene. The area of "arbitrariness" has shrunk. Edgeworth rounds off his argument:[28]

> Taking account of the two processes which have been described . . . we see that in general for any number short of the *practically infinite* (if such a term be allowed) there is a finite length of contract curve . . . at any point of which if the system is placed, it cannot by contract or re-contract be displaced; that there are *an indefinite number of final settlements*, a quantity continually diminishing as we approach a perfect market.

We are now ready to take up the question, What welfare implications are involved in the idea of exchange in general? We do this in Chapter 17.

QUESTIONS

1. How is Victoria's better set B_{V0} related to the trading set?

2. Under what conditions can both Victoria and Disraeli gain from exchange?

3. What is the relation between the trading set and the set of efficient trades?

4. How do prices arise out of the exchange situation?

5. What is the relation between trading curves and equilibrium prices?

6. What is meant by the indeterminacy of bilateral exchange? How is this related to the concept of monopoly?

[27]*Ibid.*

[28]*Ibid.*, pp. 38-39. Italics are in the original.

7. What is meant by the core of an economy? What is a blocking allocation and how is it related to a core allocation? What is the set of viable allocations?

8. In an economy with four traders, what can be said of any two couples of traders?

9. In what circumstances can Sheila gain by joining a coalition with Harry and Stanley?

10. What happens to the contract curve as more couples are added to an economy?

17
CORE
AND
CONFLICT

Conventional introductions to economics often contain lengthy eulogies of the benefits of exchange and the advantages of competition. These passages are not destitute of any grain of truth. However, on the one hand, the element of truth is hopelessly swamped in a mass of tangled claims, mostly unwarranted or inconsistent; and on the other, the very informality and vagueness of these arguments make them seem like pious incantations, deference to the sacred cows of a *status quo* that today's undergraduates find even more boring than wicked.

At a more sophisticated level, a theory of allocation is offered, with theorems that are in fact major theorems of welfare economics,[1] whether or not they are explicitly

---

[1]See E. J. Mishan, "A Reappraisal of the Principles of Resource Allocation," in his *Welfare Economics, Five Introductory Essays*, Random House, Inc., New York, 1964, p. 155.

expressed in welfare theoretic language. At this point I shall consider three welfare claims about exchange mechanisms and the allocations that these mechanisms produce.

THE EXCHANGE OPTIMUM   The exchange optimum has been effectively discussed by E. J. Mishan:[2]

> If individuals place different relative valuations on the same range of goods, some at least can profit by exchange until the rate of substitution between pairs of goods is the same for each individual in the community. Irrespective of the distribution of welfare, a movement to or towards an exchange optimum is an unambiguous *actual* improvement in the welfare of the community. In other words, some people will always be better off—and no one will be worse off—if exchange between individuals of their initial product endowments is permitted.

This requirement, that the rate of substitution be the same between any two commodities for any two people, is equivalent to the requirement that all exchanges be on the contract curve. Thus we may state the first of what are often called the two rules for optimal resource allocation:

Rule 1: An allocation is an optimal allocation if and only if it is a member of the set of efficient trades.

This way of stating the rule may bring out its dependence on the theory of exchange and, ultimately, on the axioms upon which the analysis of exchange rests. A set of efficient trades requires a trading set, for which the intersection of the better sets must contain more points than t_0, the point of no trade. For this situation, the preference rankings of the consumers must obey the axioms of choice and consumption theory; and exchange will be impossible, and therefore the concept of optimal allocation will be meaningless, unless each trader has a commodity to offer that other traders *desire*. Many of the very poor in a real society are poor precisely because they cannot offer any commodity (or, realistically, type of labor) that the market *wants*. The Axiom of Dominance, assumed to simplify the analysis, automatically rules out this case, since it implies that any trader prefers larger quantities of *either or both* of the only two commodities in the model. The use of horseshoe-shaped curves, as allowed by the Axiom of Insatiability of consumption theory, would have

---

[2]*Ibid.*, pp. 177-178. Italics are in the original.

implied that more of *some combinations* of the two commodities is always desired. Had we allowed the curves to
close within the box, we would not have implied that Vicky
had *zero* desire for Dizzy's goods, or vice versa. But in a
real society, there are people whose plight is just that *no
one wants anything they have to offer.*

The first allocation rule, "an allocation is optimal ⇔
it is a member of the set of efficient trades," is not thereby
proved *false* if applied to a theory *based on an axiom set
adequate to support it.* What we have shown is that a particular real-world situation must not be naïvely assumed
to offer a model for such a theory.

If this be granted, we may agree with Mishan as to
the validity of Rule 1 for a theory based on our present
axiom set. Notice some things that this rule *does not* require. Most surprising, perhaps, is that it does not require
any approximation on the part of the economy to its competitive core. It does not require any number of competi-
tors at all—Vicky and Dizzy would optimize by obeying
it, even in their case, which is bilateral monopoly. All
that the rule requires is tangency of the respective indifference curves, which is precisely the property of the *whole*
contract curve within the limits of the trading set. Any
arbitrary allocation on the contract curve is an *optimal*
allocation within the meaning of the rule.

I end with a pleasant but practical illustration of the
use of this rule in economic policy, as a theorem in applied
welfare economics. William Baumol writes:[3]

> Whenever it is necessary to restrict the use of a number
> of commodities, it is better to do so by means of a system of
> point rationing, in which each consumer is assigned an equal
> number of points to be used by him as he prefers, rather than
> the more usual method of assigning an equal amount of each
> good to each consumer.
>
> Thus, if each consumer is, for example, assigned 1 pound
> of beef and 1 pound of lamb per week, in an ordinary rationing
> procedure, the result is necessarily disadvantageous both to con-
> sumers who prefer beef and to those who prefer lamb. If, on the
> other hand, each consumer is given ten points and told that he
> must give up five points with every pound of meat he purchases,
> beef lovers will get their two pounds of beef and lamb eaters
> their two pounds of lamb. . . .

[3]William J. Baumol, *Economic Theory and Operations
Analysis*, 2d ed., Prentice-Hall, Inc., Englewood Cliffs, N.J., 1965,
pp. 372-373.

This theorem on rationing illustrates how relatively innocuous marginal optimality Rule 1, which requires equality of marginal rates of substitution for all consumers, can help lead to significant policy conclusions.

EQUILIBRIUM SYSTEM OF PRICES

Rule 2: Every equilibrium system of prices is a Pareto optimum, and every Pareto optimum a possible pricing equilibrium.

Only a sketch can be given here of an area of theory that has received much rigorous formal development in recent years. Intuitively, following Edgeworth, an allocation off the contract curve cannot be a final allocation. So the set of efficient trades defines a set of possible prices which are equilibrium prices. Notice that once again this is true not only of perfectly competitive core allocations. It is a property of a contract curve in any exchange situation. Any pricing system representing a point on the contract curve represents a *stable* equilibrium in the sense that there is no incentive for both parties, or all parties, to move from it.

Notice the limits of the sense in which these equilibrium points are optimal. Contrast the two ends, C and C_1, of the contract curve. An allocation at C will be highly favorable to the youths (to use the illustration of Chapter 16), whereas one at C_1 will be highly favorable to the maidens. Yet both are "optima" in the relevant sense, namely, that all parties cannot be made better off. This is, of course, Pareto optimality. All final allocations of a system of free exchange are Pareto-optima.

OPTIMALITY THEOREMS ON THE CORE OF AN ECONOMY

Here we come to the question: What optimal properties can be attributed only to the competitive core of an economy? To begin with, the arbitrariness, that admittedly characterizes bilateral exchange, and all exchange between the few, is supposed absent from core allocations. As we have seen, from a competitive core allocation, it is impossible for a subset of traders to combine and get a better allocation.

This has a suggestive ring about it, and smacks of the "best of all possible worlds." It must immediately be qualified in four ways.

Problems of convergence   Only the merest hint has been given in this book of the problems of specifying the possible paths of *convergence* to the core. Any approach to realism introduces vast complexity, and the use of simple models for the theory inevitably entails missing most of the problems that must be solved if the picture is to bear any resemblance to a possible real situation.

Problems of the multiplicity of equilibria   The competitive equilibrium need not be *unique*: the core may contain more than one point. This may be proved by showing that trading curves may cut more than once, and each cutting will be a point of the contract curve. To keep the treatment as light as possible, I have refrained from going into this; but the result must at least be mentioned now, since it affects our estimation of the competitive core.[4] A situation with more than one possible equilibrium in the core leaves open "the possibility of violent swings from one equilibrium to another."[5]

The existence problem   The existence of competitive equilibria can be proved within a static theory of pure exchange without implying that such positions will continue to exist when the theory is changed in ways intended to make it approximate more closely to reality. When, for instance, the theory is expanded to include a treatment of production or is made fully dynamic (we have already noticed the issue of convergence), the existence of an equilibrium may be called in question.

Welfare implications of the competitive core   The gist of the matter is that the core allocations are optimal, a competitive price system is efficient, only *given* the initial distribution of commodities between the exchanging parties. As Peter Newman put it:[6]

If that is unfair, no amount of economic and social "efficiency" in the exchange mechanism will do more than make the best of a bad job—and even that cautious assertion about the

---

[4]The classic reference is Alfred Marshall, *The Pure Theory of Foreign Trade*, 1879—a book, by the way, in which Marshall was highly original. See the contemporary discussion in Peter Newman, *The Theory of Exchange*, Prentice-Hall, Inc., Englewood Cliffs, N.J., 1965, pp. 93-99.

[5]John Chipman, "The Nature and Meaning of Equilibrium in Economic Theory," in *Functionalism in the Social Sciences*, American Academy of Political and Social Science, Monograph 5, Philadelphia, 1965, p. 55.

[6]Newman, *op. cit.*, p. 122. This passage could hardly be more eloquent.

merits of the Hidden Hand may not really be valid. In any actual situation it might well be that, by any reasonable ethical standards, a coalition of those less well endowed with this world's goods should block an allocation on the contract curve, and a competitive core allocation, with everyone playing the market mechanism game according to the rules, would frustrate this desirable change. If equilibrium is just equilibrium, then the *status quo* is most certainly just the *status quo*.

There is one other topic, which can be said to be concerned with welfare applications of the Edgeworthian theory of exchange, with which we shall end this chapter. It is obvious that, for the people whose relations we have been analyzing, what is exchanged need not be physical goods. Even within the customary notation of economics the commodities at issue may be services. Clearly, the Edgeworthian theory is quite general and is independent of what in any concrete case is being exchanged. Edgeworth considered his theory of pure exchange as part of mathematical psychics and thought of the latter as a moral science, concerned with analyzing the best allocation of the ultimate good, which for him was, of course, pleasure. This aspect of his work, like a number of others, lay ignored for many years after the fall of utilitarianism. The logical structure of his argument was eventually seen as subject to such a general interpretation even apart from utilitarian assumptions. The credit for seeing this belongs to Kenneth Boulding.

CONFLICT AND COOPERATION

As Boulding puts it:[7]

The general theory of preference can take care of benevolence and even malevolence just as well as it can deal with selfishness. If we identify the welfare of another as our own, we can take care of this in formal theory by simply supposing that the preference function that governs our behavior has goods possessed by others in its domain as well as goods that we possess ourselves. If we make a gift, it is presumably because we prefer the distribution in which we have less and another more to the one from which we started. There is nothing irrational in this; indeed, because community is one of the supreme achievements of man, it is highly rational.

To return to our youths and maidens; if, as the choice of example implies, they have a positive interest in each

[7]Kenneth Boulding, "The Basis of Value Judgments in Economics," in Sidney Hook (ed.), *Human Values and Economic Policy, a Symposium*, New York University Press, New York, 1967, p. 69.

other's welfare, the situation will look like that shown in Fig. 17-1. (To show this situation I have for the moment dropped the Axioms of Dominance and Insatiability.)

Of the contract curve CC_1 which gives the set of efficient trades, only a subset from y to m will remain a set of conflict positions. This is because (bless their hearts) the maidens' indifference system would *prefer not* to push the youths farther back toward their origin. I have done the youths the credit of assuming that their system will likewise close around an optimal area, y. As Boulding puts it,[8] "the preference here is for a *distribution* of the com-

[8] Kenneth Boulding, *Economic Analysis*, 4th ed., Harper & Row, Publishers, Incorporated, New York, 1966, vol. I, *Micro-Economics*, p. 628. Italics are in the original. It is possible to misunderstand Boulding's meaning by misconstruing "satiety." A situation in which one is physically glutted is clearly a model for the theory of closed indifference curves, but it is not the only valid model for this theory. A closed indifference curve, like *any* indifference set, is simply an equivalence set of the P relation—a set whose elements are equally preferred. Nothing is implied about the *motive* for which the elements are so ranked. The appearance of closed curves may indicate that we would prefer to have some optimal quantity of two things because more would be physically repellent or, equally well, closure may reflect our desire for what we regard as an optimal *distribution* of things between ourselves and others. This is the situation in Fig. 17-1.

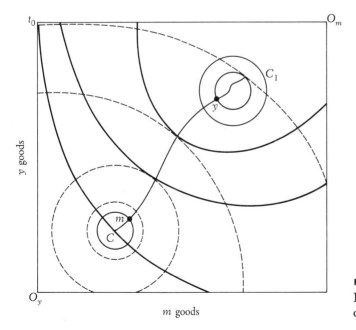

FIGURE 17-1

Exchange with an element of altruism

modities, not for possession alone. If the parties are highly altruistic, so that each worries about the poverty of the other, the indifference curves may exhibit a maximum point within the box."

At the limit, where the two optimal points became identical or, if areas, had an intersection, all conflict would disappear, and one might describe the situation as perfect love.

In essence, Edgeworth saw this, but his exposition uses the language and axioms of utilitarian ethics. He notes[9] that if we suppose our people to be

... actuated in effective moments by a sympathy with each other's interests (as even now in *domestic*, and one day perhaps in *political*, contracts), we might suppose the object which X (whose own utility is P), tends—in a calm, effective moment—to maximize, is not P, but $P \pm \lambda \Pi$; where λ is a *coefficient of effective sympathy.* . . . What, then, will be the contract curve of these modified contractors? *The old contract curve between narrower limits.* . . . As the coefficients of sympathy increase, utilitarianism becomes more pure . . . *the contract curve narrows down to the utilitarian point.*

The "utilitarian point" was the point on the contract curve that produced the greatest possible total utility of the contractors. Obviously, this requires quantitative, measurable utility, as well as interpersonal comparisons. Yet the structure of Edgeworth's argument can be expressed by means of our concept of two closed indifference systems with optimal areas or points approaching, and, in the limit, identical.

Notice that to permit discussion of these matters we have had to allow *closed* curves. This implies, as noted above, that the Axioms of Dominance and Insatiability have to be abandoned for analyses of this type. This is just what one would expect after all, since the discussion has taken us more and more in the direction of general choice theory—an analysis of what Edgeworth calls "sympathy" can hardly avoid this—and for general choice theory we never expected an Axiom of Dominance or of Insatiability to hold. Thus we see that it is impossible to discuss the ultimate significance of Edgeworth's analysis in any

[9]Francis Y. Edgeworth, *Mathematical Psychics*, Kegan Paul, Trench, Trubner & Co., Ltd., London, 1881 (reprinted by Kelley & Milman, New York, 1954), note to p. 53. Italics are in the original.

terms more restricted than the general theory of choice. He begins with the nature of contract and ends with the structure of love.[10]

We shall not be so close to Francis Edgeworth again in these pages. He was, I think, very much a man for all seasons—a passionately believing utilitarian and therefore indeed a man of the nineteenth century, yet a man with a vision that extends not only to our present but also into our future: how many Californian hippies have yet ventured a formula for the maximum ecstasy of a perfectly loving group?[11] He belonged to the past in that his mathematical method was still Newton's great method of fluxions—indeed he was probably the last man to have a love affair with the infinitesimal calculus. Yet he belonged to the mathematical future of economic theory in that he essayed, in the concept of mathematical psychics, nothing less than a general theory of choice. He is of the past in dismissing as sterile George Boole's algebra of classes,[12] which was to form the backbone of computer science. Yet he is of the future in his insistence on what he called "unnumerical mathematics" and his vision that social science would yield mathematical structure. "For this same symbol speech, so harsh and crabbed as compared with literary elegance, is gifted with

AVE ATQUE VALE

[10]See the profoundly interesting comments of Kenneth Arrow on the concept of extended sympathy in the appendix to the second edition of *Social Choice and Individual Values* (John Wiley & Sons, Inc., New York, 1963, pp. 114-115) and also in "Public and Private Values," in Hook (ed.), *op. cit.*, pp. 19-20. Arrow regards the concept of extended sympathy as offering the possibility of an escape from the difficulties confronting the formulation of a social welfare function. The argument as stated by Arrow uses a concept of appraising other people's states of well-being, which is adapted from my work, *Scarcity and Evil* (Prentice-Hall, Inc., Englewood Cliffs, N.J., 1961). Problems possibly underlying Boulding's interpretation of choice theory are noted by Ernest Nagel in "Preference, Evaluation and Reflective Choice" in Hook (ed.), *op. cit.*, pp. 81-84. Nagel implies that the attempt to treat, for instance, benevolence, within choice theory may give rise to what we have called the "incomparability issue." I shall discuss all these matters at length in *Axiomatic Choice Theory* (to be published by McGraw-Hill Book Company, New York).

[11]Edgeworth's formula is to be found in the note to p. 53 of *Mathematical Psychics*.

[12]Francis Y. Edgeworth, *Papers Relating to Political Economy*, Macmillan & Co., Ltd., London, 1925, vol. II, p. 290.

a magical charm to win coy truth; the brief and broken language which the love of abstract truth inspires, no doubt foolishness to those who have no sympathy with that passion."[13]

He lived on into the 1920s, but his most future-anticipating work was in his own nineteenth-century past, his youthful essay into mathematical psychics. The late Lord Keynes, in his charming biographical sketch, notes that Edgeworth never (again) essayed any long work but published only short scientific papers. Keynes, who knew Edgeworth well, suggests that shyness at having been laughed at for the emotional fire of his early work prevented Edgeworth from ever exposing himself again. But, if he could have anticipated his reception by today's young scientists, he need have had no fear. Keynes describes[14] how, "once when I asked him why he had never ventured on a Treatise he answered, with his characteristic smile and chuckle, that large-scale enterprise, such as Treatises and marriage, had never appealed to him. It may be that he deemed them industries subject to diminishing return."

QUESTIONS

1. Can individuals always benefit by free exchange?

2. In what situations might one say that the concept of optimal allocation becomes meaningless?

3. What is the bearing of the Axiom of Dominance in the welfare theorems deducible from exchange theory?

4. Are only core allocations Pareto optimal?

5. "Every equilibrium system of prices is a Pareto optimum." Criticize the welfare implications of this assertion.

6. Discuss the welfare significance of the concept of extended sympathy.

[13]Edgeworth, *Mathematical Psychics*, p. 86.

[14]John Maynard Keynes, *Essays and Sketches in Biography*, Horizon Press, New York, 1956, p. 108.

18

DEMAND MAPPINGS AND CORRESPONDENCES

Any point in the commodity two space within the Edgeworth box of Chapters 16 and 17 can be interpreted in
the following ways. From the point of view, say, of a particular youth, any such point represents a decision with
two aspects: an ordered couple, made up of a willingness
to *offer* a certain quantity of y goods, combined with the
demand for a certain quantity of m goods. A decision on
the youth's part to take up a particular point in the two
space is at once the choosing of a particular commodity
bundle and the choosing to supply a particular quantity of
his own goods (or, as it will become in production theory,
his factor services).

The decisions of youths and maidens about their
optimal positions in the two space are simultaneously decisions to demand and decisions to supply. The decision

space is *at one and the same time* a demand decision space and a supply decision space.

The point of equilibrium, where the trading curves cut, thus conveys all the following information: It is the one fixed point, out of the set of all youth demand/supply decisions, that is also an element in the set of the maiden demand/supply decisions. That there must be at least one such point in common to the set of youth decisions and the set of maiden decisions is a fundamental theorem in mathematical economics.

GENERAL EQUILIBRIUM

The equilibrium point, it must now be observed, gives a completely *general* specification for the equilibrium of all youths and all maidens—that is to say, for our whole exchange economy. (Suppose the economy to have been worked down through the forming and dissolution of blocking coalitions to its competitive core.) A theory that represents equilibrium as a property of all elements in the economy, considered at once in all their mutual relations, has long been called a "general equilibrium theory."

Conventional texts, under the influence of Marshall, tend to approach the general equilibrium of an economic system only indirectly, and they therefore give the impression that there is something esoteric or sophisticated about the whole idea. Actually, the sophisticated and, in a sense, artificial approach is to hold constant all but two variables in the system and concentrate on the analysis of the behavior of just these two. It is not an invalid move: all science must do this on occasion. I mean simply that the most *natural* theoretical expression, of a mutually dependent system, is surely a picture of the *whole system in its interconnectedness*.

Since we shall introduce some of the most famous concepts of so-called particular equilibrium analysis and since these were once opposed vigorously to the general equilibrium structures and were presented as superior rivals, some account of the once-opposing points of view is obviously necessary. The position is analogous to that which faced us over the issue of utility theory. There we had to discuss old issues, not because any mathematical economist still seriously disputes them, but simply to explain how the present situation arose.

Neither general nor particular equilibrium theories are new. An elaborate account of the general equilibrium of an economic system was presented by Leon Walras, of the school of Lausanne, as early as 1874.[1] The analysis of the equilibrium of particular elements of an economy had been outlined mathematically by Cournot in 1838[2] and was elevated by Alfred Marshall into the self-conscious method of his whole approach.

I think it cannot be denied that Marshall was actively hostile to general equilibrium theories, and that his powerful influence drew attention and interest away from them for many years. This element was central in his well-known hostility to mathematical methods in economic theory, a hostility often explicitly expressed. There is a paradox here. Marshall's attitude was not that of a non-mathematical mind—quite the reverse: he had been Second Wrangler at Cambridge. Indeed, part of his objection appears to be that *as a mathematician* he found the general equilibrium theories of his day cumbersome and inelegant. Recent work on issues connected with general equilibrium[3] has considerable elegance and power, purely in terms of mathematical structure. But to a professional mathematician, these qualities were not evident in the early general equilibrium theory. The development of mathematical economics was probably delayed by the contempt Marshall felt for its adolescent struggles.

Marshall's finer moral qualities joined forces with his mathematical esthetic to reinforce the effect. He writes that he was compelled into economics by the miseries he saw on walks through the slums. Abandoning the beauty and exquisite structure of pure mathematics, he turned to economics, strictly for its quick usefulness in aiding enlightened social policy. His compulsion led to the development of a hasty, intellectually sloppy empiricism and to an impatience with logical niceties or prolonged abstract argument—a stifling of the very graces his mind clearly originally possessed. Thus also John Donne, in his later life as a divine, rejected the beautiful erotic poetry of his

[1]Leon Walras, *Elements d'Economie Politique Pure*, 1874.

[2]Antoine Augustin Cournot, *Recherches sur les Principes Mathematiques de la Théorie des Richesses*, 1838.

[3]For a highly readable survey of this, see James Quirk and Rubin Saposnik, *Introduction to General Equilibrium Theory and Welfare Economics*, McGraw-Hill Book Company, New York, 1968, *passim*.

youth, and St. Augustine strove to extinguish the delicate sensual awareness of his mind. Conversions, I fear, often have this destructive effect.

However, certain characteristics of the age in which he lived to some extent lent rational justification to Marshall's attitude. For one thing, he wanted to be widely read, and he lived at a time when the business community was not the sophisticated, mathematically literate audience that it is becoming today. Moreover, he wanted to produce results whose applications could easily be seen; and *applying* economic theory, in an age before the computer revolution, meant doing so in your head: it meant rule-of-thumb, rough guesswork, much use of judgment, and a definite limit to the amount and complexity of calculation that could profitably be undertaken. Marshall looked at the cumbersome equations of Walras and concluded with justice that they were too intricate and too complicated a tool to be used on daily issues of policy in his world. Meanwhile, classical mathematics and the science based on it, offered an obvious expedient: The device of holding all elements in the system but one pair constant and watching the results of the changes in one of the variables being studied upon the other.[4]

It is now time to introduce a concept that became a typical tool of Marshallian economic theory, although its introduction is actually due to Cournot—the concept of the demand function. Before we consider demand functions, we must make explicit a few notions that have underlain our discussion at many points but with which we have not hitherto come to terms.

RELATIONS AND MAPPINGS

Return for a moment to the concept of a relation R, which holds between the set of all x and y such that $x\,R\,y$. The domain of the relation is the set of all x, such that for some $y\,(x, y) \in R$. Let us suppose, with Patrick Suppes, that "L" is the relation that consists of all ordered couples (x, y) where x loves y. Then the domain of L, is the set of all those who love at least one person.

The counterdomain, or range, of a binary relation R is the set of all y such that for some $x\,(x, y) \in R$. So the

---

[4]Partial derivatives are surely one of the most naturally applicable of the concepts of analysis.

counterdomain of the relation L is the set of all those who are loved by at least one person.

In this chapter, we shall be concerned with a particular proper subset of the set of binary relations, those commonly called "functions" or "mappings." We shall use the latter terms as synonyms. These are relations such that for each element in their domains there is one *unique* element in their counterdomains. A function, or mapping, R is a binary relation such that:

Definition 18-1:   R is a function $\Leftrightarrow x R y \,\&\, x R z \Rightarrow y = z.$

If X is the domain of such a relation and Y the counterdomain, the function "f" is spoken of as a *mapping* of X to Y, which may be written "$f: X \longrightarrow Y$." A function "f" is said to *map* its domain onto its counterdomain (or range). The set of elements into which X is mapped by f is called its "image" under f. Think of a globe, and a representation of the globe on the plane of the page of an atlas. The representation of the globe on the page is a *mapping* of points on the globe to points on the page. A point x on the globe is taken to a point y on the page—y is the image of x under the mapping f. The point y may therefore also be written as "$f(x)$" to stress this. We now consider certain important cases of mappings.

These cases are easy to visualize if we keep to finite sets. In Fig. 18-1, we shall accordingly confine ourselves to two finite sets, a set "D" of drinks whose members are represented by triangles and a set "G" of girls whose members are indicated by asterisks. Figure 18-1a represents the important case of a *one-to-one* mapping: Each drink is taken to exactly one girl, and there is a drink for every girl and a girl for every drink. Figure 18-1b shows a mapping of D *into* G. Every drink goes to a girl, but there is one girl left out. Finally, a mapping of D *onto* G is shown in Fig. 18-1c. Here a drink is taken to every girl, but as it happens two drinks go to *one* girl. Notice that a mapping onto is not necessarily therefore a *one-to-one* mapping.

Now, suppose we decide to make the drinks larger, by taking a pair of glasses and pouring the contents of one into the other. In this way we get the mapping of a set *onto itself* as in Fig. 18-2.

Finally, we consider a relation that is not a mapping. We may illustrate by going back to the relation "L." We have two finite sets, Y a set of youths and M a set of

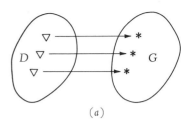

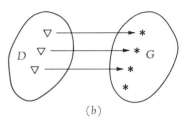

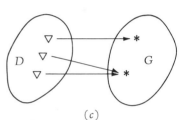

FIGURE 18-1

Mappings from D to G:
(a) one-to-one mapping;
(b) mapping into;
(c) mapping onto

FIGURE 18-2

$f: D \longrightarrow D$

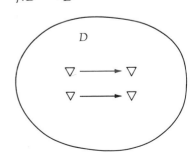

maidens. Consider the possible case of the relation L in Fig. 18-3. The behavior of y_2 shows that the relation L is not a mapping.

Recall at this point the definition of a mapping given earlier in this chapter. Given the nature of L, if $x \mathrel{L} y$ and $x \mathrel{L} z$ it is clearly not necessarily the case that $y = z$. So L is not a mapping. This is true of many relations, the classic case being a relation like "brother of."

In the neoclassical tradition, it is a salient characteristic of the relation assumed to hold between any price and the quantity demanded at that price that this relation is assumed to be a mapping. This assumption was made by both the general-equilibrium school of Lausanne and the partial-equilibrium school of Marshall, and the idea is due originally to Cournot. Stated in Marshallian, partial-equilibrium terms, the quantity demanded "q" is some function "f" of the price "p" of the good. In conventional notation, $q = f(p)$. If "Q" is the set of all nonnegative quantities of the good and "P" is the set of its prices, we may translate this into mapping notation as f maps P to Q, $f : P \longrightarrow Q$.

Since Hicks, demand functions have themselves been derived from sets of tangencies between indifference curves and lines indicating relative prices. That this relation will in turn be a mapping depends crucially upon the assumption of classical, strict convexity of the indifference curves.

Since the Edgeworth-box constructions of the theory of exchange described in this book were constructed under the restrictions imposed by two special axioms (the Axioms of Dominance and of Strict Convexity), demand curves can be derived from them that graph the traditional demand function, as it has been from Cournot to Hicks. The

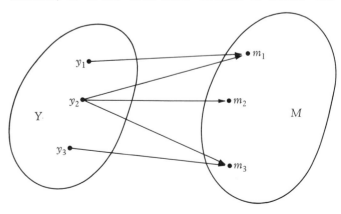

FIGURE 18-3

A relation, L, that is not a mapping

derivation, which is Hicksian, is a mapping of a set of points from the trading space of exchange theory to a price / quantity space, which is the space of demand theory.

We shall thus consider first in this chapter the neoclassical theory of demand functions. We shall then, in the last section, relax the assumptions of strict convexity and dominance, restoring indifference curves to their freedom as the boundary points of weakly convex better sets. We shall find that the treatment of demand then requires the introduction of the notion of demand *correspondences*.

Since we shall be concerned in particular with mappings from *points* representing prices to *points* representing quantities, a few words are in order concerning the real line and the real plane. We said in a previous chapter[5] that the points on a straight line could be *identified* with the set of all real numbers; we may now express this by saying that there is a *one-to-one* mapping between them. The set of points defined by this one-to-one mapping is the real line, and it is called the "graph" of R, the set of all real numbers.

Likewise, there is a one-to-one mapping between the Cartesian product set $R \times R$ (the set of all real numbers multiplied by itself) and the set of all points in the plane.

We may now construct the space relevant to our discussion of neoclassical demand theory. Place two replicas of the real line perpendicular to each other at the zero point of each. We shall call these the "vertical axis" and the "horizontal axis." Let all nonnegative amounts of some commodity be identified with points on the horizontal axis starting from O and all nonnegative prices of that commodity with the points on the vertical axis starting from O. Any combination of a price and a quantity that sells at that price will be a point in the plane, such as x_0 in Fig. 18-4.

The point x_0 in the demand space is an ordered couple (p, q), composed of the price p and the quantity that is demanded at that price q. The demand mapping is a subset of the Cartesian product set $P \times Q$. Its *graph* is a set of points in the demand space. If we assume continuous divisibility of both the commodity and the monetary unit, the graph of the demand mapping will, as we shall see, be a continuous curve on Hicksian assumptions. We already have continuously divisible commodities; we can assume

[5]See Chapter 13, pp. 133-134.

THE HICKSIAN DEMAND MAPPING

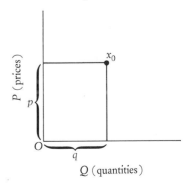

FIGURE 18-4

The demand space

that the set of prices is identified with all nonnegative amounts of one of these commodities (if you feel like being traditional, say gold). We shall identify the demand mapping with its graph and speak of it freely as the demand "curve." So far, we have been slipping along with an undefined intuitive notion of what is meant by the "continuity" of a mapping. I shall, however, give a sketch of the broadest notion of continuity. Consider two sets A and B and a mapping f of a point a_0 of A to a point b_0 of B (Fig. 18-5). Let $N(b_0)$ be any arbitrary neighborhood of b_0. The mapping f is said to be *continuous* at a_0 if there exists a neighborhood $N(a_0)$, such that the image of every point in $N(a_0)$ is contained in $N(b_0)$.

We shall now describe the Hicksian derivation of the demand curve. I propose to derive this curve from the Edgeworthian exchange situation, so we return to this to look for what we need. Consider the two points x_1 and x_2 in Fig. 18-6. These points are tangencies between Disraeli's indifference curves (I_{D1} & I_{D2}) and different rates of exchange between his goods and Victoria's. Recall that x_1 and x_2 are points on Disraeli's trading curve, which shows the set of all offers of his goods and demands for Vicky's goods that he will make.

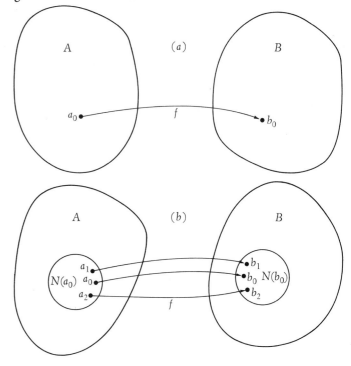

FIGURE 18-5

The continuity of a mapping, $f : A \longrightarrow B$: (a) a mapping f, from A to B; (b) its continuity, where arbitrary points a_1 and a_2 in a neighborhood of a_0 have images b_1 and b_2 in $N(b_0)$

We are interested at the moment in only some of the information summarized in points like x_1 and x_2. We are concerned with the fact that they show the amounts of V goods Disraeli will demand at different slopes of the exchange line. As we know from Chapter 16, any slope of the exchange line can be translated into an absolute price, so many "guineas."[6] So every point like x_1 can be interpreted to give us an ordered couple (p, q) consisting of a guinea price and a quantity of V goods q demanded by Dizzy at that price.

Furthermore, the Axiom of Strict Convexity ensures that as the exchange line rotates about t_0, showing continuously changing prices, there will be a continuously changing quantity demanded. The trading curve, which is the set of all these points of tangency, is a continuous function, so the demand curve will also be a continuous function for all prices at which Disraeli trades.

Identifying the set of all nonnegative prices for V goods with the vertical axis of Fig. 18-4, each price p is taken to some nonnegative quantity of V goods q. The demand function f maps prices into quantities of V goods.

The graph of f will be a curve like D in Fig. 18-7. The function f will be identified with its graph, the curve D, and we shall normally speak of the demand *curve*.

Nothing has been said so far about the shape or the behavior of this curve D. We now turn to investigate this question, subject to the neoclassical assumptions on which the curve was derived.

Our new curve shows simply one relationship extracted from the whole complicated system of relationships involved in Edgeworthian exchange theory: The dependence of the quantity of a good demanded upon its price. At first sight, this might seem to be simply a loss of generality at no gain in usefulness. A little consideration will show that this is not so, however. We can use the partial concept to analyze a single aspect of economic equilibrium—the dependence of demand upon the price of the good in abstraction from all other properties of the economy. Even our pure exchange economy had a number of aspects that are not now being actively used. But theories closer to the real world would clearly have many more: they would involve some effort to show the dependence of the demand for a

[6]For continuity, we must suppose that prices may be expressed as any fraction of a guinea.

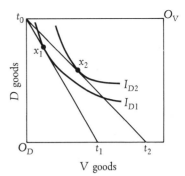

FIGURE 18-6
Points on Disraeli's trading curve

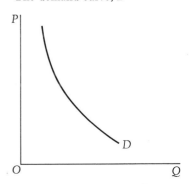

FIGURE 18-7
The demand curve, D

particular good upon the prices of all other goods, upon incomes, upon changes in tastes, upon changes in production and in the supply of the factors used in producing goods, and so on. Walrasian general equilibrium theories attempted much of this. But we are now following the Marshallian method of abstracting a particular relationship and studying it, making *the assumption* that all other factors that might affect the demand for a particular good remain unchanged at some fixed value.

The use of this technique will enable us to treat such matters as the theory of decision making by a firm, the theory of production, which would become very complicated if we insisted on a full general-equilibrium analysis at all points. We must now investigate some properties of the demand curve.

The first point of interest can be very simply stated. We have derived a demand curve for one person. We need for most purposes of economic theory the so-called *market* demand curve—that is, a curve showing the amount of the good that would be demanded at each price by the whole society. The way to obtain this curve seems obvious— simply find out how much would be demanded at each price by each individual, and add these amounts. Clearly, it is this market demand curve that is of interest to a producer.

Two comments must immediately be made, however. First, no econometrician trying to calculate the market demand curve for a product would think of trying to find out thousands of individual demand curves, then adding them. He would go after the market demand curve directly—indeed, such information as he can get is likely to bear on this and not on individual behavior.

So our need to know whether individual demands can legitimately be added is not an *econometric* need—it is not the result of efforts to test or to apply mathematical economics. It arises from our theoretical desire to see that our structure is consistent: In what *models* can we legitimately speak of an aggregate demand function for a particular good?

You may see the problems if I put it that we could certainly aggregate all the demand curves for individual youths in the Edgeworthian model of an economy with many traders.[7] Why?

---

[7] See pp. 173-177.

Essentially because they are simply replicas of the *same person*—they have identical *tastes* and *incomes*. The moment we relax this requirement and allow into the model people who differ in various respects, the possibility of meaningfully adding individual demands grows less. As to the problems that arise over *income*, consider a possible case where a good is demanded by consumers who fall into two categories: A's, who consume the good but also sell it and B's who consume it but do not sell it. If the group demand curve of the B's for the good shifts to the right and if this shift increases the income of the A's (who regard the good as an inferior good), the A's may in turn demand less of it for themselves, so that their demand curve would shift to the left. So the demands of the A's and the B's are not independent of one another and cannot meaningfully be simply summed.

Problems over *tastes* can be illustrated by the important case of fashion goods: a consumer's demand curve for a good may shift simply *because* other people are buying it. He may feel that it is very "in"—or, on the other hand, he may feel that it has been overdone.

This latter problem, over tastes, can be avoided by an axiom that is interesting because it comes up again in a number of contexts—notably in fitting a production theory into our total picture of an economy. This axiom is an assumption that a decision maker values states of the economy solely in terms of the commodity bundle that he receives, irrespective of the commodity bundles assigned to other consumers (or the pattern of production in the economy, if the model contains producers). The *state of the economy* is thus the set of all decisions to consume or exchange (or produce, if production is introduced). The concept of selfishness, in terms of which the axiom is sometimes stated, requires that a consumer be willing to rank two states of the economy as indifferent if and only if he can obtain the same commodity bundle in each and to rank one state as preferred if he can obtain a preferred bundle in the latter state.[8]

Clearly, such an axiom would enable us to assume that individual demand curves could be treated as independent, as far as problems over the interaction of *tastes* are concerned. The price paid, however, would be colossal.

[8]The concept is discussed in Quirk and Saposnik, *op. cit.*, pp. 16-17, 28-29.

A consumer must be supposed indifferent between a state of the economy in which thousands starved to death and one in which everyone was prosperous, as long as his commodity bundle remained the same. This would empty the theory of consumers' behavior of any possible welfare-theoretic significance—a high price to pay for removing *one* of the difficulties concerning the aggregation of demand curves. (Difficulties over changes in income distribution, remember, would still remain.)

We shall return to the question of an axiom of this kind in Chapter 20, where it comes up again over the effect of production decisions.

SHIFTING DEMAND CURVES

It is important to distinguish clearly two different things that are often confused in the use of such phrases as "a change in demand" and "an increase in demand." In Fig. 18-8, the movement from x_0 to x_1 is a movement *along* one demand curve. If the whole curve is to shift, say from D to D_1, some variable in the whole system of general equilibrium and outside the particular price quantity relationship, must be allowed to change. At D_1, more is being demanded at *every* price. This could be due to a change in income, in other prices—even in season: consider the demand curve for bikinis.

Even the phrase "movement along a demand curve" could be misleading. Remember that the demand curve is simply a set of ordered couples, each containing one price and one quantity, such that at that price that quantity will be bought. A point like x_0 specifies one price/quantity pair, and x_1 another. The points do not represent progress through time. The *only* sense in which time enters into the matter is that the demand curve shows how much would be bought at different prices at some point of time.

This characteristic of the demand curve raises problems about the empirical application of the concept. Producers and others are extremely interested in knowing the forms of the demand curves for particular commodities. The fact, however, that the relevant curve at one moment need bear no relation to the curve at another makes statistical investigation difficult. The obvious approach is to take price/quantity data for a period and plot them on a graph. In Fig. 18-9, x_0, x_1, and x_2 represent quantity sold in successive months at the prices represented by their position on the graph.

FIGURE 18-8

Shifting demand curves versus a movement along a demand curve

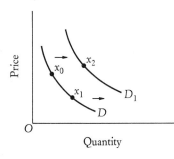

Suppose one tries to fit the curve "D" and imagines that this is approximately the true curve. In fact, x_0, x_1, and x_2 may be points on quite different curves, ruling at the different points of time. To avoid this problem, more sophisticated methods have been developed to deal with the question of *indentification* of particular demand curves.[9] A glance at Fig. 18-9 will show how disastrously wrong any decision making about optimal output by a producer would be if based on the false demand curve yielded by naïve statistical methods.

We now turn to a fundamental property of demand curves, first systematically analyzed by Marshall.

A typical task undertaken by classical mathematical analysis when applied to science was the elucidation of the ways in which the rate of change in a variable y was effected by changes in another variable x, upon which y was dependent. The Marshallian concept of *elasticity* of demand is wholly in this tradition. It is a measure of responsiveness of quantity demanded to changes in the price of the commodity.[10]

The most obvious such measure would be the change in absolute quantity demanded in response to a given change in price. But commodities are measured in different units. How do you compare an increase in the demand for ocean racers amounting to ten yachts with an increase in the demand for surfboards amounting to a thousand boards? Similar problems arise in comparing price changes directly. A ten dollar drop in the price of a surfboard might make it a bargain and significantly increase the demand for it, whereas, a change in building costs of several thousand dollars might result in no change in the size of orders to build a 40-foot ocean racer. These considerations led Marshall to develop a concept of *proportionate* elasticity, measured by the relation of the percentage change in quantity demanded to the percentage change in price of a good. We may therefore write:

[9]The econometric techniques are described by William J. Baumol, *Economic Theory and Operations Analysis*, 2d ed., Prentice-Hall, Inc., Englewood Cliffs, N.J., 1965, chap. 10 and appendix.

[10]Or to changes in income or in some other variable affecting demand, singled out for analysis.

THE CONCEPT OF ELASTICITY

FIGURE 18-9

True and false demand curves

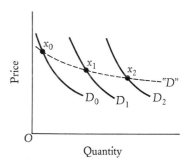

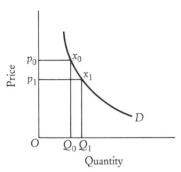

FIGURE 18-10
Arc elasticity

Price elasticity of demand =

$$-\frac{percentage\ change\ in\ quantity}{percentage\ change\ in\ price}$$

The minus sign which is put into the definition as a matter of convention serves the following purpose: Normally a rise in price will lead to a drop in quantity demanded, so that the fraction will be a negative number, and a minus sign is needed to make it positive. It is purely a matter of convenience that one should arrange things so that elasticity should appear as a positive number. For the change in quantity write ΔQ. Then the percentage change in quantity is

$$\frac{\Delta Q \cdot 100}{Q}$$

the percentage change in price is

$$\frac{\Delta P \cdot 100}{P}$$

so we get elasticity (written "e") as

$$e = \frac{100\,\Delta Q}{100\,\Delta P} \cdot \frac{P}{Q}$$

which reduces to

$$e = \frac{\Delta Q}{\Delta P} \cdot \frac{P}{Q}$$

ARC ELASTICITY AND POINT ELASTICITY

The following question arises about the formula given. In Fig. 18-10, does one express elasticity in terms of percentage change in the *initial* quantity Q_0, before the price is changed, or in terms of the quantity demanded after the price change, Q_1?

The custom is to use the average of the two quantities. How meaningful this average will be clearly depends on how small a change in quantity is studied. Ideally, we want a measure of the elasticity at any *point* on the demand curve. Analysis provides us with the exact notion required.

Let the arc of the demand curve between x_0 and x_1 be made smaller and smaller. The limit of the arc elasticity, as $Q_1 - Q_0$ approaches zero, is the point elasticity.[11]

[11]Point Elasticity: $\dfrac{dQ}{dP} \cdot \dfrac{P}{Q}$

One can describe point elasticity geometrically in the following way. In Fig. 18-11, AB is the tangent to the demand curve D at point x_0.

The slope of AB at x_0 is $\Delta P/\Delta Q$ and is represented by $x_0 C/CB$. So we have $\Delta Q/\Delta P = CB/x_0 C$. Now P/Q is $x_0 C/OC$. So point elasticity is

$$e = \frac{CB}{x_0 C} \cdot \frac{x_0 C}{OC} = \frac{CB}{OC}$$

In principle, elasticity can vary between zero and infinity. A demand curve of zero elasticity appears geometrically as a vertical straight line (see Fig. 18-12a). It represents the case where no change in price calls forth any change in quantity demanded. One would not expect to find this in real life, since, for one thing, income sets an upper limit to the price people can pay. A demand curve might, however, have a stretch for which it ran vertically. A medicine, for example, might be bought on a physician's advice even if its cost increased considerably. But more of it would not be bought if its price dropped. The opposite extreme is a curve of infinite elasticity, which shows as a horizontal straight line (Fig. 18-12b).

A demand curve of infinite elasticity implies that there exists some price at which an unlimited quantity can be sold, whereas above this nothing can be. Empirically unlikely, this case nevertheless describes the situation which an individual producer may face in the important case of perfect competition theory, where a producer is supposed to assume that he cannot affect the ruling price but can sell all he can produce at that price. The nearest thing to this in real life is perhaps a small farmer who can sell all he can produce at a given ruling price, but can sell nothing if he tries to raise the price. But it is only the demand curve for the product of an individual farmer that is horizontal—the demand curve for the agricultural product of all the farmers is downward sloping.

The case of unitary elasticity (Fig. 18-12c) arises where throughout the curve, all proportionate changes in price result in equal proportionate changes in quantity demanded. It is natural to imagine at first that a linear demand curve will have the same elasticity throughout its length. This is so, however, only in the extreme cases of zero and infinite elasticity. In every other case the elasticity is dif-

IMPORTANT CASES OF ELASTICITY

FIGURE 18-11
Point elasticity

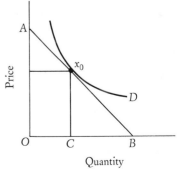

ferent at every point along the linear curve. While the absolute rate of change of P and Q remains the same, these are different *proportions* of continually changing total quantities and prices. The convexity to the origin of the curve of unitary elasticity may be explained as follows: As price drops by equal units, greater and greater *proportional* changes in price occur. Therefore, as quantity increases, it must increase by larger and larger *absolute* amounts to keep the proportionate change in quantity equal to that in price.[12]

Demand curves of unitary elasticity throughout their length are rather unlikely, but a part of the curve may well be of unitary elasticity. The concept, however, has a theoretical usefulness: It serves to divide demand curves into those of *less than* unitary elasticity (known as *"inelastic"*), and those of greater than unitary elasticity (known as *"elastic"*). We should expect commodities with which most consumers are far from satiated to have elastic demand curves, since this expectation entails that more of them will be preferred, whereas a commodity with which consumers are near satiation would have an inelastic demand curve.

ELASTICITY AND TOTAL REVENUE

We may now illustrate the motivation for investigating the elasticity of demand by showing the relation between this concept and a key concept of the theory of production, the concept of total revenue.

We may define the *total revenue* obtained by producers of a good as the quantity of the good sold multiplied by its price. Now as long as elasticity is greater than unity, a 1 percent drop in price is leading to more than a 1 percent increase in quantity sold, and total revenue is rising. When

FIGURE 18-12

Cases of elasticity

[12]It can be shown that the exact curve is that known as a "rectangular hyperbola."

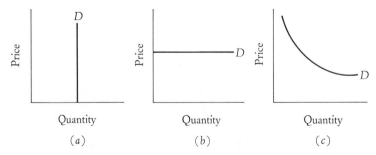

Quantity	Quantity	Quantity
(*a*)	(*b*)	(*c*)

elasticity is unity, total revenue is constant, and when elasticity is less than unity, total revenue is falling. A total revenue curve thus outlines the frontier of the area of attainable revenue from all different outputs of the commodity, as in Fig. 18-13.

Point x_0, where total revenue is 1,200 for 100 units, thus maximizes total revenue. This is in turn the quantity of output for which elasticity of demand is unity. The total revenue set, thus derivable from the demand curve, is of obvious interest to producers.

So far we have confined ourselves to discussing the elasticity of demand for a commodity in response to changes in *its* price, with all other prices—as well as incomes, tastes, and the distribution of incomes—being assumed constant. But one can get an elasticity concept by allowing any one variable to vary, all the others being held constant, and observing the effects of the variations upon quantity demanded.

In particular, the *cross elasticity* of demand is defined as the percentage change in the quantity of X demanded, divided by the percentage change in the price of Y, where Y is some other commodity. Cross elasticity can have any value from plus to minus infinity. When its value is zero, the two commodities are unrelated goods. When it is positive, the two commodities are substitutes for each other: an increase in the price of Scotch will induce people to drink more bourbon. The percentage change in the price of Scotch and the demand for bourbon will be in the same direction. On the other hand, complimentary commodities have negative cross elasticities. An increase in the air fare from Copenhagen to Malaga will decrease the demand for bikinis in Copenhagen, and a decrease in the air fare will increase it. The change in air fares is accompanied by change in the demand for bikinis in the opposite direction, so the cross elasticity will be negative.

The notion of cross elasticity is sometimes used to define the concept of an *industry*. For any x and y, x and y are produced by the *same* industry, if and only if their cross elasticity is positive and high. But how high? No hard-and-fast rule can be given: it depends on the problem on hand. There may be a high cross elasticity between convertibles and station wagons, and between station wagons and jeeps. Are convertibles and jeeps then in the same

CROSS ELASTICITY AND INCOME ELASTICITY

FIGURE 18-13

Total revenue set

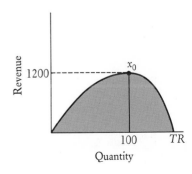

industries or different? The cross elasticity concept alone will not tell how to decide this issue.

Income elasticity is defined as percentage change in quantity demanded divided by percentage change in income. An increase in income will usually lead to an increase in quantity demanded, so income elasticity will usually be positive. For some goods, however, this need not be so, and this fact was recognized by Marshall, who described the extreme case (where an increase in income leads to an actual *shrinking* of quantity demanded) as the case of inferior goods. The discussion of the effects of changes in income leads to an important distinction and its analysis, which was presented by Sir John Hicks.

INCOME EFFECTS AND SUBSTITUTION EFFECTS

Since the time of Hicks it has been usual to analyze the effects of a change in a consumer's income or in the price of one commodity upon the consumer's situation and therefore upon his optimizing decisions, in terms of two separate categories: the income effect and the substitution effect. A manner of analyzing these effects, due to Hicks, follows:

Suppose the consumer's income to shrink, as in Fig. 18-14. Notice that the frontier of the smaller attainable region is parallel to that of the larger—that is, *relative* prices of the two commodities making up income in the model are the same. The path traced out by the set of all tangencies[13] between an indifference curve and a frontier, for some level of income, is the *Hicksian income consumption curve*. It shows how consumption of the two commodities brownies and milk will vary at all different levels of income for some given pair of *relative commodity prices*. It isolates the pure *income* effect upon consumption, relative prices being constant. Now to isolate the pure *substitution* effect.

FIGURE 18-14
Hicksian income consumption curve

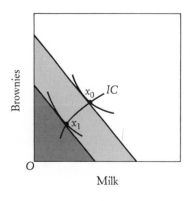

Allow the frontier of the consumer's attainable region to swing from F_0 to F_1 in Fig. 18-15, showing a rise in the relative price of the horizontal commodity. This will force the consumer from x_0 to x_1, the most preferred position he can now attain. Since this is a position on a lower indifference curve I_1, we may say with Hicks that his income has

[13]We may say "tangencies" since the Hicksian analysis, like that of Edgeworth, rests on Axioms of Dominance and Strict Convexity, and we may as well present it in its classical form.

fallen. We could restore him to the former level of income, while maintaining the change in relative prices, by shifting the frontier out to F_2, keeping F_2 parallel to F_1 to retain the same relative prices. At F_2 the consumer is in equilibrium at x_2, which is a point on his original indifference curve I_0. Hicks is treating any two points on the same indifference curve as giving one the same income. The move from x_0 to x_2 is then the pure *substitution* effect of the changes in price.

Thus any change in the price of one commodity, all other variables in the system held constant, can be analyzed into two elements, the income effect and the substitution effect.

We may now use these results to investigate the so-called law of demand. This is sometimes expressed by saying that more of the commodity will be bought at lower prices or, in terms of the shape of the curve, that demand curves slope downward to the right. This way of putting things, however, rules out the possibility that the demand curve might have a stretch or stretches over which price elasticity was zero—that is, where the curve was vertical. Any way of formulating laws about demand involves making decisions about what to include in the normal case.

The demand curve we have derived from the trading curve contains, as we can now see, both substitution effects and income effects. Hicks derived a similar demand curve, from what he called a *price consumption curve*. The latter was the locus of points of tangency between a consumer's indifference curve and lines representing different relative prices; thus it was, from the present point of view, structurally similar to our trading curve. Hicks now produced what has become a classic argument about the properties of his demand curve. The gist of the argument was that the substitution effect of a fall in the price of the commodity must be to increase the quantity demanded and of a rise in price to reduce it. The proof of this was an example of an explicit use of the strict convexity property of indifference curves (Fig. 18-15a).

A change in relative prices, income held constant, from F_0 to F_1 shows that strict convexity entails an increase in the consumption of the commodity whose price has fallen from OA to OB.[14] That this conclusion need not fol-

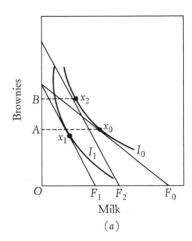

(a)

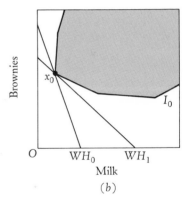

(b)

FIGURE 18-15

Hicksian substitution effect (a) and a contrasting contemporary case (b)

---

[14]Remember that this is what is implied by a change in the slope of the "price line" (Hicks' term for the wealth constraint).

low from the weak convexity axiom of contemporary consumption theory will be seen from Fig. 18-15b. Here the change in relative prices indicated by the swing from WH_0 to WH_1 leads to no change in the consumption of either commodity.

Arguing that the substitution effect, taken alone, must lead to a downward-sloping demand curve, Hicks then asked whether or not the income effect would reinforce this slope. He concluded that it would, except in the case of an inferior good, for which no more might be bought at higher levels of income and in fact *less* might be bought. The classic case is a good like potatoes which people buy less of when their incomes rise above a certain point. Even with negative income effects, however, Hicks concluded that the demand curve would still be conventionally shaped unless the negative income effect should be sufficient to *outweigh* the positive substitution effect.

The Hicksian conclusion was that demand curves will be conventionally shaped (slope downward to the right) except in the case where extreme negative income effects outweigh the substitution effect. The matter can be carried a little further. It can be argued that a demand curve, if it is to show the dependence of quantity demanded solely on the changes in the price of the good, should be adjusted to abstract from the income effect of these price changes; therefore, such a curve, since it shows only substitution effects, must necessarily be conventionally shaped. However, unless we have an Axiom of Strict Convexity, this conclusion does not follow. The price of a good can fall to some extent without any increase in the consumption of the good. So such a demand curve could have vertical stretches.

We are now ready to conclude the chapter with a brief look at those contemporary demand relations usually referred to as "demand correspondences."

DEMAND CORRESPONDENCES

To see the motivation for concluding in this manner, relax the two Axioms of Dominance and Strict Convexity, assumed in order to generate a simple Edgeworthian exchange theory, and restore the indifference curves to the freedom that they enjoyed under Axioms of Insatiability and Weak Convexity. Consider the attempt to derive a

demand curve from the relationship between such indifference curves and a wealth hyperplane, which is allowed to
swing so as to show changing relative prices.

As may be seen from Fig. 18-16, the weak convexity
of B_0 allows the wealth hyperplane WH_0 to be supporting
to B_0 throughout the infinite set of points in the closed
interval from x_0 to x_1 (*closed* because it includes the limit
points x_0 and x_1), which we shall write $[x_0, x_1]$. Now, if
"p_0" is the price represented by this slope of the wealth
hyperplane, there is no mapping f that takes p_0 to some
unique quantity: At p_0 any quantity in the closed interval
$[q_0, q_1]$ may be demanded.

At some prices (slopes of WH), there *is* a unique
quantity of commodity S demanded: where the wealth
hyperplane is supporting to a single point of a better set,
as with WH_n and B_n at x_n. At this price, the quantity q_n
of commodity S is uniquely demanded.

That is the problem. Now we turn to the method of
tackling it. If with each element p of a set P is associated
a *nonempty* closed subset $N(q)$ of a set Q, a *correspondence* (or set-valued mapping or multivalued mapping, or
point-to-set mapping) f from P to the set of subsets of Q
is defined.

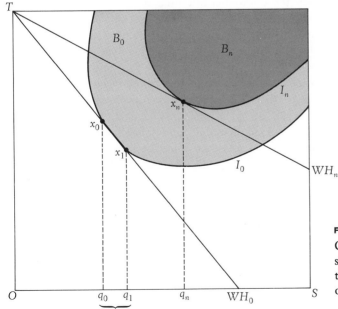

FIGURE 18-16

One price, represented by the
slope of WH_0, associated with
the infinite set of quantities
of commodity S in $[q_0, q_1]$

Suppose that you are crossing the Atlantic in a small sailboat, headed for Portugal. You might stay clean shaven (highly inconvenient, it is so hard to shave), grow a full beard, or settle for some intermediate growth. Call this set of actions "A." Let "a_0" be staying clean shaven, "a_2" be growing a full beard, and "a_1" be some intermediate stage of hairiness. When you arrive, you hit the season at Estoril. Now, let the set of girls in Estoril be "G," and suppose there is a nonempty subset of G (one of whom is bound to respond) attracted by action a_0, another subset attracted by any action a_1, and still another subset drawn out of the woodwork by a_2. Then we have a correspondence, or set-valued mapping, or multi-valued mapping, f, from any element a of A to some member of a nonempty subset of G. Manifestly the relation between price and quantity where an indifference curve has linear segments is a correspondence. Notice that the fundamental idea of a correspondence, like the idea of a single-valued mapping, can be stated in terms of finite sets. As *continuity* is not necessary to the notion of a single-valued mapping, so what is called "upper semicontinuity" is not necessary to the notion of a correspondence.

Now a demand correspondence is sometimes illustrated as in Fig. 18-17. But this "demand curve" will not bear the traditional interpretation. Traditionally, any point on a demand curve, say a, maps a single price p to a single quantity q. This is a way of saying that if the price is p, the quantity q *will be sold*. Therefore, to draw the horizontal stretch of demand curve from a to b implies that at price p there is infinite elasticity between these points. This means that if a supplier offers *any* quantity in the closed interval $[q_0, q_1]$ at price p, that quantity will sell.

But all that the indifference-curve situation entitled one to assert was that, since the wealth hyperplane is supporting to B_0 for the relevant linear segment of B_0, the consumer might (indifferently) decide to choose any particular quantity in the closed interval $[q_0, q_1]$ at price p. If he happens to choose q_0, for instance, a supplier who assumed he could sell q_1 will be left with stock on his hands.[15]

Suppose that you have bought a small-sized bikini in France, intending to give it as a present to some girl of

FIGURE 18-17

$f: p \longrightarrow [q_0, q_1]$ interpreted as leading to a demand curve, D, with an infinitely elastic segment

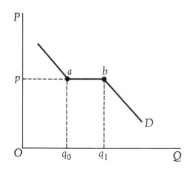

[15] This argument was developed in discussions with A. Anastasopulos.

the right size. Suppose that three girls of the right size come to swim in your pool and that they know you have decided to give the bikini to one of them but that you do not mind which one. There is then a set-valued mapping from the bikini to the set of three girls. What is a girl entitled to assume?

Surely only that she *may* get the bikini.[16]

QUESTIONS

1. Suppose that the friendliness of a Danish girl whom you have just met in Pedro's depends on her whole life history up to then, together with your conversation, behavior, and the weather that evening, as well as the food, wine, and service at dinner. What would be the Marshallian approach to analyzing the situation? What can be said for, and what against, this point of view?

2. What subset of binary relations are mappings? Distinguish mappings *onto* from mappings *into* a set. Are mappings from a set P onto a set S necessarily one-to-one? Can they be one-to-one?

3. Outline the concept of a continuous mapping. What reasons are there for treating the demand function as a continuous mapping?

4. How may demand curves be derived from trading curves? Do demand curves give more or less information?

[16]The only text I know of in which set-valued mappings and the whole significance of demand and supply correspondences in mathematical economics are discussed at an undergraduate level is Quirk and Saposnik, *op. cit.*, chaps. 2 and 3. In this book the authors associate demand correspondences with demand curves having infinitely elastic segments, like that in my Fig. 18-17. We have since agreed in discussion that this will not do. For the rest, their treatment is amazingly clear and simple, especially on the difficult question of the "upper semicontinuity" of correspondences. An informal, very clear graduate-level treatment will be found in Kelvin Lancaster, *Mathematical Economics*, The Macmillan Company, New York, 1968, "R9 Point-to-Set Mappings," pp. 342-353. The mathematics is briefly treated in Gerard Debreu, *Theory of Value: An Axiomatic Analysis of Economic Equilibrium*, Cowles Foundation Monograph 17, John Wiley & Sons, Inc., New York, 1959, pp. 5-6, 17-19. An excellent formal mathematical source is Claude Berge, *Espaces Topologiques et Fonctions Multivoques*, Dunod, Paris, 1959; English translation, *Topological Spaces*, The Macmillan Company, New York, 1963.

5. Define and distinguish *arc* elasticity of demand and *point* elasticity. In what cases may more than one point on a demand curve have the same elasticity?

6. Distinguish the important cases of elasticity. Why are demand curves of unitary elasticity not linear?

7. Define and distinguish cross elasticity and income elasticity. What bearing does cross elasticity have on the distinction between complimentary and substitute commodities?

8. Analyze the consequences of a price change in terms of Hicksian income and substitution effects.

9. Does a pure substitution demand curve necessarily follow the law of demand?

10. In what circumstances is the demand function a set-valued mapping, or correspondence?

11. If a supplier knows that a price p_0 is mapped to a closed interval $[q_0, q_1]$, what quantity can he count on being able to sell?

19

SUPPLY AND EQUILIBRIUM IN AN EXCHANGE ECONOMY

The reader who is blessed with a sense of structure might be expecting at this point to find a chapter symmetrical with the previous one and entitled "Supply Mappings and Correspondences." And indeed we shall shortly make a number of moves that look symmetrical with those in Chapter 18. We shall derive a supply curve from the general picture of exchange and show that it has properties —such as elasticity—that formally resemble those of demand. The point of view from which demand and supply curves may be regarded as symmetrical is well expressed by R. G. D. Allen:[1]

It is appropriate, in some problems, to represent the conditions of supply of a good in a way analogous to those in demand. Suppose, for example, that a market consists of indi-

---

[1]R. G. D. Allen, *Mathematical Analysis for Economists*, The Macmillan Company, New York, 1966, p. 121. Italics are in the original.

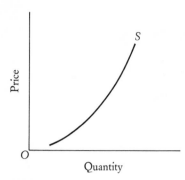

FIGURE 19-1
A supply curve

viduals who bring fixed stocks of various goods to a market place for exchange amongst themselves. If there is pure competition among the individuals, market prices (in money terms) of all goods being given, then each individual will determine by how much he will increase or decrease his stock of any one good. If he wishes to increase his stock, he forms part of the *demand* for the good; if he decreases his stock, he contributes to the *supply*. Then, if all prices other than that of the good concerned are fixed, the total demand and the total supply of the good are defined, by addition over the whole market, as dependent upon the price. The demand and supply functions are exactly similar, supply being negative demand.

As is implied by Allen's argument, a supply curve can be derived from the trading curve of exchange theory in an analogous manner to that in which we derived the demand curve. A trading curve is a set of ordered couples, one element in each couple being a demand and one element being an offer. If the set of demands for all prices can be abstracted, so can the set of offers. The set of all Q, such that Q is a quantity offered at some price P, is then our supply curve. One takes each (p, q) from the Edgeworth box to a price/quantity two space (Fig. 19-1).

The shape of the supply curve, indicating that at higher prices more will be offered, follows here simply from the theory of exchange. The owners of a good will offer more of it as its price rises—that is, in terms of the theory of exchange, as its price rises *relative* to that of the commodity they are demanding, as the rate of exchange moves in their favor.

**THE ELASTICITY OF
SUPPLY**

Furthermore, various concepts of elasticity can clearly be formally applied to the supply curve. Price elasticity of supply, for instance, is percentage change in quantity supplied over percentage change in price. As in the case of demand, this may be calculated for an arc or at a point. Again, one may distinguish the limiting cases of zero and infinite elasticity, respectively Fig. 19-2a and Fig. 19-2b.

FIGURE 19-2
Limiting cases of
elasticity of supply

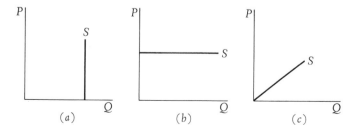

The case of supply fixed irrespective of price is actually an empirically important one, being the basis of the analysis of non-supply-regulating incomes, a topic that we shall deal with when we come to the question of supplies of factors of production.[2]

Notice that with supply curves the case of unitary elasticity is *linear*, as in Fig. 19-2c. A supply curve of unitary elasticity is any straight line outward from the origin. As with demand, one uses the case of unitary elasticity as a dividing line between elastic and inelastic curves.

So much for the properties common to demand and supply curves. Now we turn to correspondences.

As we have seen, in any model for Edgeworthian exchange theory, any point on Disraeli's trading curve is an offer to supply his goods as well as a demand for V goods. So, on the Axiom of Strict Convexity, there is a supply function f, which takes each price p to a quantity offered q. But if you look at Fig 19-3, you will see that relaxing the Axiom of Strict Convexity has the consequence that a particular price p_0 may be mapped to a closed interval of quantities supplied, say $[q_1, q_2]$.

So the supply curve may look as it does in Fig. 19-4.[3]

SUPPLY
CORRESPONDENCES

[2]See Chapter 22, pp. 272-275.

[3]See James Quirk and Rubin Saposnik, *Introduction to General Equilibrium Theory and Welfare Economics*, McGraw-Hill Book Company, New York, 1968, p. 49.

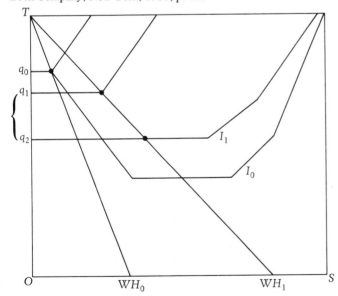

FIGURE 19-3

A supply correspondence, a set-valued mapping, f, from p_1 (slope of WH_1) to a closed interval of quantities,
$f : p_1 \longrightarrow [q_1, q_2]$

You will immediately ask: Why can the set-valued mapping $f : p_1 \longrightarrow [q_1, q_2]$ be represented in this case of *supply* by an infinitely elastic stretch of supply curve? Ask yourself the economic meaning of an infinitely elastic stretch of supply curve like that in Fig. 19-4. It means that the supplier is *willing* to supply *any* quantity from q_1 to q_2 inclusive.

So much for the superficial similarities and differences of demand and supply curves. Now we must go behind the curves and compare the decisions that underlie them.

THE CHARACTER OF DECISIONS TO SUPPLY

The demand curves of Chapter 18 are derived from properties of an Edgeworth box construction which are in turn deduced from the axioms of choice theory and of consumption theory.

The situation for the supply curve is very different. The only decisions to supply so far covered are of a very special type: namely, those where the decision turns on whether to offer a quantity of a good in exchange or to consume it oneself. Now, *some* important supply decisions have this form. The most obviously important case is the decision to supply labor: one can sell his time in return for purchasing power over other goods or he can consume it himself as leisure. In principle, one can make decisions of this type wherever one has a good that he can either consume himself or exchange. A small farmer, producing mainly for subsistence, can decide whether to market some of his produce in return for the power to buy goods from a town. At unfavorable relative prices, he can consume his produce himself. In today's world, labor is probably the only empirically important case in a developed economy.[4]

So far, we have a theory of supply decisions *only* for situations in which these are an aspect of consumption and exchange decisions: we are beginning to feel acutely the lack of a *theory of production*. To explain the most important factors underlying the supply curve in a developed economy we need a theory of production decisions and a theory of cost.

It is time to give up our assumption of a pure exchange economy and to introduce next an axiomatic theory

FIGURE 19-4

A supply curve S, graphing a supply correspondence

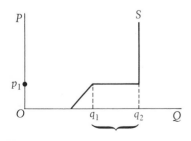

[4]Not everyone can vary even his supply of labor. In most industrial jobs, one can choose only the standard work week or not working.

of production decisions, developed by adapting and adding to our existing axiom set. These axioms will be presented in Part 5 of this book, beginning in Chapter 20.

In the meantime, lacking the full understanding of the factors underlying the supply curve, which must wait until later, we may nevertheless sketch the general outline of the notion of equilibrium price as the intersection of the demand and supply curves.

In Fig. 19-5 the curves are drawn as straight lines, specifically to draw attention to the fact that no claim is being made that their exact form reflects any empirically important concrete case, only their general relations being important for the moment.

Out of the set of price/quantity couples demanded and the set of all couples offered, there is one couple represented by x_0, which is the intersection. Quantity Oq_0 at price Op_0 is both demanded and supplied. This is the equilibrium quantity and price.

What guarantee do we have that there will exist a point x_0, at which demand and supply are equal, at which there is zero excess supply and zero excess demand, so that the market is cleared?

In the simple case before us the answer is not too far to seek. Since the trading curves of the theory of exchange have a fixed point—at which offers and demands are equal—so will the demand and supply curves that are simply derived from them. The intersection of a youth's trading curve and a maiden's trading curve define the point, which is at once a youth's demand for m goods and a youth's supply of y goods and also a maiden's demand for y goods and the maiden's supply of m goods. This point is simply taken to a two space representing the demand and supply for m goods and to another two space to represent the demand and supply for y goods.

A GLANCE AT THE EQUILIBRIUM OF DEMAND AND SUPPLY

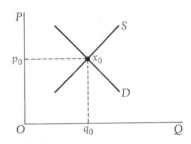

FIGURE 19-5
The equilibrium price p_0 and quantity, q_0

As theories of an economy become more complicated than our Edgeworthian theory of pure exchange and as they approach more closely to real life, the *existence* of an equilibrium comes to stand in need of proof. Such proofs do not attempt to delineate the equilibrium or to show that only one equilibrium is possible. They aim simply to show that a system satisfying certain axioms must *have* at least one equilibrium. Existence theorems in mathematics and

EXISTENCE THEOREMS

science serve the important function of showing that search for solutions to some problems is not futile simply because there was no solution to be found.

We have seen one important instance of an existence theorem in these pages, namely, Kenneth Arrow's proof of the nonexistence of a social welfare function upon certain axioms. This is a *negative* existence theorem. A proof that something does *not* exist can be highly important. If it is the case that no Swedish girls go to Estoril, knowing this may save weeks of wasted effort.[5]

QUESTIONS

1. In what sense is the derivation of *supply* curves from a model for Edgeworthian exchange theory symmetrical with the derivation of the demand curve?

2. Compare supply correspondences with demand correspondences. Draw the graph of a supply correspondence. What interpretation is presupposed of the closed interval $[q_1, q_2]$ to which some price p is mapped?

3. Describe the properties of the concept of elasticity of supply. What are the important cases of supply elasticity?

4. What are the similarities and contrasts of supply elasticity and demand elasticity?

5. What underlies the supply curve in a pure exchange theory? In what sense is the theory of supply trivialized by the absence of a theory of production?

6. What guarantees that the existence of an equilibrium point for demand and supply can be derived from the properties of the pure exchange theory?

[5]The problems posed by existence theorems proving that a competitive equilibrium will exist in a given model for a general equilibrium theory upon given axioms cannot very well be meaningfully discussed below a certain level of complexity and formality. However, any reader of this book should be able to handle Tjalling Koopmans' beautifully written *Three Essays on the State of Economic Science* (McGraw-Hill Book Company, New York, 1957). The excellent survey of the whole area in Quirk and Saposnik (*op. cit*) is more formal but should be still within reach.

Part 5
Production Theory

20
AXIOMS
OF
TRANSFORMATION

The youths and maidens in our model for the Edge-worthian theory of a pure exchange economy were endowed with a fixed initial holding of y goods and m goods. We explicitly abstained from investigating how they came to be in possession of the initial stocks. We simply thought of them as thus endowed by, so to speak, nature. It was, after all, an Arcadian scene, a world free from "dark satanic mills," very much to the taste of William Blake.

In the world we live in, most of the things we want do not exist by acts of nature but must be consciously produced; and the supply of them that is forthcoming depends on the decisions of the producers, while these decisions in turn depend largely on the cost and effectiveness of the factors which must be used in production. This was well known to the classical English political economists.

We shall now begin to approach somewhat nearer to reality by constructing, as a model for choice theory, an explicit theory of production. Even this theory, however, will offer only a highly simplified picture of reality. It will, however, be an axiomatization of currently received production theory.

THE TRANSFORMATION RELATION "T"

Producing, in the widest sense, is a matter of *transforming* something, x, into something else, y. A commodity may be transformed by being physically changed, as wood and nails are made into a table; but it may also be transformed by being transported from one place to another, by being made available in any way, by having its accessibility increased—as when a book is translated from one language into another or information is processed by an electronic system. For any x and y where x may be transformed into y we shall write, following a notation introduced by S. Afriat, "$x \, T \, y$."

To assert "$x \, T \, y$" is to claim that "were the agent in the economic state defined by possession of x, it would be possible by available means, to attain the state y. These means might be the exchanges which take place between agents, or through markets, or in the input-output of industrial processes permitted by technology."[1]

Notice that pure exchange can be regarded as a case of transformation. A moment's reflection will show the truth of this: the youths certainly transformed their offering into m goods, and the maidens likewise.

The transformations considered from now on may be thought of as including exchanges, but they are free to take any form allowed by the axioms imposed below upon the relation "T." This relation will be adopted as a primitive. It is the only primitive concept that we shall need to add in order to axiomatize the theory of production. Our first requirement is for an axiom guaranteeing that the set of possible transformations is not empty. We accordingly assume that at least one element in the attainable set of general choice theory may be transformed. This may be thought of as an axiom assuring the Existence of Productions:

Axiom 14 $\exists \, x \, \exists \, y \, (Ax \, \& \, x \, T \, y)$

[1] Sidney N. Afriat, *Economic Transformation*, Krannert Institute Paper No. 152, Purdue University, November, 1966, p. 2. For a striking analysis of the concept of the production of scientific and other work as instances of transformation, compare Louis Althusser, *Pour Marx*, and *Lire Le Capital*, Hadamard, Paris, 1965.

Some elements in the attainable set may be transformed into y. The set of all productions y is written "Y," and is clearly a proper subset of the attainable set A.

A producer may be an individual, a partnership, a corporation, a scientist, an Israeli Kibbutz, a Yugoslav workers' cooperative, a government servant, an artist giving instructions to some engineer, or, for that matter, an electronic brain. For the purposes of the theory, a producer is simply anyone who transforms some x into some y: "an economic agent whose role is to choose (and carry out) a production plan."[2]

The introduction of production into a theory is sometimes heralded by the adoption of an axiom asserting the existence of producers or of production decisions. Producers are sometimes formally distinguished from other economic agents, such as consumers.[3] We realize, of course, that what is being distinguished is the role of making production decisions, and that this and other roles can coexist in one person in real life.

Here, however, I shall take the position that the only new primitive notion needed to introduce production explicitly into the theory is the relation "T." Production is introduced explicitly, in terms of the primitive notion of a transformation, by Axiom 14. There is no need to assume that transformations are due to a special class of agents.

The phrases "production decision" or "choice of a production plan" or "choice by a producer" will be used only for stylistic variety; they will stand simply for the choice to *transform* some $x \in A$ into some possible y. Clearly, if x is an element in the attainable set and if x may be transformed into $y, y \in A$. In other words, the set of all possible y, written "Y," is a proper subset of the attainable set. The set Y, such that $Y \subset A$, will be called the "production set."

Since the production set is a subset of the attainable set of choice theory, we shall assume that production theory is a model for the theory of choice and that therefore the

PRODUCTION DECISIONS AND THE AXIOMS OF GENERAL CHOICE THEORY

[2]Gerard Debreu, *Theory of Value: An Axiomatic Analysis of Economic Equilibrium*, Cowles Foundation Monograph 17, John Wiley & Sons, Inc., New York, 1959, p. 37.

[3]*Ibid.*, p. 39; Tjalling C. Koopmans, *Three Essays on the State of Economic Science*, McGraw-Hill Book Company, New York, 1957, p. 44.

seven axioms of general choice theory apply to production decisions. Their relevance in this particular context may bear a little exploration, however. The assumption of the Axiom of Comparability[4] implies, in the present context, that received production theory, such as that about to be described here, cannot handle problems of production decisions that may arise through there existing plans which the producer, for any reason, finds incomparable. That such decisions are empirically possible and may be important is not denied. However, they cannot be handled within the axiom set of existing decision theory.

The Axiom 2, the Axiom of Transitivity, is relevant in the following way. It is just as necessary that decisions about production plans should be consistent as that any other decisions should be. If a production y_2 is preferred by a producer to a production y_1, and y_1 to another y_0, then we need to be able to infer that $y_2 \, P \, y_0$.

Finally, the remaining axioms of pure choice theory, as applied to production decisions, simply require these decisions to be in accordance with the ordering system discovered by applying the first axioms. These decisions are required to be optimal—producers are required to pick an element in the maximal set of their ordering, whatever the criteria may be that have led them to order plans in a given way.

We have thus, so far, an axiom introducing transformations, and the seven general axioms of choice theory, assumed to apply to these decisions. As in the case of consumption decisions, the reader would expect that special axioms, too restrictive to be a part of general choice theory, will now be needed to generate a production theory of recognizable character. This is indeed the case. It may further be suspected that at least some of the axioms upon the production set will show structural similarity to some of those upon the consumption set.[5] This also is true: We shall run up against issues concerning the concepts of continuity and—above all—convexity once again. I shall pay a great deal of attention to these similarities of form, since one of the things which I am most concerned to make vivid is the underlying unity of the character—and problems—of mathematical economics.

[4]See pp. 80-82.

[5]For the axioms on consumption sets recall pp. 130-147.

If we did not already have them in our model, consumers or, if you like, consumption decisions, would have to be explicitly introduced.[6] As it is, we already have consumers, making consumption and exchange decisions. They are assumed to continue to do so, subject to the axioms of choice and of consumption theory. The theory of production must assume, for example, that complete satiation will not suddenly appear and that the properties of the preference ordering of consumption theory, like convexity, will continue to hold.[7] One might put the point by saying, simply, that the axioms of consumption are *ipso facto* axioms of production theory. They help to define the logical world about which production theory has been written. We have therefore numbered the first axiom of production theory as our Axiom 14.

It is customary to add a new kind of commodity to those appearing in the commodity set of consumption theory. These are *input* commodities, including all resources withdrawn from nature and all kinds of labor. They may be assumed to be owned by consumers in a private ownership economy, but this is not essential to the theory. However they are *owned*, they must *exist* if production is to be possible. (It is not assumed that they can be consumed only by producers: leisure, as we have seen, can be regarded as a way of consuming labor by its owner, and a piece of land can also be consumed by its owner, by using it as a private estate.)

We, however, already have inputs, simply by virtue of Axiom 14: If there exists some attainable x, such that x can be transformed into y, this is already to say that x is an input and y an output.

Nor need we specify that all inputs come from the attainable *commodity* set of consumption theory: some may well be such as not to count as commodities until the possibility of *transforming* them is opened. Our inputs are simply drawn from the attainable set of general choice theory, of which they are clearly a proper subset.

THE PRODUCTION SET
AND THE AXIOMS OF
CONSUMPTION THEORY

[6]As they are in Koopmans' Axioms One and Two (Koopmans, *op. cit.*, p. 44).

[7]The Axioms of Strict Convexity and of Dominance, introduced for Edgeworthian exchange theory, will not be needed essentially in production theory. They do not, however, act as restrictions on it—they are simply without effect. Nonsatiation and weak convexity are alone relevant.

We next need to add an assumption upon preference orderings to those already adopted in the theory of consumption; there are new elements in our world whose effect on preferences had not previously been considered. For one thing, consumers must decide what inputs to offer, including inputs for which they may have no personal use in direct consumption if they withhold them. Hitherto we have considered, in the theory of exchange, only the case where they offer something that they will otherwise consume. For another thing, there is a new set of decisions, production decisions. These may affect consumers' preferences. For the moment, we shall simply eliminate such crosscurrents by an axiom. This is in fact done by received production theory, but we must immediately insist on the limiting effects of the move. The assumption that the decisions of producers has no effect on consumers' preference structures is often untrue. Manifestly, the whole character of our life, in the real world, is affected by the productive processes that are used. In particular, the welfare implications of the theory are seriously impaired by this assumption of zero interdependence[8] between consumption and production decisions. The assumption is made simply to give a picture of received production theory, but its limiting effects on the empirical realism of the theory must not be forgotten. Subject to this, we shall assume an axiom which we shall describe as the *Neutrality of Transformations*. We postulate that consumers judge transformations solely by their inputs and outputs—the *processes*, or *activities*, as such do not give rise to preferences. If any x may be transformed into any y by the use of any of several processes, or activities, these activities will be judged indifferent just in case their inputs are indifferent and their outputs are indifferent:

[8]The distinction between the private cost of a productive process—i.e., the inputs that the producer has to pay for—and the social cost of the process—i.e., its private cost plus concealed damage to the rest of society—was one of Pigou's most fruitful insights. Any amount of alienation and general human misery can be ignored by the dodge of judging a productive system simply in terms of the inputs producers have to pay for its (private) costs and its outputs. Claims about welfare, about the size of a national product, or about growth or progress that ignore these issues should be regarded as highly suspect. See the discussion in Koopmans, *op. cit.*, p. 41, and reference given there.

Axiom 15   *Any two transformations are indif-ferent ⇔ their inputs are indifferent and their outputs are indifferent.*

Taken this way, Axiom 15 amounts to assuming part of what is contained in Quirk and Saposnik's Axiom of Selfish-ness.[9] But since our theory makes no distinction between the *persons* involved in production and those involved in consumption, it is in the cards that any consumer may be involved in any productive process. So no matter how *selfish* he was, he presumably would alter his preference ordering if the existence of a transformation made *him* suffer. So it is better to interpret our Axiom 15 as an assumption that all transformations are, so to speak, morally and aestheti-cally "clean." Need I point out again that in the world we live in this is most notoriously not so?

Received production theory, however, depends on the assumption that all transformations are regarded by all con-sumers as clean transformations in the sense of Axiom 15. Theorems showing conditions under which production optima can be attained particularly depend, for their force as welfare theorems, upon this assumption. Two arrange-ments of production activities in a society may be equally efficient in terms of their use of inputs and delivery of outputs in the ordinary sense. But one of them may be considered "dirty" by a particular group, who will then cer-tainly not regard the two productive arrangements as indif-ferent. Axiom 15 assumes that this issue does not arise for any transformation.

We have now prepared the ground for the considera-tion of a set of axioms specifically on the transformation relation, whose form was developed by S. Afriat. The first of these, the Axiom of Procession, may be written:

Axiom 16 $x \, T \, y \, \& \, y \, T \, z \Rightarrow x \, T \, z$

This axiom asserts that T is a transitive relation. Notice that transitivity is thus assumed to hold not just for production *decisions* (this is already covered by Axiom 2 of general choice theory) but also for the production *processes*, or *activities*. "The axiom states that the result of a proces-sion of possible transformations is a possible transformation.

[9]See the discussion in Chapter 18, "Demand Mappings and Correspondences," pp. 199-200.

This axiom is inseparable from the concept of a transformation."[10] Thanks to Axiom 16, we shall be able to ignore intermediate stages of production and intermediate commodities, like special grades of steel, made by one industry to be used by another, in our general elementary production theory. (A special study of the relations of industries of different levels would require further assumptions.)

In a somewhat similar spirit we adopt as our Axiom 17 the following Axiom of Additivity, in a notation due to S. Afriat:

Axiom 17 $x_0 \, T \, y_0 \, \& \, x_1 \, T \, y_1 \Rightarrow$
$$(x_0 + x_1) \, T \, (y_0 + y_1)$$

As Koopmans puts it speaking of a similar axiom that he adopts,[11] "the implication of this postulate is one of non-interaction between productive processes. Given the resources required for each of the two methods of production, both can be engaged in simultaneously without either one of them effecting the outcome of the other." Variants of this axiom are adopted by Afriat, Koopmans, and Debreu.[12] As in the case of the Axiom of Procession, the Axiom of Additivity is a very natural assumption for a simple theory of production.

Theories of production have always made some such assumption to rule out certain of the complexities of actual productive structures. In particular it was felt to be important to be able to assume that individual transformation activities can be *added* together to form an activity that is their simple sum—that activity a_1 added to activity a_2 forms simply $(a_1 + a_2)$ and not some obscure activity that has resulted from unforeseen interactions between a_1 and a_2. In real life, many productive activities are (to use the Hicksian language) technically complimentary or substitute, so that a_1 and a_2 carried on together give a result different from the simple sum of the value of a_1 taken alone and of a_2 taken alone. The formalists, of course, are perfectly well aware of this. Koopmans immediately points out that

[10]Afriat, *op. cit.*, p. 16. I am indebted for many happy hours spent discussing choice theory with Sidney Afriat. Needless to say Sidney Afriat is not to blame for any misunderstandings of his axioms of transformation on my part.

[11]Koopmans, *op. cit.*, pp. 74-75.

[12]Afriat, *op. cit.*, pp. 16-17; Debreu, *op. cit.*, p. 41.

both within a firm and between firms, interaction between activities actually takes place. "Economic literature abounds with examples of interaction, such as water and air pollution, drawing on subsoil water or oil, effects of deforestation on water runoff, etc."[13]

These interactions[14] again provide a basis for a famous distinction of Pigou's welfare economics, that between private and social cost. Pigou rightly saw that an activity may cost more to society than it does to its proprietor, since it may have damaging side effects on other activities or directly on other people. In the spirit of Pigou, one cannot stress too much the necessity for making the Axiom of Additivity explicit, if one is to use it at all. Received production theory has in fact assumed it, because of the simplification of structure that it makes possible, and welfare theorems proved with the aid of received production theory therefore hold only (among other things) *to the extent that this axiom is empirically true*. In particular, as Koopmans points out, the proof that perfect competition allocates resources Pareto-optimally in an economy with production activities depends on this axiom.

Two rather straightforward axioms, motivated by the same desire to simplify the structure of production so as to facilitate its handling, may now be introduced. We begin with an Axiom of Annihilation:

Axiom 18 $x \, T \, 0$

This axiom, whose form above is due to Afriat, asserts that anything may be transformed into nothing. In the real world, a factory or an apartment building, say, cannot be instantly and costlessly transformed into nothing. The axiom eliminates "stickinesses" of this kind, important though they are in reality, from our formal theory. Compare the Axiom of Free Disposal of Debreu:[15] "If a total production has all of its outputs null, it is possible." It is a consequence of Axiom 18 that $0 \, T \, 0$—that nothing may be transformed into nothing. This is noted by Koopmans and Afriat to be a consequence of various axioms in their sys-

[13]Koopmans, *op. cit.*, p. 75.

[14]Also interactions between productive processes and consumers' preferences of the type ruled out in our theory by Axiom 15 above, see pp. 227, 199-200, and footnote 8.

[15]Debreu, *op cit.*, p. 42.

terms and is elevated into the status of a special axiom on its own by Debreu, to the effect that 0 is an element in Y, what he calls the "possibility of inaction."[16]

I have stressed the unanimity on this point, and in particular the seriousness with which it is treated in Debreu, because I think it is exactly the sort of point about a formal axiom system that looks misleadingly trivial at first glance. In fact, it is extremely important, both empirically and to the mathematical structure.

Empirically, authors have wanted the theory of production to be able to cover long-run decisions—in which no commitment of input factors, no structure of plant, and no choice of processes is *fixed* and in which decision is open on every production, including the question of producing at all. So the production set must contain all possible productions, and the null production must be one of them. Mathematically, failure to notice that a production set must include its origin is a misunderstanding of the structure of these sets that proves highly nontrivial.[17]

We now add an axiom asserting the impossibility of free production: No positive output can be produced without using up some input.

Axiom 19 $0 \, T \, y \Rightarrow y = 0$

As Afriat puts it,[18] "possible transformations suffer from the restriction that, with them, there can be no gain without a loss, no output without an input." This appears in Debreu as his Axiom (c), on the Impossibility of Free Production, and also in Koopmans.[19]

We are now at a turning point. Our axiom system for the most general production theory is almost complete. We need simply two more, highly important assumptions. These assumptions have a special character. All the axioms, up to now, leave open several possible interpretations of our theoretical system. The remaining assumptions will bring us to terms on this issue.

ASSUMPTIONS UPON SCALE   The issue to which we now turn is so fundamentally important to the theory of production that assumptions—

[16]*Ibid.*, p. 40.

[17]Koopmans, *op. cit.*, pp. 24-25.

[18]Afriat, *op. cit.*, p. 23.

[19]Debreu, *op. cit.*, p. 40; Koopmans, *op. cit.*, p. 79.

even if not formalized axioms in the sense of contemporary mathematics—have been made about it at least since the days of the classical English political economy. In a sense, this line of thought goes back to David Ricardo.

On the axioms so far assumed, the production set Y_j of individual producer j and the total production set Y, may have any of the forms shown in Fig. 20-1.

The figure shows possible cases of the production of the jth producer of one commodity, measured up the vertical axis, produced by a process using one input measured along the horizontal axis. Since an input is a *loss* of a commodity, input amounts are measured to the left of the origin 0, so the production set shows possible *gains* (vertical) of the output commodity in return for various *losses* (horizontal) of the input commodity. The production set Y_j therefore does not appear in the nonnegative quadrant of the space, where any point represents a positive quantity of both commodities. (For n inputs and n outputs, the equivalent of the nonnegative quadrant in an "n" space is called the "nonnegative orthant.")

Figure 20-1a represents the case of increasing returns, Fig. 20-1b represents decreasing returns, Fig. 20-1c represents constant returns, and Fig. 20-1d represents a productive process which at first shows increasing returns as

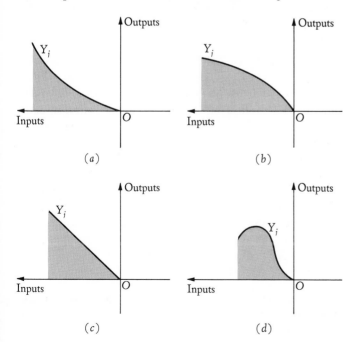

FIGURE 20-1

Possible cases of return to scale

the scale of operations is increased, then constant, and finally decreasing returns.[20]

From the point of view of empirical realism, the situation shown in Fig. 20-1*d* is probably the most valid picture of a typical production set. Indivisibility respecting plant and equipment would probably mean that advanced technology cannot be used for various small outputs, hence one would expect increasing returns until the operation was of technically optimal size. Further expansion might be accompanied by constant returns until the operation became unwieldy (again perhaps due to indivisibility), after which decreasing returns might be expected from any further expansion.

It was usually felt that the situation of Fig. 20-1*d* was too complex a case to attempt to build into an elementary theory of production. The problem was to find what assumptions would give the maximum gain in structural simplicity for the minimum loss in realism.

The classical move, from the nineteenth century right down to the end of the forties (and in textbooks down to today) was to rule out the case of increasing returns (Fig. 20-1*a* and, of course, Fig. 20-1*d*, since it contains a section which has increasing returns). The contemporary way of making this move is to assume an axiom such as the following, which is Debreu's Axiom (f),[21] of Convexity,

Axiom 20 Y_j *is convex.*

In Figs. 20-1*b* and 20-1*c*, where returns are decreasing and constant respectively, for changes in scale, the production set Y_j is a convex set; in Fig. 20-1*b* it is strictly convex. So the effect of Axiom 20 on the empirical cases we can cover is to rule out the case of increasing returns. Certainly this limits the empirical realism of the theory. Increasing returns obviously exist—we have heard of General Motors. Several points must, however, be made. To begin with, the limitation is not peculiar to contemporary axiomatic, formal production theory. Large parts of classical economic theory depended from the beginning on this assumption; the axiomatization merely makes it explicit and forces it continually on our attention. To take what is perhaps the most typical instance, the classical theory of com-

[20]For further discussions of returns to scale see the latter part of Chapter 21, pp. 254-260.

[21]Debreu, *op. cit.*, p. 41.

petition is inconsistent with increasing returns to scale. Firms would grow until they became monopolies.

A more formal point arises over the issue of indivisibility. It may be hazarded that many of the cases of increasing returns to scale that are found in real life are ultimately due to the fact that some process or piece of equipment comes only in a certain minimum size. Elephants and oil refineries have both figured as factors of production, and both come only in minimum sizes. But insofar as increasing returns are due to indivisibilities in the factors of production of this type, the assumption of a convex (and therefore connected) production set already rules out this ground for expecting the existence of increasing returns in the theory. In other words, it can be argued that if increasing returns are to be considered, the way to do this is to introduce a discontinuous production set. But if continuity assumptions have already been made for production theory, then this in effect rules out increasing returns.

What must be admitted is that *mathematically* even the newest theory is not in shape to handle the case of increasing returns, being heavily dependent on convexity: "The convexity assumption is crucial because of its role in all the existing proofs of several fundamental economic theorems."[22]

So far, our axioms give a picture of production that covers both classical and contemporary theory. If we introduce one more axiom, we can limit our system so as to make it represent the structure of most recent theories of production—such as those of Koopmans, Debreu, and Afriat. Also, we can begin to show how these new theories diverge from classical production theory. We accordingly introduce (in a form due to S. Afriat) an Axiom of Proportionality (constant returns to scale), which asserts that where lambda is any nonnegative number, if $x \, T \, y$, then $(\lambda x) \, T \, (\lambda y)$. Where two operations are similar, and differ only in scale, in the ratio given by λ, the axiom asserts that they are both possible:

Axiom 21 $x \, T \, y \, \& \, \lambda \geqq 0 \Rightarrow (\lambda x) \, T \, (\lambda y)$

Geometrically, if y is possible, so are $2y$ and $3y$.[23] Notice the shape of the production set—the shaded area in Fig. 20-2; notice also that it reaches a point in the origin 0.

[22]Debreu, *op. cit.*, p. 41.

[23]Koopmans, *op. cit.*, p. 75.

FIGURE 20-2
Production set under Axiom 21

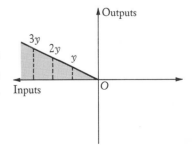

This follows from the assumption that the null production is a member of the production set. Because of its shape, the production set under Axiom 21 is known as a *convex cone*. Observe that *"convexity"* has here its set-theoretic sense of *weak* convexity.

This convex cone is the principal character, indeed the hero, of contemporary *linear* production theory.[24] It represents the simplest form (mathematically) that a production set can assume and enables us to bring to bear on both the theory and its applications the powerful tools of contemporary linear algebra—and the computer.

THE R-EQUIVALENCE SETS OF THE TRANSFORMATION RELATION

We end this chapter by noting certain properties of the relation T that are significant. Eggs can be transformed into scrambled eggs, but scrambled eggs cannot be transformed into eggs. Coded messages, however, can be *unscrambled*, and many chemical processes can be run either way. We may define the reversible transformation relation, "R," in terms of our primitive relation T, as follows:

Definition 20-1: $x \, R \, y \Leftrightarrow x \, T \, y \, \& \, y \, T \, x$

By definition, the relation R is symmetric. It is reflexive (like "$=$," T is a relation everything bears to itself, and therefore so is "R"). And since T is transitive, so is R. Therefore, R is an equivalence relation.[25]

The set of all inputs and outputs may now be partitioned into R-equivalence sets, and these sets may be simply ordered by T.

This relation T, which holds between the R-equivalence classes, is the one-way, irreversible, case of transformation which we normally think of as *production*. There is thus no need to introduce an Axiom of the Irreversibility of Productive Processes, as is sometimes done.[26]

The axioms of transformation so far assumed will prove adequate to enable us, in Chapter 21, to sketch a theory of production which is similar in outline to those of Debreu and Afriat. It will enable us to distinguish properties common to classic and contemporary production theory from the properties peculiar to contemporary models, such

[24]That is, where the production set is bounded by straight lines.

[25]Recall the discussion of equivalence relations in Chapter 9.

[26]For instance, by Debreu, *op. cit.*, p. 40.

as that of Koopmans. The axiom sets of Debreu and Afriat are so constructed as to cover both classical and contemporary production theory. As we shall see, this turns on the consideration that neither of these writers assumed an axiom limiting the set of possible activities or processes to the case of a *finite* set.[27] Koopmans, who does assume as an axiom that there are only a finite number of processes, will serve as our main example of what is characteristically new in production theories since 1950.

1. Mention some features of our economic experience   **QUESTIONS**
    that might remain in a world without production.
    What features would *not* remain?

2. What are the properties of the transformation relation "T"?

3. Describe the bearing of the axioms of general choice theory upon production decisions.

4. If we had not generated the theory of consumption, how would this affect our axiom set for production?

5. What are inputs, what characteristics do they have, and how can they be introduced into our theory?

6. How might the preference orderings of consumption theory be affected by the introduction of production into the theory, and how do we allow for this axiomatically? What effects does the relevant axiom have upon the welfare implications of the theory?

7. What may be transformed into nothing according to the axiom set offered in Chapter 20? What simplifications of empirical fact arise in this connection?

8. What possible cases of production are ruled out by the assumption of convexity in the production set? Does the assumption of proportionality add any further restrictions?

9. If we allowed, in our theory, for some productive processes using equipment which came in fixed (large) indivisible units, what would be the effect of this upon our axioms? If we rule such indivisibilities out, what can be said in mitigation of the resulting unrealism of our theory?

10. What is the significance of the equivalence sets of the T relation?

[27]Afriat, *op. cit.*, p. 41.

21
PRODUCTION
AS AN
EFFICIENT COMBINATION
OF
PROCESSES

Production theory brings us, once more, face to face with the central concept of this book, which is that the core of economic science is a *general theory of choice*.

I shall take the view that *all* decisions by a producer that are aimed at optimizing subject to constraints are relevant to the economic theory of production. Surprisingly, this assumption was not always made. The issue, however, turns on one's fundamental view of the scope and character of economic science. If you think that economics is concerned with explaining the pricing mechanism, you may assume that producers have somehow set their own houses in order, that they have somehow solved all their internal optimizing problems, and that they have discovered the most efficient combination of processes, or activities. On these assumptions, you then study their reaction to

prices in a market. This latter adjustment—to the market—
and only this is then supposed to constitute the economic
theory of production.

However, if you think that economics is about optimizing as such, entirely irrespective of what is being
optimized and whether or not the things at issue appear
in a market and show in prices, your view will be very
different. A general theory of choice, applied to production,
would concern itself with all production decisions. All of
the decisions of the jth producer would be elements in his
production set, Y_j. This is the point of view that will be
adopted here. The optimizing of a producer will be considered in the first instance as the choice of an efficient
combination of processes.

This point of view is part of a new tradition that has
developed since about 1950.[1] Neoclassical economic theorists ignored these problems as being none of their business.
They never learned the lessons of Lord Robbins' *Essay on
the Nature and Significance of Economic Science*, that is,
that *any* problem about the optimal use of scarce resources
to achieve given ends is a problem in economizing. The
new theory fulfills the program of the *Essay*.

Sir John Hicks, surveying the changed scene for the
American Economic Association and the Royal Economic
Society, remarks that "if we take the famous definition,
given so many years ago by Lord Robbins—'the relationship between ends and scarce means that have alternative
uses'—economics, in that sense, is very well covered by the
linear theory."[2]

There is a certain irony in all this. Granting the
appeal of the view of economic science put forward in this
book on grounds of strict logic or even granting that the
present view best expresses the content of recent axiomatic,
mathematical formalizations of economic theory, you may
yet not be ready to rush forward in defense of the claim
that the view of economics offered here is the most *practical*
that one could find.

However, we are going to do just that. The theory of

[1]The (now classic) source is Tjalling C. Koopmans (ed.),
Activity Analysis of Production and Allocation, John Wiley & Sons,
Inc., New York, 1951.

[2]Sir John Hicks, "Linear Theory," in Norman S. Buchanan
(ed.), *Surveys of Economic Theory*, The Macmillan Company,
New York, 1966, vol. III, p. 111.

production that develops naturally and necessarily from the new point of view has exactly the structure to exhibit the problems of optimization that press most immediately upon producers in the world of experience, and this theory generates the mathematical concepts that have been found to work in their solution.

PRODUCTION AS AN OPTIMAL COMBINATION OF PROCESSES

We shall accordingly introduce contemporary production theory by the addition to our general set of production axioms of one further special axiom. This axiom, as was remarked at the end of Chapter 20, simply involves an assumption limiting to a *finite* set the set of alternative *processes*, or *activities*, open to a producer. Any transformation may require one or more processes, or activities. A particular process, written "P_1" is distinguished from another process "P_2" through the fact that P_1 uses some input x_1 in a different proportion to P_2. A process, or activity, is thus way of combining inputs in order to transform them into outputs. The notion of "process" will at this point be introduced as a primitive. The possibility of combining, say, two inputs x_1 and x_2 in any proportions whatever thus implies that there are an infinite set of processes $\{P_1, P_2, \ldots \}$. The special character of contemporary production theory will be exhibited by introducing the assumption that inputs can be combined in production in only a finite number of ways, i.e., that the set of processes is a finite set $\{P_1, P_2, \ldots P_n\}$. We thus adopt an Axiom of the Finiteness of the Set of Processes:

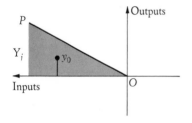

FIGURE 21-1
Production set for one input, one output, and one process

Axiom 22   *The set of processes is finite.*

To begin with, notice that if there are any two processes available to a producer, they may be combined at any scale of input for each process to produce any desired output. This follows from the Axiom of Additivity.[3]

FIGURE 21-2
Production set with two inputs, x_1 and x_2, one output, and one process

If a producer, j, has available to him only one process, which consists in transforming one input into one output, his production set Y_j is the shaded cone (Fig. 21-1).

His *efficient* production set is the boundary of Y_j, the line OP. This result is standard, that is, if he is producing at a point such as y_0 within the set, he is not maximizing output for the given input level. The line OP is known as a "ray" and also as a "half-line." It forms the boundary of

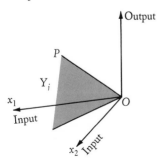

[3]See Chapter 20, pp. 228-229.

the attainable production set. If he must use two inputs to produce the *one* output but can combine them in only one way—that is, one process—his production set is as in Fig. 21-2.

Looking down on Fig. 21-2 from above and turning the diagram around so that we can begin to notice structural similarities to the diagrams in choice theory and consumption theory, we get Fig. 21-3.

Now to introduce a finite set of processes. The efficient set associated with each process will be a ray like OP. Take the simplest case, in which the set of processes has only two members. We then get two rays, OP_1 and OP_2, as in Fig. 21-4.

To show the structure of production decisions, we shall now increase the supposed number of basic processes to four. Needless to say, this is still a gross simplification of anything one is likely to find in an empirical situation, but it is enough to exhibit the most elementary properties of the situation. We continue to assume that there are only two inputs and one output. We can thus remain within three-dimensional geometry.

To begin with, we need a small piece of formal apparatus. We have assumed in Chapter 20 that producers' decisions obey the axioms of general choice theory. Once we know *how* the producers *order* outputs, we can apply our axiom set to the structure their decisions must exhibit. We have not, however, tied down the general axioms of production theory by constructing them on the basis of any one narrow concrete assumption as to what *criteria* will make producers order one output above another. It is nowhere assumed in Chapter 20 that there is any one criterion or any one set of criteria such that *all* production decisions order outputs, as more or less preferred, in terms of this criterion or set of criteria. This is parallel to our refusal to accept the utilitarian notion that all choices are ordered in terms of the criterion "quantity of utility." Our axioms of transformation presuppose that all production decisions can be ordered, but they do not presuppose the concrete criterion or criteria in terms of which this ordering is carried out.

The classical English political economists, from Adam Smith on, assumed that producers order alternatives solely in terms of money profits resulting from their adoption. The

CHOICE AMONG PROCESSES

FIGURE 21-3
The efficient·production set for two inputs, x_1 and x_2, one output, one process, rotated and seen from above

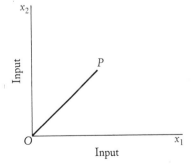

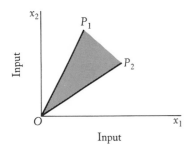

x_2

P_1

P_2

Input

O x_1

Input

FIGURE 21-4

Efficient production set with
two inputs, x_1 and x_2, one
output, and two processes

neoclassical, utilitarian, economists treated money profit
maximization as the equivalent, in production decisions, of
utility maximization in consumption decisions. Utilitarianism does not *entail* this view, as was indicated by
Edgeworth in numerous passages throughout his writings.
Despite their differences, however, the neoclassical school
deriving from Marshall and the general equilibrium theorists deriving from Walras and Pareto, were at one in
accepting money profit maximization as the sole criterion
for ordering a production decision. The assumption is still
found in the picture of a private-ownership economy offered
by Gerard Debreu as a model for his theory. Here, however, things are a little more complicated. Profit maximization is not introduced until his axiom set for producers is
completed, and it is *not* given the status of an axiom of the
system.[4] Furthermore, his first picture of equilibrium is
given for economies involving production and consumption
in general, and "private ownership economies," with the
assumption of profit maximization, are introduced with this
description:[5] "A special class of economy is then considered, namely, the private ownership economy, where consumers own the resources and control the producer. Given
a price system, each producer maximizes his profits."

Observe that we have followed Debreu in constructing our production axiom set so that it applies to any
economy, and in not making profit maximization an axiom
of production theory.

As has been known for some years, the work of
Baumol and others has cast doubt on the empirical realism
of the profit-maximizing assumption, even for private-
ownership economies. Subject to reaching a minimum level
of money profits, producers probably optimize in terms of
a number of criteria, such as size, public image, pleasant-
ness of operation, avoidance of strain, and so on.

For present purposes, we shall make what is perhaps
the simplest possible assumption about ordering of choices
by producers: of any two elements in the production set,
they prefer the one that represents a larger output of the

[4]Gerard Debreu, *Theory of Value: An Axiomatic Analysis of
Economic Equilibrium*, Cowles Foundation Monograph 17, John
Wiley & Sons, Inc., New York, 1959, p. 43.

[5]*Ibid.*, p. 74. The section in which private ownership economies are explicitly introduced begins on p. 78.

commodity being produced. Writing ">" for "larger than," we may frame a special axiom, needed to generate the most elementary case of contemporary production theory, in the form of a First Criterion of Producer's Orderings:

Axiom 23 $y_1 \, P \, y_0 \Leftrightarrow y_1 > y_0$

Obviously Axiom 23 is extremely weak—it would not be strong enough to serve as a criterion for ordering in a model for production theory with even two outputs. Suppose y_0 gave you more of one output, and y_1 more of the other. However, it will do for a one-output model, and it is not our purpose to tie ourselves to an axiom stronger than necessary. Once two or more different outputs are considered, something like the profit-maximizing assumption is obviously needed. But this, in turn, is an inadequate assumption, as has already been noted, for a theory that attempts to come close to the behavior of producers in the real world.

We now have the piece of apparatus we needed to exhibit the ordering of production decisions for our elementary case of two inputs and four processes and one output. The entire production set Y_j of the jth producer may be ordered into indifference sets. Each indifference set contains all those points in the production set representing outputs of *equal* size. For this reason, they are sometimes known as "equal product" sets or "isoproduct" sets. For any arbitrary unit of output represented by a point y_0 in the production set, the indifference set of which y_0 is a member will be the isoproduct set I_0.

We may now depict the technology of our simple transformation situation and the optimizing decisions that pertain to it. We assume that there are four processes, each absorbing the two inputs x_1 and x_2 in some fixed proportion. These four processes are shown by the rays OP_1, OP_2, OP_3 and OP_4 in Fig. 21-5.

The isoproduct sets show how much of each of the inputs x_1 and x_2 are required to produce a given amount of the output. Notice that if I_1 represents one unit of output and I_2 represents two units, the distance from the origin along any ray to the intersection with I_1 is equal to the distance from I_1 to I_2. This reflects the Axiom of Proportionality—constant returns to scale.[6]

[6]See last chapter, pp. 233-234.

FIGURE 21-5

Production set with four processes, showing isoproduct sets

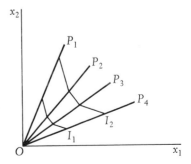

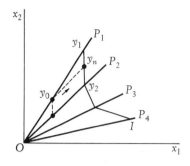

FIGURE 21-6
Combination of two processes

The isoproduct sets are made of three linear segments, reflecting the effect of the Axiom of Additivity:[7] that is, any two processes can be combined in any proportion. A point such as y_n in Fig. 21-6 then has the following interpretation.

It represents combining amount Oy_0 of process P_1 with amount y_0 to y_n of process P_2. It does *not* mean that there is a process running along a ray from O to y_n.

The notion of a set of processes, of what is called "the technological base," should now be getting clearer. Rays from O such as OP_1 and OP_2 depict processes, but there is no such ray from O to y_n. The point y_n is a possible combination obtained from adding different amounts of two processes carried out with given output levels.

One process might combine input factors so as to use one man per machine. Another process, less up to date, might combine *two* men and one machine. There might, technologically, be *no* intervening combination. But both these processes can be *used* in any proportion to produce a given output, and they are both included in the technological base, or set of processes.

Since there are no new technological possibilities between two rays, the surface of the production set in three dimensions shows flat facets between these rays, indicating that the two processes represented by the bounding rays of any facet can be combined with constant effectiveness in any amounts. For the same reason, the segments of the isoproduct sets between two processes are linear. Such a cone, with a finite number of flat facets, may be called a finite cone, as long as we remember that what is finite about the cone is its number of *flat sides*, not the number of *points* in it—these, as a result of our continuous divisibility assumptions, are an infinite set[8] (an effect of the Axiom of Proportionality, as will be recalled from Chapter 20).

We may now introduce the concept of an "independent and efficient" process. Each of the processes in the technological base, so far described, has these two properties: They are "independent" if each can be used alone

[7]See pp. 228-229.

[8]The term "finite cone" is David Gale's (*The Theory of Linear Economic Models*, McGraw-Hill Book Company, New York, 1960, pp. vii, 51-59).

and "efficient" if doing so could lead the decision maker to an optimum. It turns out that if the four processes are independent and efficient, any isoproduct set formed from points on the rays will be a convex set (Fig. 21-7).

Suppose, for example, that y_3 lay above the line joining y_2 and y_4, as in Fig. 21-8. Then a combination of y_4 and y_2 would be more efficient than y_3, since it would need smaller inputs for the unit output. It further follows that the only efficient combinations are of processes adjacent to one another: y_1 and y_2 can be combined, or y_2 and y_3, but not y_1 and y_3, for y_2 uses fewer inputs than any point on the straight line joining y_1 and y_3. We may now say that "basic" processes or "processes in the technological base," are those that are independent and efficient. Finally, any combination of inputs represented by a point within the cone P_1OP_4 is a *possible* combination of processes. It is perhaps misleading to draw the isoproduct sets as is often done in texts, so as to make them look like conventional indifference curves (Fig. 21-9). The point is that outside the cone the additional amounts of input x_1 or x_2 are redundant and make no contribution to output—there is no process that can use up the extra amount of x_1 at a point like y_n in Fig. 21-9. Given the Axiom of Annihilation, or Free Disposal,[9] such redundant inputs may not *interfere*, but they represent no new technical opportunities.

No position like y_n outside the cone is a meaningful output combination. All the output combinations are contained in the finite cone,[10] and the producer's optimizing decisions can now begin to be shown. These decisions involve eliminating inefficient combinations. A combination like y_1 and y_3 is inefficient, as we have seen. The same is true of combinations of three or more processes: in the case we are considering, these are *possible* but inefficient.

In Fig. 21-10, combinations of y_1, y_2, and y_3 are equivalent to points inside the triangle defined by y_1, y_2, and y_3 as corners. But any combination of either y_1 and y_2 or y_2 and y_3 uses fewer input resources.

The only efficient combinations are therefore y_1 and y_2, y_2 and y_3 or y_3 and y_4.[11]

[9]See Chapter 20, pp. 229-230.

[10]See R. G. D. Allen, *Mathematical Economics*, 2nd ed., The Macmillan Company, New York, 1965, pp. 338, 623.

[11]*Ibid.*, pp. 623-624.

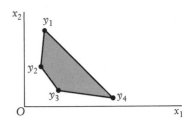

FIGURE 21-7

An isoproduct set for a unit of output

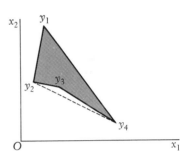

FIGURE 21-8

The isoproduct set of Fig. 21-7 supposed nonconvex

FIGURE 21-9

Conventional representation of isoproduct sets

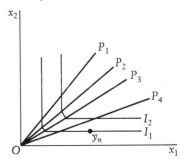

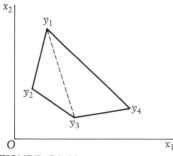

FIGURE 21-10

Inefficiency of combinations
of three or more processes

Given the Axiom of Proportionality,[12] that what is true of one level of output is true of any level, we can generalize and express our result as governing efficient combinations, not simply for unit output but for the whole length of the process rays throughout the cone. This may be expressed by saying that only combinations lying on a single facet of the finite cone are efficient.

So far we have analyzed only the structure of the technology, and no mention has been made of the constraints upon the carrying out of activities.[13] What we have in effect are sets of indifference sets of inputs. We do not know what point on a particular indifference set will be chosen or whether it will indicate the use of a single process or of a combination of two adjacent processes. Nor do we know what indifference set the producer can reach—up to what *level* he can acquire the inputs to produce output—what is the limit of his *attainable* production set.

OPTIMIZING SUBJECT TO CONSTRAINTS

Suppose that there are fixed available amounts of one or both of the two input factors. This could be the result of a physical limitation, such as the size of the available warehouse space, the capacity of machinery, or the amount of land available for cultivation. Or it could be a credit limitation or an instruction to a producer who was part of some integrated production system, such as a subsidiary of a large corporation or a plant manager in a socialized economy, or to the director of a research project limited by funded resources from government or foundations. First

[12]See Chapter 20, pp. 233-234.

[13]I shall use the word "activity" as a synonym for "process," simply for stylistic variety. This seems reasonable, since in the literature the phrase "linear activity analysis" of production is used to refer to just such an analysis of production in terms of a finite faceted convex cone. Koopmans, in particular, in early work, used the term "activity" for what we are here calling a "process." In *Three Essays on the State of Economic Science* (McGraw-Hill Book Company, New York, 1957), he suggested reserving the term "activity" for a particular *point* on a process ray: "The activity *a* will be called the *defining* or *unit activity* of the process (*a*), the scalar λ the *level* of the activity λa" (pp. 76-77, italics are in the original). On this usage the points y_1, y_2, y_3, and y_4 are unit activities of the processes P_1, P_2, P_3 and P_4 respectively. I shall not, however, adopt this usage. I shall use the term "activity" not for one level of output, but as a synonym for a whole process ray.

consider the case where one factor is available in unlimited quantities but the other only within some fixed limit OA (Fig. 21-11).

The optimal point will be at a corner, such as y_1. Here the resource (the straight line AB) constraint is a supporting hyperplane to the isoproduct set I_1. Observe that with one constraint *only one process* is needed. There is no need to mix activities. But now look at the case where there are two constraints, AB and CD (Fig. 21-12).

Here y_0 is a mixture of two processes, P_2 and P_3. Of course, y_0 *might* fall at a corner, but it *need* not. Where there are two inputs, as in our very simple model, there are at most two constraints, and one may need to combine at most two processes. It can be shown that the number of processes combined need never be larger than the number of constraints.

In Fig. 21-13, the producer's attainable set of input combinations, the rectangle $OABC$, often called his "feasible region," intersects the isoproduct set I_1 in a boundary point, y_4, so y_4 is possible.

The producer may not be able to use up all of one available factor when the outer corner of the producer's feasible region lies outside the finite cone representing his production set (Fig. 21-13). Of the input x_1 that is available to the producer, an amount AD is unused. Notice that in this case only one process P_4 is used.[14]

[14]William J. Baumol, *Economic Theory and Operations Analysis*, 2d ed., Prentice-Hall, Inc., Englewood Cliffs, N.J., 1965, pp. 286-287.

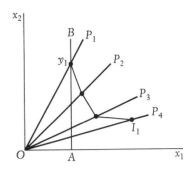

FIGURE 21-11

Optimizing subject to one linear constraint

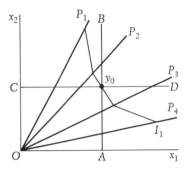

FIGURE 21-12

Optimizing subject to two constraints, AB and CD

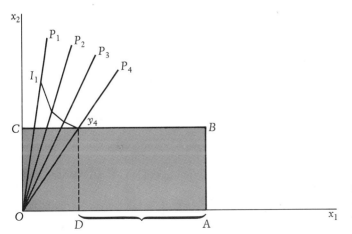

FIGURE 21-13

Case of one input (x_1) not utilized to availability limit

The producer may be subject to a simple wealth constraint similar to that introduced in the theory of consumers' behavior. Suppose that he is told that he can have 1,000 units of input x_1 or 500 units of input x_2 or any combination *at that rate* within these limits. This defines the familiar attainable region of consumption theory with its linear frontier, WH (wealth hyperplane, or price line, or rate of exchange), between x_1 and x_2 (Fig. 21-14).

Notice that only one process, P_3 is used. If the rate of exchange WH swung, indicating a change of relative prices of inputs, till it lay along the line $y_2\, y_3$, either process P_2 or P_3 or any combination of them, would be optimal. *Relative input prices would have to change considerably before process P_2 would be substituted for process P_3.* This is an important consequence of the assumption that there are a finite number of processes, that the production set is a finite cone, and that the isoproduct sets are therefore weakly convex.[15]

Thinking of a private-ownership economy, it is natural to interpret Fig. 21-14 as depicting the situation of a producer acting in a perfectly competitive manner. Like the traders in the picture of the competitive core,[16] this is a producer who assumes that his decisions as to how much of an input or output to buy or sell cannot affect the ruling prices of the market where he buys his inputs and sells his outputs.

This interpretation in terms of perfectly competitive producers adjusting to prices appearing in a market is by no means the only possible or the only important interpretation of the theory of optimizing that we have just considered:

FIGURE 21-14

Optimizing constrained
by a budget

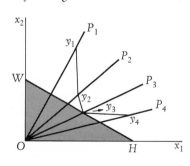

[15]Compare this result with the results that follow upon the contemporary assumption of weakly convex indifference sets in consumption theory. Neoclassical strict convexity meant that the choosing agent had a definite and continually changing marginal rate of substitution as one moved along one of his indifference curves. Therefore, *any* change in relative prices meant a new tangency, and the substitution of some of the (now) cheaper commodity (or input) for some of the (now) dearer. But on contemporary weak convexity assumptions, wealth hyperplanes representing widely different relative prices may all be supporting to an indifference (or isoproduct) set in a corner point like y_3 in Fig. 21-14. See pp. 152-154, 206-208.

[16]See pp. 172-177.

There are many allocation problems involving multiple objectives for which no market evaluations exist to establish comparability, while at the same time several scarce primary resources are required to serve these objectives. Problems of this kind arise particularly in connection with governmental tasks, such as resource development, municipal services, or national defense.[17]

Koopmans mentions a device for handling such problems which illustrates the point at issue. The gist of this is that the supreme policy-making authority present producers in charge of parts of the establishment with a set of relative prices at which they will trade different inputs and different outputs (which need not be physical goods but may be purpose attainments of various kinds). These relative evaluations can, of course, be revised in the light of experience.

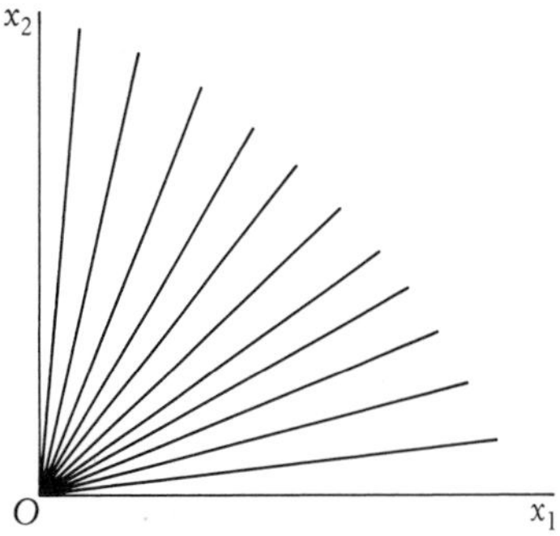

FIGURE 21-15
Production set approaching
the neoclassical model

The neoclassical theory of production can be generated from our axiom set in two stages, by relaxing in turn two of our axioms.

First of all, if we relax the special axiom postulating a Finite Set of Processes assumed in this chapter, the production set may be imagined to change in the following manner (see Fig. 21-15).

Suppose the number of process rays to approach infinity. To allow an infinite set of process rays is tantamount to assuming that the two inputs x_1 and x_2 can be combined with continuously varying resulting outputs, in any combination whatever. The production set now occupies the whole space $x_1 O x_2$, and it is no longer a cone with a finite number of flat facets. It now curves smoothly, as in Fig. 21-16.

This smooth surface is a particular case of the production surface of neoclassical theory.

For the moment we shall consider only one of its properties. To do this we move into position to look down on it from above, as in the case of the finite cone, and notice the form of the isoproduct sets. These are now smooth curves, exactly like the indifference sets of consumption theory (Fig. 21-17).

In other words, these isoproduct curves are *strictly* convex. This is the property I want you to concentrate on.

NEOCLASSICAL AND CONTEMPORARY THEORIES OF PRODUCTION

FIGURE 21-16
Production set with continuous
substitutions of inputs
and continuously varying output

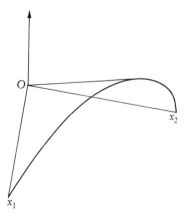

[17]Koopmans, *Three Essays on the State of Economic Science*, p. 100.

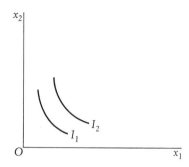

FIGURE 21-17

Isoproduct set in neoclassical theory

FIGURE 21-18

Marginal adjustments between wealth constraints and isoproduct curves

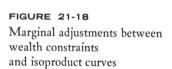

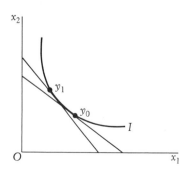

The whole distinction between the linear activity analysis of production and the neoclassical theory lies in this property. To see what it implies, we need to introduce a wealth constraint, delimiting the producer's attainable region, and consider what analysis of his decisions is offered by neoclassical theory.

The neoclassical theory was extremely simple. The producer is optimizing if and only if he is at the point of tangency between the wealth constraint and the highest attainable isoproduct curve. *This is a straight application of the classical Edgeworthian decision rule for optimizing in a choice space with smooth, strictly convex indifference curves and a limited attainable region.* The neoclassical theory is pure Edgeworthian choice theory.

Suppose the producer to be at equilibrium initially at y_0 (Fig. 21-18). Allow relative prices of inputs to vary slightly, so that the wealth constraint swings, giving him a tangency at y_1. Now, suppose y_1 to be as close to y_0 as you please. No matter how close these two points are, it is supposed by the neoclassical theory that the producer will move to y_1 when prices change. He is assumed to be able to adapt his productive technique continuously so as to take advantage of the smallest marginal change in relative input prices. How does this affect his technology? *We are not told.* However he does it, there is assumed to be an optimal way of combining inputs and he is assumed *to have found this out and to be using it.*

What we are being offered is a general choice theory combined with *the most stringent continuity assumptions possible upon the technological choice space.*

The effect is to reduce the theory of production decisions to the tangency rule and in fact to eliminate any consideration whatsoever of the problem of choice among technologies. The hard crystalline structure of the producer's decision situation has been sandpapered down till none of its edges show.

I cannot resist two comments of a rather "philosophy of science" tone at this point. The first is that pure science makes bad engineering. One strong argument for purifying the general theory of choice, formally axiomatizing it, and letting it have an independent existence as pure science, is that people will be less tempted to offer results that are properly regarded as results in pure choice theory as if they were contributions to (for instance) a theory of production decisions. The implications of strict convexity, such as the tangency optimizing rule, are theorems in Edgeworthian pure choice theory. If the structure of the production set reduces to these forms, we do not need a special theory of production. All we need is to refer to the results of Edgeworthian choice theory. It is notorious in the profession of economics that production managers, engineers, industrialists, and others interested in a usable production theory never got any joy out of the neoclassical production surface. Surely this is less than surprising: its structure is such as to assume all their problems solved.

Now my second "philosophy of science" comment. This can be expressed in terms of the issue as to the appropriate choice of axioms or in terms of the appropriate choice of mathematical structure for a theory. The two approaches converge. From the beginning of our study of choice theory, continuity assumptions have been an issue. Clearly they are an issue here. We made, in Chapter 20, certain continuity assumptions upon production decisions, specifically, the Axiom of Proportionality. We assumed, however, in this chapter, the finiteness, the discontinuity, of the technological base. Drop *this* discontinuity and you emasculate production theory. Notice that in a particular *application* of choice theory *certain* continuity assumptions may be needed (and justifiable) for simplicity, whereas others may destroy the specific properties of the area being investigated.

This may also be expressed by saying that a particular mathematical method may make it impossible to see the crucial issues in a scientific area. Notice that the concept of *marginal* change applies nontrivially throughout the smooth production surfaces of neoclassical theory. A continuously changing marginal rate of technical substitution can be found for all movements along a production indifference curve, strictly comparable to the marginal rates of personal substitution of consumption indifference curves. The slope of the isoproduct curve at any point indicates the rate at which one input must be increased to compensate exactly for a decrease in the other input, so as to leave output constant. Do I need to say what is skulking behind all this? Edgeworth's true love, the differential calculus.

Of course, the whole "marginalist" point of view (as the neoclassical theory has been called) also reflects a position about what problems economic theory should tackle.

If, as was pointed out at the beginning of this chapter, you think that the job of economic theory is simply to explain market behavior, you will feel that you have adequately covered the *relevant* production decisions if you have explained how producers' decisions to buy inputs and sell outputs will be changed by changes in market prices. Neoclassical economics was not really interested in the decision problems of a producer as such, except insofar as these issued in changed purchases or sales on a market. Producers' outputs, added together, gave you the supply curve of the industry, and this was all that the neoclassicists were after.

A production theory derived, by the imposition of special axioms, from a general theory of choice, will obviously take the opposite point of view. Commenting on the analysis of the choice among a set of processes, which is the core of the activity analysis approach to production theory, Koopmans makes some observations that I cannot resist quoting at length:[18]

The choice of the best modes of operation and the best combination of such processes is indeed one particular manifestation of the general problem which forms the recurrent theme of economics: the best utilization of scarce means for given ends. The insights into this general problem that economics has gained primarily by the study of allocation through a price system and a market mechanism are relevant also to allocation problems arising within the productive establishment. Where exchange and pricing do not exist as market phenomena, they may still be useful as constructed conceptual aids to decision making.

Finally—and this is perhaps the most important consideration—even with regard to the allocation problems of an entire economy there are good reasons for starting with the construction of models of production possibilities before institutional assumptions are specified. In the modern world largely the same fund of technological knowledge and experience is utilized under an amazing variety of institutional arrangements, ranging all the way from American corporate and individual enterprise to Soviet communism. Within Western "capitalism," governmental and private enterprise operate side by side in different or even in the same industries. Within the private "sector," the problems of explaining how production tasks are distributed between different firms, and of recommending how they could best be distributed, belong to one of the most challenging and least clarified

[18]Koopmans, *Three Essays on the State of Economic Science,* p. 71.

areas of economics. There is therefore a need for the evaluation
of institutional arrangements as well as for the prediction of
production capabilities in any particular institutional setting.
To make progress in these various directions, it may help to
start from models that formalize nothing but the range of technological alternatives open to a producing organization, whether
an individual, a plant, a firm, a governmental agency, or society
as a whole. In this way the character and range of possible decisions are clarified before the decision makers, their functions
and their incentives enter upon the stage of the analysis.

He continues:

. . . the [linear] activity analysis model . . . can be looked upon
as one step in that direction. It represents technological possibilities by a set of postulates that are perhaps as simple as they
can be chosen and yet permit useful analysis, applicable rather
well to some situations, only in rough approximation to a wider
range of phenomena, and not at all to some other situations.

The fact that the model is devoid of "institutional" specifi-
cations contributes to its flexibility of interpretation.

This remarkable passage was published in 1957. The
following year, Dorfman, Samuelson, and Solow, in what
has come to be regarded as a fundamental work, sum up
their position on these issues:[19] "Our point of view, then,
will be that the essential choices made by a firm do not deal
directly with levels of input and output, but rather concern
the extent to which 'different ways of doing things' are
used." They explain that by "a way of doing things" they
mean a process, or activity.

Finally, a point of enormous importance in applying
economic theory: Wherever production problems are even
approximately a model for the theory of linear activity
analysis, the powerful computational methods known as
linear programming can be applied to their solution, and
these methods have proved eminently suitable for high-
speed electronic computation.

When we began comparing contemporary and neoclassical production theory, I said that this could be done
by relaxing two of our axioms, one by one. So far, we have
relaxed only the special axiom, assumed in this chapter, of

**THE GENERAL CASE OF
NEOCLASSICAL
PRODUCTION THEORY**

[19]Robert Dorfman, Paul A. Samuelson, and Robert M. Solow,
Linear Programming and Economic Analysis, McGraw-Hill Book
Company, New York, 1958, p. 132. Compare Allen, *op. cit.*,
pp. 618-620.

the Finiteness of the Technological Base. By relaxing this axiom, we turned the finite cone of activity analysis, with its flat facets, into a smooth conic surface, with continuous possibilities of factor input substitution throughout, giving us a sample case of a neoclassical production surface. Observe that we did not need to change any of the axioms of Chapter 20—as we remarked there, that set of axioms is adequate to generate both contemporary and neoclassical theory.

The case of a neoclassical production surface with which this leaves us is still conic (though continuously curved) in form. This is a consequence of the Axiom of Proportionality, which ensures that changes in scale of inputs result in proportionate change in output—constant returns to scale. An element of linearity remains: We still have a cone, though a smooth one.

As it happens, the case in which the production set is a continuously curved cone has greatly interested neoclassical economic theorists,[20] for several reasons. For one thing, it was sometimes suggested that, for decisions made with a sufficiently long-term viewpoint, under conditions in which all productive equipment can be changed and nothing is fixed, constant returns to scale may not be a bad general hypothesis. There is also some empirical evidence that the total production set for the American economy may be approximately of this form.[21]

Moreover, the simple linear relationship between input size and output size implied by the assumption of constant returns to scale allows this conic production surface to retain some of the advantages characteristic of a linear theory.

I shall present some of the key concepts of neoclassical production theory in terms of this simple case of constant returns to scale, in which they stand out most vividly.

TOTAL AND MARGINAL PRODUCTIVITY AND VARIABLE RETURNS TO A SINGLE INPUT FACTOR

As has already been remarked in this chapter, the neoclassical assumption of continuous possibilities of input

[20]Referred to in neoclassical literature as the case of a linear homogeneous production function, it gets a great deal of attention.

[21]See P. H. Douglas, "Are There Laws of Production?" *American Economic Review*, vol. XXXVIII (1948), pp. 1-41; Robert M. Solow, "Technical Change and the Aggregate Production Function," *Review of Economics and Statistics*, vol. XXXIX (1957), pp. 312-320.

substitution leads to theoretical concepts motivated by the underlying mathematical structure of the theory. These concepts bear more than a family resemblance to certain notions of neoclassical utility theory. Instead of a total utility curve, we get a total product curve; and just as a marginal utility curve may be derived in neoclassical general choice theory, so also may a marginal product curve be derived from the total product curve in neoclassical production theory. This will be shown here simply in terms of the geometry, but the reader should be alerted to the fact that all the important concepts are simply the fundamental (classical) mathematical concepts underlying the structure of neoclassical economics, in "production theory" clothes. It is like Estoril in World War II, with every *maitre d'* a spy underneath his bland exterior. The truth about these concepts has been laid bare in R. G. D. Allen's older book, *Mathematical Analysis for Economists.*

Geometrically, then, the total product curve is obtained in this way: At any fixed distance from the origin, take a slice through the production surface parallel to one axis.[22]

The cross section of the production surface shown in Fig. 21-19*a* is reproduced as the total product curve, *TP* in Fig. 21-19*b*. It depicts the maximum physical output that can be obtained for every different level of input of one factor x_1, the other being held constant. Observe that as we add increasing amounts of the input factor that we are varying to the fixed amount of the other, we get increasing amounts of output; but the total product increases at a decreasing rate and eventually levels off. This is to say, the *marginal* physical product resulting from increasing amounts of one input factor, the other held constant, eventually declines.

The property of (eventually) diminishing marginal productivity is the neoclassical version of a concept going back to David Ricardo: the so-called law of diminishing returns to the use of a factor. The classical Ricardian example cites the effects of adding more and more labor to the cultivation of a fixed piece of land. Returns in output will increase as more labor is added, but they are likely to increase at a decreasing rate and ultimately more men will add nothing to the output and may even diminish it by

[22]See Baumol, *op. cit.*, p. 254.

FIGURE 21-19

Derivation of the total product curve

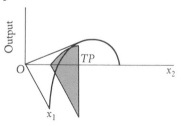

(*a*)

(*b*)

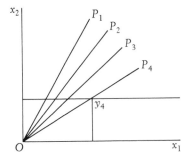

FIGURE 21-20

Ricardian diminishing returns
in linear activity analysis

getting in the way. The "law" is simply a highly plausible empirical assumption.

Observe that the curve of marginal physical productivity is only assumed to be *eventually* declining. The neoclassicists did not assume that marginal productivity must be declining from the beginning. (Contrast their assumption about marginal utility.) If the total product curve is rising at an increasing rate, the marginal product curve derived from it will be rising. A section of total product curve that is rising at a constant rate will show in a horizontal stretch of marginal product curve. When the total product curve is rising only at a declining rate, the marginal product curve is declining.

Distinguish carefully between the concept of decreasing returns from the increased use of one input, all others constant, and the concept of decreasing returns *to scale* of operations, with *constant* input combinations. The smooth convex cone of neoclassical theory with constant returns to scale shows eventually diminishing marginal products for variations in the use of any one factor, the other being held constant.

Our activity analysis model was based on constant returns to *scale*, but it exhibited the phenomenon of diminishing returns from the increased use of any one input. This is easily seen in Fig. 21-20.

For some fixed level of use of input x_2 and any level of input x_1, process P_4 can be used to the level indicated by output point y_4. But since any process, such as P_4, requires inputs in a constant proportion, there is no possibility of using larger quantities of x_1, together with the same fixed quantity of x_2, in turning out larger outputs by means of process P_4.

**THE GENERAL CASE OF
THE NEOCLASSICAL
PRODUCTION SURFACE**

So far, we have discussed neoclassical production theory for the special case in which the production surface is a smooth cone.

However, the most characteristic form assumed by the production surface in neoclassical theory was not conic at all. Indeed, one might say that it had no definite shape, within certain very wide limits. I am about to present a version of neoclassical production theory in which the shape of this surface is tidied up a little.

The question obviously arises: Why am I entitled—and why is it a good idea—to present the neoclassical theory strapped, so to speak, into a Maiden Form bra, instead of *au naturel?* The answer is that the slightly restricted structure I am about to offer is sufficiently close to the natural form of neoclassical production surfaces to enable one to derive all their important characteristics *save one*—and this latter has a special status. Furthermore, all the characteristics that can be derived from the slightly restricted structure are consistent with a convex production set and are therefore consistent with all the powerful theorems of mathematical economics *which depend upon convexity.* Obviously, I am placing on the production surface the restriction that *it cannot have concave areas,* in order to retain the convexity property that is the fundamental structural characteristic of the production set under the axioms of Debreu or Afriat.

Let us explore the axiomatic implications of the move I am advocating. The Axiom of Proportionality must be dropped to get *anything approaching* the general case of a neoclassical production surface. Typically, these surfaces show increasing returns to scale for various small outputs (below a certain size technology is supposed to be inefficient); then for some variations in output, returns may be constant; and finally they are supposed to be decreasing as the scale increases. The figure is usually drawn something like Fig. 21-21.

Two lines of equal height, depicting input combinations that yield equal product, I_0 and I_1, are drawn showing the derivation of isoproduct curves. Visibly, this surface can be a mix of every case of returns to scale: increasing, decreasing, and constant. Linearity has disappeared except for short stretches of output variation. The restriction I wish to impose excludes the case of increasing returns to scale—to eliminate areas of concavity. The Axiom of Proportionality still must be relinquished in order to generate this case; but since on my suggested restriction returns are supposed either constant or decreasing and since the former implies weak convexity and the latter strong convexity in the production surface, we still retain Axiom 20, the Axiom of Convexity.[23]

If we adopt this move we can still obey Axioms 1 to 20 inclusive (confining ourselves to a theory that can be formalized to the most rigorous standards of contemporary mathematics), yet generate a production surface on which

[23]See Chapter 20, pp. 232-233.

FIGURE 21-21

Typical neoclassical production surface

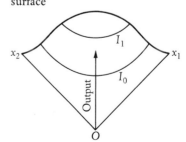

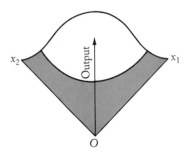

FIGURE 21-22
The limits of increasing returns
in a typical neoclassical
production surface (increasing
returns rule over the
shaded area)

can be exhibited all the properties (save the treatment of increasing returns) of neoclassical production theory in its most general form.

Remember, as was remarked when Axiom 20 was discussed, neoclassical theory *itself* depends heavily upon the exclusion of increasing returns. This was particularly true of the principal model for neoclassical theory—the perfectly competitive economy. Very roughly, the neoclassical position was that, if a producer encountered increasing returns to scale, he would find it profitable to increase his size till his share of the market became substantial, giving him the power to change ruling prices and therefore making him no longer a perfect competitor—one who takes prices as beyond his control.

You may ask at this point why, if the neoclassicists themselves had difficulties over increasing returns, they did not exclude it altogether from their production surfaces. The answer is worth pondering, since it throws a strong light on the contrast between the contemporary, formalist, axiomatic theory and the traditional methods. Look again at the neoclassical production surface on which increasing returns to scale appear: notice that in Fig. 21-22 they appear only over a range of *very small* levels of output.

From their point of view, the neoclassicists could make this small concession to realism at no theoretical cost, since their only worry was to avoid the admission of increasing returns to scale leading to big monopolistic firms. To the contemporary formalist, things are very different: if he seeks this small extra realism, he pays the price of dropping Axiom 20. The production set is then no longer a convex set; therefore, all the theorems on convex sets upon which so much mathematical structure depends are now no longer open to him. So a mathematically more naïve theory can, in a sense, afford to be more "realistic": it has less at stake. Since it has no formal theorems that depend crucially on certain structures having simple forms, traditional theory can afford to be generous and cavalier about its basic structures assuming complicated forms.

This illustrates a phenomenon that is often noticed when a scientific area is first being formally axiomatized. To the traditional, intuitionist mathematician, the formalist appears to be fussing over axiomatic precision only to produce a theory that in the end fits "reality" less closely than the traditionalist's more loosely constructed theory. What the traditionalist forgets is that the greater "realism" of his theory is merely a reflection of his not attempting to give it the kind of rigorous structure that could lead to powerful theorems and to the possibility of rich computer applications.

Models for the theory of linear activity analysis can easily be made to look like childishly simplified pictures of economic "reality" by any traditionalist with a malicious wit; but the axioms of activity analysis lead to theorems whose computer applications, as linear programming, have been highly successful throughout industry, science, and government, wherever situations suitable for their use arise.

Formal, symbolic languages can be shown to lack much of the richness and delicacy of a natural language like English, but the computer revolution would have been impossible without them. Formalist mathematicians may sometimes sound as if their exquisite criteria of satisfactory axiomatic structure sprang from a mathematical aesthetic worthy of Oscar Wilde; but do not forget that in science handsome is as handsome does, and formalized structures are likely to be computer-feedable.

For these reasons, I shall present neoclassical production theory in this chapter subject to the restriction that the production set is a convex set. The production surface will then look somewhat as in Fig. 21-23.

The reader, facing this surface, may feel like asking, "Haven't I seen you somewhere before?"

A fair answer might be: "Well, you saw my sister."

Since neoclassical production theory shows the continuous dependence of the attainment level of a single goal upon the size of a set of inputs, the resulting surface (abstracting from the case of increasing returns) will closely approximate that of neoclassical utility theory. As was remarked earlier in this chapter, neoclassical production theory *is* just Edgeworthian choice theory applied virtually without modification to production decisions.

In two respects, however, the shape of the production surface may differ from that of the utility surface, as usually drawn. First, we are imposing upon the production set only the restriction of *weak* convexity: returns to scale over some range of input variation may be decreasing *or constant* (whereas the neoclassical utility surface was constructed on the assumption of universally *diminishing* marginal utility, and hence was strictly convex throughout).

FIGURE 21-23

Neoclassical production set, restricted by the Axiom (20) of Convexity

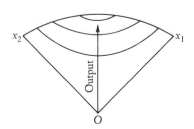

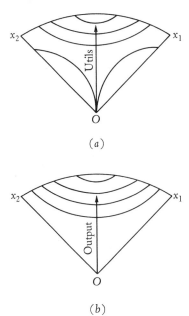

(a)

(b)

FIGURE 21-24

Possible utility surface (a)
and·production surface (b)

FIGURE 21-25

General case of neoclassical
production surface, viewed from
above and showing ridge lines

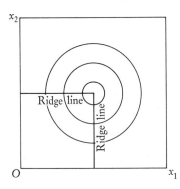

The second difference arises over the fact that the utility surface may show positive heights (amounts of total utility) for the consumption of one commodity alone (movement along one axis alone), whereas I have drawn the production surface on the assumption that the use of one input alone yields no output. Contrast the two figures in Fig. 21-24.

If you choose to assume that one input alone can yield positive output, the production surface can look like the utility surface of Fig. 21-24a. This assumption need not be absurd. If we think of production as, say, carpenters producing chairs, then a carpenter alone, or wood alone would produce no output. But not all transformation is like this, and where there are many inputs, outputs may be possible in a subspace of the production space. This only looks unreasonable in the *two-input* case, since we feel intuitively that you can't get output from one of two inputs taken alone. But if input axis x_1 is allowed to stand for a whole group of inputs and input axis x_2 for another whole group, positive outputs may be possible using amounts of the x_1 group or of the x_2 group of inputs alone.

If we now put in some isoproduct curves and look from above at the hill formed by our production surface, its contours may be projected onto the floor of the diagram, and the isoproduct curves look exactly like the closed indifference curves of choice theory (Fig. 21-25).

Notice that in Fig. 21-25 I have drawn complete, closed production indifference curves. We know how to interpret closure in an ordinary indifference curve. The question arises: how is it to be explained in the case of isoproduct curves? This issue did not arise as long as the neoclassical production surface that we were discussing was based on the assumption of constant returns to scale because such surfaces formed a cone, rising continually up in the product axis. However, in the general case now being considered, the surface reaches a peak, where the maximum product is attained. Strictly speaking, the curves close *completely* only if the marginal product of all combinations of *both* inputs becomes negative—that is, if both inputs, after a certain point, lead to a diminution in output if used in larger quantities, no matter how they are combined. One can consistently take the case in which the marginal products of the two inputs in some combinations simply *ap-*

proach zero at infinity, which still gives you diminishing returns to scale. But I have drawn the case which seemed more generally likely—as well as easier to draw!

Whatever about closing, the isoproduct curves certainly are bound to show segments in which an individual input is redundant.[24]

For the sections of curves labeled "*a*" in Fig. 21-26, x_2 is redundant—more of x_1 is needed to keep on the same isoproduct curve as further additional quantities of x_2 are added. This implies that x_2 is being used more than optimally. The same is true of x_1 for sections of curve labeled "*b*." Optimal combinations of x_1 and x_2 are those lying between the lines AB and BC, in the darkly shaded bottom left-hand segment of the figure. This is the equivalent in neoclassical production theory of the Hicks-Allen effective region of an indifference-curve diagram. Clearly, a rational producer will not knowingly choose to be at a point outside the segment bordered by the lines AB and BC. These lines are known as "ridge lines." They indicate the edge, the frontier beyond which the use of one particular input ceases to be effective.

Finally, an important concept can be derived by introducing a wealth constraint, showing the constraint upon the amounts of each factor input that the producer can acquire during, say, a given period. In Fig. 21-27, three positions of a constraint showing constant relative prices are given.

The locus of all points of tangency between an isoproduct curve and a wealth constraint shows along what path of input combinations the producer will travel if his buying power is increased at constant relative prices. The curve OE is such a curve and is called the "expansion path." Clearly, this is the production-decision equivalent of the Hicksian income-consumption curve.

Now, since the slope of an isoproduct curve at any point indicates the technical rate of substitution of one input for the other at that point, it can equally be said to indicate the ratio of the marginal product of one input to the margi-

[24]It should be noted that the neoclassical production surfaces of Fig. 21-25 and Fig. 21-26 are inconsistent with retaining Axiom 18, the Axiom of Annihilation. Sections of isoproduct curve labeled *a* and *b* in Fig. 21-26 imply that it is costing something to *dispose* of a redundant input. See Chapter 20, pp. 229-230.

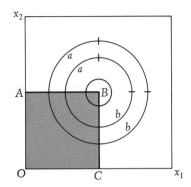

FIGURE 21-26

Sections of isoproduct curves in which a single input is redundant

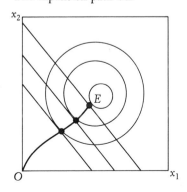

FIGURE 21-27

The expansion path OE

nal product of the other input at that point. So tangency of an isoproduct curve to a budget constraint line implies that

$$\frac{MPx_1}{MPx_2} = \frac{\text{Price of } x_1}{\text{Price of } x_2}$$

(remember, the slope of the budget-constraint gives the ratio of input prices).

This rule, which the expansion path follows, of keeping the ratio of marginal products of inputs equal to the ratio of their prices, was the core of the neoclassical theory of optimal production decision making. This concept of the expansion path will lead us naturally, in Chapter 22, into the theory of the costs of input factors, which will in turn lead us to the question of the supply of factors and to the considerations that cause variations in factor supplies.

QUESTIONS

1. "Technical optimizing decisions are the job of production engineers, and do not concern the economist." Criticize in terms of the structure and concepts of axiomatic choice theory.

2. What is the significance for contemporary production theory of the assertion that the production set is a finite cone?

3. Is it axiomatic in contemporary production theory that producers maximize profits? What institutional circumstances are presupposed by contemporary production theory?

4. What is the relation between an ordered set of indifference sets in general choice theory and an ordered set of isoproduct sets in production theory?

5. If two processes are "combined," does that mean that a third process is being used?

6. In a model with two inputs, one output, and four processes, prove that if the four processes are independent and efficient, any isoproduct set formed from points on the rays will be a convex set.

7. In the model of Question 6, prove that any combination of three or more processes, though possible, must be inefficient.

8. If a producer is optimizing the production of one output, with two inputs subject to two linear constraints, what maximum number of processes need he use and why? Will both inputs be used up to the limit of their availability?

9. If a producer is optimizing subject to a budget constraint, how many processes will he use? If he is using one process P_3 and relative input prices change marginally, what will he do?

10. What change in our axiom set will generate an important special case of neoclassical production theory? What form does the production set now take?

11. Discuss the significance of the concept of marginal change, contrasting the properties of the neoclassical production set with the finite cone of linear activity analysis.

12. What change in our axiom set is required to generate the general case of neoclassical production theory? What form does the production surface now take? How close can we come to traditional neoclassical statements of production theory without abandoning all the properties of the axiomatic theories of Debreu and Afriat?

13. What lessons can be learned from production theory about applying general choice theory to special decision situations? In particular, discuss the concept of continuity.

22
THE
CONCEPT
OF
COST

The concept of cost is fundamental to economic science, as it is to the very notion of economizing in ordinary language. Indeed, the word "cost" is ordinarily used in a way that closely approximates what has come to be the usage of mathematical economics: we say, "What you have chosen to do has *cost* you her love" and "A democracy can fight a war only at the *cost* of impairing its definitive freedoms." When we speak like this, we recognize that the cost of attaining a goal is the other goals that have to be sacrificed to attain it. This simple notion is the core of the contemporary scientific concept of cost. Stated choice-theoretically, the cost of choosing an element in the maximal set is any member of the next most highly ordered set, which has been forgone. The cost of Marina is Karen.[1] This is the

[1]Or, if you want to bring the situation nearer to contemporary America, the cost of Marina and Marie is Karen.

concept of opportunity cost: The cost of one choice is what you give up—your next most highly ordered alternative.

It will be recalled that the concept of cost was in fact built into the axioms of transformation: there is *input*— nothing can be produced without sacrifice of something which is used up in the productive transformation.[2] The cost of production follows directly from the fact of scarcity. The fact that productive resources are scarce and that they have alternative uses implies, as was pointed out by Lord Robbins, that they must be economized. To the extent that they are used to produce one desired outcome, they are withdrawn from another.

Despite the reasonableness of this view and its closeness to ordinary language, it was not adopted from the beginning by economic theory. In fact, its final adoption involved a dispute that may seem very strange to anyone who comes fresh to the issue and sees the concept of opportunity cost as a natural inference from the axioms of general choice theory. What may seem even more strange is that in at least one important area of economic science the controversy did not die out until the sixties.

Once more, we face an issue concerning the history of science. We could take a ruthless contemporary view and let the past bury its dead. As usual, to do so would render unintelligible a good deal of highly important writing, including some relatively recent work. In the case of the theory of cost, however, there is another reason for looking briefly into the past. It happens that the earliest scientific views on the subject are not as silly as they once were thought, and they illustrate some issues of highly contemporary interest. Once more, therefore, I ask your pardon for playing historian.

For our purposes, we may begin with David Ricardo. Ricardo made the famous assumption that the costs of production could be regarded as proportional to labor input. This was sometimes interpreted as implying that doses of labor caused some strange metamorphosis of material things. Subject to correction by learned historians, I doubt that Ricardo intended anything of the kind. Consider for a moment an activity-analysis interpretation of his theory of cost as proportional to labor input.

THE RICARDIAN SINGLE-INPUT MODEL

[2]See the discussion of Axiom 19, on the Impossibility of Free Production, p. 230.

Since output is assumed proportional to labor input in turning out any one product, labor must be being combined with all other input factors in some fixed proportion at all levels of output. Each process is thus defined by the amount of labor input it requires to produce a given output. Therefore, we may describe two processes as distinct if they use a different amount of some one single input (which we shall treat as equivalent to Ricardo's "labor") to attain a given output. Consider a classic problem in the programming of shipping movements. A shipping company has in a set of ports ships that have been unloaded and are ready to go to sea to pick up cargo. Assume that there is no cargo in these ports, so the ships must be sent somewhere to pick up cargo. Suppose that there is another set of ports where cargoes are available. Each possible *transformation* of a ship from one of the first set of ports to one of the set where it can take on a cargo is a productive process. The cost of the process is the number of days a ship must spend at sea. The company's problem may then be expressed: Move all the ships to ports where there are cargoes for them, subject to the requirement that *ship-days at sea* be minimized. Intuitively, you might say that the answer is obvious: Send the ships on the shortest passages. But consider the following trivially simplified case. There are ships in Lisbon and in Liverpool. They are needed in Bordeaux and Bombay. Suppose Lisbon-Bordeaux is two ship-days and Lisbon-Bombay is ten, while Liverpool-Bordeaux is three ship-days, and Liverpool-Bombay is fourteen. Then, although Lisbon has an *absolute* advantage in both processes, it has comparative advantage in the transformation Lisbon-Bombay. A linear program of the whole shipping problem would (and in practice continually does) make this kind of move wherever there was a *comparative advantage*. As it happens, Ricardo used his concept of cost to state the theory of comparative advantage quite clearly in the first edition of his *Principles*.[3]

Ricardo stated his concept of comparative advantage in terms of international trade in physical commodities, but the generality of the notion is clear. Observe that in setting out the shipping problem we have retained his assumption that cost can be handled in terms of one variable input factor—in our case the number of ship-days at sea. Of

[3]Robert Torrens also stated this concept clearly around the same time in his brilliant *Essay on the External Corn Trade*.

course, those who go to sea (and even some landlubbers) realize that every ship is unique. She is a mysterious, feminine being, and she differs in everything—even the cost of keeping her going—from all other ships. But the hard fact must be faced that, in complicated cases, a linear programming solution that is based on the assumption that ship-days at sea are equivalent units of cost will give one a better result (in terms of ultimate cost to the company) than any attempts to route the ships by intimate knowledge, instinct, and rule of thumb. All this notwithstanding the drunken (and therefore wasteful) sea cook on the *Liverpool Lovely* and the intimate problems of the first mate of the *Bombay Duck.*

No doubt the historians will be about my ears for making Ricardo look like an anticipator of linear programming, but consider the evidence and see if you can really deny that he was close to some of the core insights underlying the linear activity analysis of production.[4]

REAL COST – THE MARSHALLIAN REFORMULATION

By the time Alfred Marshall began to write his *Principles*, a reaction had set in against Ricardo. The whole classical school of English political economists had made an article of faith of what, in Ricardo, was probably simply an assumption for a first theory of production, namely, the treatment of cost in terms of a single input. They had also followed him in another assumption, of even wider and more daring scope.

Ricardo had no explicit choice theory; he could have found the beginnings of one had he looked in certain late eighteenth century French authors, in particular Turgot and Condillac. Ricardo, however, followed Adam Smith; and Smith, who had known the French school, had failed to understand this aspect of their work.

The question was, without a theory of choice (and therefore without a theory of demand), how to explain relative prices. Ricardo made the daring assumption that the price of a unit of any output commodity depended simply on the amount of the input, labor, needed to produce it.

Is this necessarily absurd? Assume the axiom set of linear activity analysis, in particular the Axiom of Propor-

[4]This issue will be discussed at length in a companion volume by the present author, *Theory of International Trade: An Axiomatic Introduction to Interacting Economic Systems* (to be published by McGraw-Hill Book Company, New York).

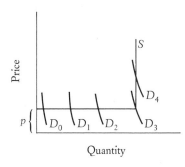

Price

S

D_4

$p\ \Big\{$ D_0 D_1 D_2 D_3

Quantity

FIGURE 22-1

A case of demand and supply on
Ricardian labor cost assumptions

tionality (constant returns to scale). Add Ricardo's axiom
that output is proportional to input of one single factor—
call it L. Assume, as is reasonable, that there is some
physical limit to the possible output of each final commodity, beyond which production cannot be carried. At
this point, the supply curve S, for any given commodity
turns vertical. Then, for all positive outputs less than this
limit, relative prices will be determined solely by the relative amounts of L needed to produce a unit of output. The
implications of all this show rather clearly in a conventional supply-and-demand diagram (Fig. 22-1).

As demand shifts from D_0 to D_3, price remains constant at the initial level, p, simply because, within the
constraint limit, any quantity is forthcoming at constant
cost—the supply curve is infinitely elastic. But when demand shifts from D_3 to D_4 *no* further output is forthcoming and the *whole* change in price is due to the change in
demand. On this model, all relative prices in situations in
which supply is not fixed (where the physical constraint
upon output has not been reached) can be explained simply
in terms of the relative doses of the input factor needed to
produce one unit of each commodity.

(For all its quaintness, the Ricardian theory antici-
pates a sophisticated contemporary development that forms
another branch of linear theory, namely the input-output
analysis developed by W. Leontief.)

The followers of Ricardo became more and more
doubtful about a theory of prices that wholly ignored demand and ran solely in terms of labor cost. When Jevons
wrote his *Theory of Political Economy*, he dethroned cost
and enthroned marginal utility and the demand curve immediately derivable from it, as the whole underlying explanation of relative prices. In so shifting the emphasis
from cost to marginal utility, he ushered in what has become known as neoclassical economic theory.

Such was the state of affairs when Marshall began
to write. Now Marshall accepted, as we already know, the
Jevonian concept of marginal utility and therefore the importance of the demand curve. However, Marshall was
deeply a traditionalist, and, by his own admission, he was
smarting at the extreme iconoclasm with which Jevons
wished to junk the whole classical tradition, particularly
Ricardo.

Furthermore, Marshall could see clearly that Jevons
had gone too far. It was just as one-sided to say that

relative prices were *solely* due to demand as to say that they were *solely* due to supply. It was, as Marshall remarked in a famous passage, like asking which blade of a pair of scissors did the cutting. Relative prices were determined by the interaction of demand and supply. Considerations of cost of production determined the shape of the supply curve, considerations of marginal utility governed the shape of the demand curve, and price depended on their interaction.

In his restoration of the importance of the concept of cost, however, Marshall was not willing to go back exactly to the Ricardian position. It seemed clear to him that the attempt to treat cost in terms of variations in one input factor, labor, alone was too unrealistic and limiting to maintain any longer. Yet his feeling for Ricardo was strong. To show this, one need only remark that Marshall probably rejected the theory of opportunity cost (of which he cannot have been unaware) because of his desire to stay as close as possible to the Ricardian tradition.

The concept of cost as a forgone alternative was clearly stated by the Austrian school, notably by F. von Wieser, toward the end of the nineteenth century. But particularly the mathematical systems of the school of Lausanne, beginning with Walras, imply it. For Walras, all prices, of inputs as well as of outputs, are determined simultaneously; and the price of any input reflects the set of opportunities for the use of that input and the demand for each of the final goods to whose production the input can contribute.

Now Marshall, as we know, was thoroughly acquainted with the work of the school of Lausanne. He had studied their method of general equilibrium analysis and had rejected it in favor of his own partial approach. He could not do this without becoming acquainted with the notion of cost as a forgone alternative.

He turned his back on this notion, however, and offered an account of the costs of production in quite different terms. If costs could not be said to be proportional to labor, still, so the idea went, they could be said to reflect *disutility*. Production gave rise to various disutilities, and the supply curve reflected these just as the demand curve reflected the marginal *utility* of consumption. Thus the notion of costs as efforts and sacrifices—the theory, as it came to be called, of *real* costs—was built in as a cornerstone of neoclassical economic theory.

THE REAL-COST–
OPPORTUNITY-COST
CONTROVERSY

The remarkable thing about Marshallian real-cost theory is how long it held sway over Anglo-American economics. (The continent of Europe was opportunity-cost oriented from the beginning of the twentieth century.) I fear this must be attributed to the influence of the man Marshall rather than the inescapable cogency of the ideas.

From the beginning, real-cost theory ran into difficulties. For one thing, it is not a very happy explanation of production costs where human effort plays no part. The cost of using a machine to turn out one product is a matter of the alternative uses of the machine and of any other inputs, certainly *not* of the disutility experienced by the machine. This is more vividly obvious today, as we move into an automated productive system where even machines themselves are designed and built by other machines; but still, it was true, even in Marshall's day, that some costs had no relation to human disutility, just as Marshall himself had seen that not all cost was proportional to Ricardian labor input. Moreover, even for human effort itself, Marshall's theory would require that the work where marginal disutility was greatest should cost the most. Notoriously, however, some of the most unpleasant work is most poorly paid. Clearly, such labor is paid low wages, not because the disutilities are low, but because *alternative uses* for that labor are few.

Above all, however, the objection to the Marshallian concept of the disutility of effort is simply the same as the objection to his concept of quantitative utility. All the problems we have discussed that arise over the concept of utility arise equally over the concept of disutility.

By the time the Hicksian revolution had swept away Marshallian utility theory in favor of indifference-curve analysis, real-cost theory had suffered the same fate. For instance, in 1939, Hicks' great classic *Value and Capital*, which is set out explicitly in terms of Lausanne general-equilibrium analysis, contains a clear opportunity-cost approach.

In the mid-fifties, however, a last stand was made in defense of real-cost theory, which did not finally die out until the beginning of the sixties. This controversy is worth a few words, not simply because it was launched by two great economists, Jacob Viner and Paul Samuelson, but because it brought to light a genuine weakness in the existing ways in which opportunity-cost theory had been expressed.

The issues were joined in a specialized area of economic theory,[5] but they can be stated quite generally, without bringing this particular area into the picture. The gist of the matter was simply this: Suppose a society is initially producing a bundle of desired commodities on the frontier of its attainable region. If we make the drastic simplifying assumption that only two commodities are being produced, we can represent the possible combination of outputs of these two commodities in a two space. We may as well do this, since generalization to an n space will not affect the argument. Suppose that the society is producing at point x_0 on the frontier of its attainable region, as in Fig. 22-2.

I have drawn the frontier on the assumption that diminishing returns to specialization occur if the society tries to concentrate on one or the other of the two outputs. This, however, does not affect the argument. Let the frontier take any form you like.

The concept of opportunity cost may then be expressed by saying that the cost of choosing to have OA of commodity S is forgoing BD of commodity T, and the cost of having OB of T is doing without AC of S. Suppose that the technological possibilities change for some reason (the reason for the change is immaterial) so that the new frontier is the dashed line in Fig. 22-3.

The society could now move to any point on the new frontier, such as x_1, at which the opportunity costs of this decision can again be expressed as so much of S and T, each forgone in order to obtain some of the other. But suppose that instead the society chooses to stay at x_0, consuming the same amount of each of the two commodities as before, and simply taking advantage of the new technology to *work less and thus reduce the disutility of labor.*[6] It was then concluded by Samuelson and by Viner (independently) that this social choice could not be explained exclusively in opportunity-cost terms, since the society is choosing, if it remains at x_0, to consume less of *both* commodities than it needs—it could have more of either or both commodities at zero opportunity cost.

[5] The area was the pure theory of international trade. Since I shall be treating this aspect of the matter at length in *Theory of International Trade* (see Footnote 4), I shall abstract from it entirely in the present work.

[6] This argument was developed (independently) by Paul Samuelson and Jacob Viner. See references in Richard Caves, *Trade and Economic Structure, Models and Methods*, Harvard University Press, Cambridge, Mass., 1960, p. 110.

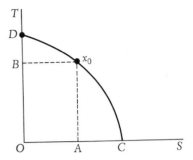

FIGURE 22-2

Society's feasible region and opportunity cost of x_0

FIGURE 22-3

A change in the feasible region

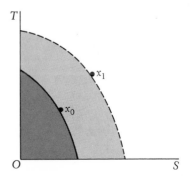

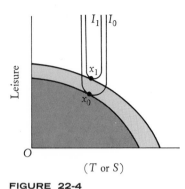

FIGURE 22-4

$x_1 \, P \, x_0$, since it contains
more leisure

The received answer is based on two results, one of mine in 1956 and the other due to J. Vanek in 1959.[7] I shall give the argument here in a form derived from our axiom set, which I did not have when I wrote in 1956.

If we retain the Axiom of Dominance, introduced to simplify the theory of exchange, the society will not settle at x_0 when the feasible frontier shifts but will move to a new point on the new frontier, such as x_1 in Fig. 22-3. This axiom, however, is too severe for present purposes, since it rules out all satiation. Let us therefore relax it, retaining only the Axiom of Insatiability of consumption theory.

If the society settles at x_0, this must mean that satiation has been reached in respect of T, of S, and of *any combination* of T and S. However, by the Axiom of Insatiability, there exists some x_1 such that $x_1 \, P \, x_0$. Actually, we already know what x_1 must represent: it is a position with more *leisure* being consumed in preference to more of any other commodity. The nested indifference "cups" are open in a dimension that represents more leisure. To show this, consider a third dimension at right angles to the plane of the page, measure leisure up this new axis, and treat this as the new vertical axes. Choose as horizontal axis either of the two axes in the previous plane of the page, as in Fig. 22-4.

Now society will move to its frontier, in the leisure dimension alone (on the Samuelson-Viner assumptions).

Hence the Samuelson-Viner attack on opportunity cost depended upon society being satiated with every one of the commodities available as well as with every combination of them. Generalizing the two space on an L space, if *any one* of the L commodities is still desired, the society will move in that dimension to the new frontier, as in Fig. 22-5. One can then express the opportunity cost of the new position x_1 as one does for any frontier position, like the original position x_0. The problem of being unable to define opportunity cost therefore arises only if social indifference curves have closed in every commodity dimension—if society has zero interest in any more of any commodity, including leisure.

FIGURE 22-5

The opportunity cost of leisure

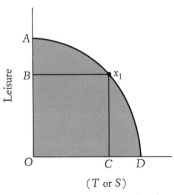

[7] V. C. Walsh, "Leisure and International Trade," *Economica*, vol. 23 (1956), pp. 253-260; Jaroslav Vanek, "An Afterthought on the 'Real Cost–Opportunity Cost Dispute,' and Some Aspects of General Equilibrium Under Conditions of Variable Factor Supplies," *Review of Economic Studies*, vol. 26 (1959), pp. 198-208.

Where leisure is the only remaining interest, opportunity cost can still be defined. Leisure is a commodity like any other. The leisure axis needs a word of explanation, however: you do not choose the origin of the diagram to represent zero leisure in the sense of working twenty-four hours a day! Make an assumption, based on whatever information is available, about what working day maximizes physical output of T or S. *That* is the origin of the leisure axis. Amounts of leisure (movements up along the vertical axis) are reduction in the working day, at the opportunity cost of lower output of T or of S. So when the feasible region expands, if the society is interested only in more leisure, it moves straight up in the leisure axis to x_1, as in Fig. 22-5.

The opportunity cost of taking OB of leisure is then CD of the horizontal commodity, and the opportunity cost of taking OC of this latter good is forgoing BA of leisure.

I think that the Samuelson-Viner argument *does* show that the theory of opportunity cost will not explain all cost phenomena unless *the commodity set is correctly defined*. If only, say, physical goods are included in the commodity set and if the society is satisfied with respect to these goods, the opportunity-cost concept will appear to break down. It seems to be generally agreed today that the concept of costs as forgone alternatives, when carefully formulated, offers a general explanation of their bearing upon economizing decisions.[8]

IMPLICATIONS OF OPPORTUNITY COST

We have been discussing this concept of cost from the point of view of a society as a whole. From this point of view, the notion of opportunity cost can be used to express welfare theorems about the optimal allocation of resources. Thus one may say that the cost to society of a

[8]The contributions of the present writer in 1956 (Walsh, *op. cit.*) and of Jaroslav Vanek in 1959 (*op. cit.*) are ably summarized in Caves, *Trade and Economic Structures . . . (op. cit.).* These results are adopted and used by Vanek in *International Trade, Theory and Economic Policy* (Richard D. Irwin, Inc., Homewood, Ill., 1962, pp. 198-205); M. C. Kemp has generalized them in *The Pure Theory of International Trade* (Prentice-Hall, Inc., Englewood Cliffs, N.J., 1964, pp. 99-107); and they have been related to subsequent developments by M. O. Clement, R. L. Pfister and K. H. Rothwell in *Theoretical Issues in International Trade* (Houghton Mifflin Company, Boston, 1967, pp. 74-77).

given use of input factors is the alternative uses of the same resources that have been forgone.

At the opposite extreme, Crusoe on his island may regard the cost of one set of uses of his time as being the alternative uses that he has not chosen.

From the point of view of the producer, the cost of a unit of input to him is what he has to pay to prevent it (or its owners) from shifting to another producer.

The welfare implications of the concept are severely limited by its ultimate dependence on the way in which outputs are *ordered*. In a private-ownership economy, the fact that tastes happen to be such that a particular commodity is highly ordered in the preference rankings of those with most money will enable its producers to bid resources away from other uses. The input factors used in producing commodities that are highly ordered by the more well-to-do segment of a population will therefore have a high opportunity cost. This does not mean that there is anything intrinsically valuable about these factors—simply that they happen to be needed to produce commodities that are demanded by those who at that moment have the means to pay. If, for instance, economic change alters the distribution of income in favor of the young, the opportunity cost of factors needed for making armchairs may go down and the opportunity cost of pop groups go up. The same would happen if the distribution of income remained the same, but tastes changed—say older people start to like pop sounds, which were previously liked by the younger. We may now introduce an old but still-important concept.

NON-SUPPLY-REGULATING INCOME

The notion at issue is due to Ricardo and Robert Torrens, but I shall not discuss its original complexities, presenting instead a simple form developed by contrast with the modern concept of opportunity cost. We may bring out the issues by considering the possible forms of a supply curve, in the light of the concept of opportunity cost. In Fig. 22-6, when the demand curve shifts from D_0 to D_1, price rises but so does the quantity supplied. This reflects the fact that input factors can be bid away from other uses at higher prices. But when demand shifts from D_1 to D_2, although price rises considerably there is no increase in supply. The supply curve is vertical. This might reflect the fact that a physical constraint or constraints prevented the production of any more output, no matter what was offered for it. Or it might simply reflect the unwillingness of the input factors to supply more of their services. This is especially likely to be the case when a crucial ingredient in the output is the input of a skilled performance of some kind: a singer can sing or a surgeon can operate only so much of the time. Indeed, at high levels of price, the supply curve may even bend backward, indicating a leisure preference on the part of the input factor. Thus for any price above P_2 the supply curve bends back toward the vertical axis. At P_3, the owners of the factor are taking advantage of the high income available to them to supply less of their factors service than they will do when their income is lower; thus they are indulging in leisure preference.

Observe that the demand curve can shift anywhere between D_2 and D_1 *without the supply changing*. The extra income earned by suppliers when the demand curve is up at a position like D_2 is therefore referred to as a "non-supply-regulating income" to indicate that this sum did not *need* to be paid to call forth the supply. We may then say that whatever element in price is *not needed* to call forth

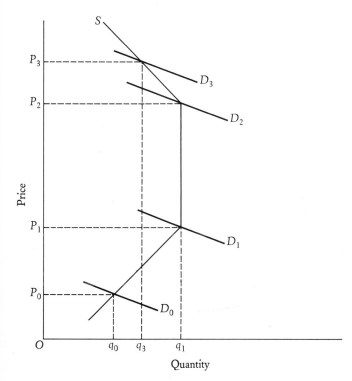

FIGURE 22-6

Supply curve illustrating opportunity cost and also non-supply-regulating income

a given supply is non-supply-regulating income, whereas whatever *is* needed to prevent input factors shifting to other uses is opportunity cost.

Since Ricardo and Torrens, the term "pure rent" has been used to refer to non-supply-regulating incomes because the phenomenon was discovered first in relation to agricultural land, which was the case analyzed by the classical political economists. Before the nineteenth century, England had been well able to feed herself; but the industrial revolution and the great increase in population and the development of new towns during the Napoleonic wars created a situation in which the British needed to import grain. Such imports were prevented by some ancient statutes, the so-called "corn laws." Torrens and Ricardo observed that, with imports prohibited and all suitable land already fully used, successive increases in demand simply raised the price of corn and elicited no increase in supply. They concluded that the corn laws were simply redistributing the country's income in favor of the richest class, the landlords, and at the expense of the poorest, the new urban industrial workers. The repeal of the corn laws was not without bearing on the power and the influence of the classical English political economy.

This was an early instance both of rigorous economic theory and also of the derivation of a welfare theorem: unless you approve of redistributing income in favor of the landlords, repeal the corn laws.

The question then arises: Can one derive a general welfare theorem concerning non-supply-regulating incomes? I abstract from this question the question of *finding out* just how much of an income is opportunity cost and how much is what Ricardo would have called "rent." It may not be at all easy to find out.

The difficulty about a general welfare theorem on these incomes is that their analytical economic character is simply that they do not need to be paid to prevent an input factor from shifting its services. Now, many input factors valued by a society may be highly immobile. They may be more immobile the more important they are. A young man can change jobs often and easily; an older senior executive is likely to lose greatly if he must do so. An elderly village schoolteacher may be so committed to the place she has lived in and worked in all her life that her willingness to leave is very low, but it would not necessarily be good social policy to start reducing her income to see at what point she threatened to move.

Notice that non-supply-regulating incomes are not necessarily *high* incomes. They have simply the property that they need not be paid to prevent the factor instantly moving off to another opportunity. Clearly, this alone is not sufficient as a basis for any welfare conclusions.

Having surveyed the phenomenon of cost, I shall now indicate how the traditional cost curves of neoclassical analysis are affected by the adoption of the axioms of contemporary production theory.

We may begin with the total-cost curve (Fig. 22-7). I have drawn it so that it is linearly related to output. This is the situation where the production set is a smooth continuous cone. Consider the concept of the expansion path introduced at the end of Chapter 21. If the production surface is a smooth cone, increasing output requires successive amounts of an input mix, increasing at a constant rate. Hence there is a linear relationship between total costs and output size.

The same is true of the activity analysis of production for which the production set is a finite cone, as long as the most economical process or combination of processes can be used. This can be conveniently shown in the course of introducing two other cost concepts that we need. First, we derive a curve of *marginal* costs from the total cost curve in precisely the same way as the *marginal* utility curve is derived from the total utility curve. Simply vary output and note how total cost changes for each unit of output. In a similar way, we can discover a concept not used in utility theory, but important in cost theory, namely, *average* cost. This is simply the total cost of an output divided by the number of units of output so as to get the cost of a unit. In the case of a smooth cone, marginal and average costs are identical (since cost is changing at the margin at a constant rate), and the curve is a straight line parallel to the horizontal axis. This is because it simply shows that unit changes in input lead to unit changes in output—constant returns to scale. Note the effect of the Axiom of Proportionality. This situation appears in Fig. 22-8 from the origin O up to point y_0. To the right of point y_0, we show how the marginal and average cost curves diverge in the

⁹See discussion, pp. 233-234, 238-239.

THE COST CURVES

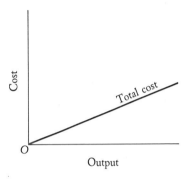

FIGURE 22-7
The total cost curve

FIGURE 22-8
Marginal and average costs under the Axiom (21) of Proportionality, and the Axiom (22) of Finiteness of the Set of Processes⁹

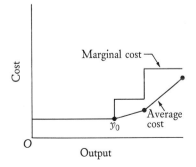

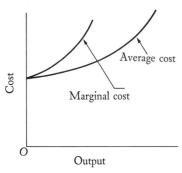

FIGURE 22-9

Cost curves in a neoclassical model under the Axiom (20) of the Convexity of the production set

THE NEOCLASSICAL COST CURVES

FIGURE 22-10

Neoclassical curves, showing increasing returns for small outputs

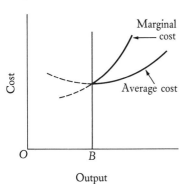

case of activity analysis, with a finite cone, once physical constraints have made it necessary to use more expensive processes.

The rising marginal cost in the case of a finite cone comes about in the following way. One process may use mainly inputs whose cost is low but which are available only for small outputs. That is, a physical constraint prevents their use when the producer wants to expand his output beyond a certain limit. He then has to shift to the next most economical process, and so on.

As soon as a point is reached where output can be increased only at increased cost per unit, marginal cost becomes separate from average cost; it then lies above average cost, and its upward movement is "pulling" average cost up after it.

So far, we have considered costs in the linear activity-analysis model of production and in the special case of neoclassical theory in which the production set is a smooth cone—constant returns to scale. Those are the cost pictures underlying theories based on the axiom sets of Koopmans, Debreu, and Afriat. We now move to the general neoclassical picture.

If we drop the Axioms of Proportionality and of Finiteness of the Set of Processes, but retain the Axiom of Convexity[10] of the production set, upon which we have based our treatment of neoclassical production surfaces, the cost curves look as in Fig. 22-9.

The marginal cost curve now shows continuous variation in response to changes in output, reflecting the shape of the convex neoclassical production surface, which is no longer a cone but some sort of dome, with ultimately decreasing returns to scale, and therefore having continuous, smoothly increasing costs for increased output. The average cost curve follows the marginal curve up.

As a matter of custom, the cost curves of neoclassical theory are normally shown U-shaped as in Fig. 22-10.

This simply reflects the neoclassical willingness to allow increasing returns to scale to appear in the shape of the production surface for initial small outputs. This shows in the cost curves as decreasing average costs for outputs less than OB.

[10]See the discussion of Axiom 20, pp. 232-233, 254-260.

In using U-shaped, neoclassical cost curves it is important to remember that one has to abandon the Axiom of Convexity on the production set, and thus all the theorems dependent upon this axiom.[11]

1. How is the economist's concept of cost related to the ways in which the word "cost" is ordinarily used? Examine the claim "the cost of Marina is Karen."

2. Does the Ricardian model of cost require the assumption that some esoteric uniquely productive quality be attributed to labor?

3. How was the Marshallian concept of cost related to the neoclassical concept of utility?

4. Need there have been a real-cost–opportunity-cost controversy?

5. What welfare theorems, if any, may be derived from the distinction between opportunity costs and non-supply-regulating incomes?

6. What are the peculiarities of the curves of average and marginal cost under the axioms of the linear activity analysis theory of production?

7. How do the cost curves look when the Axiom of Proportionality is dropped but the Axiom of Convexity retained?

[11]In particular, if a model of perfect competition is based on these cost curves, it must be remembered that none of the theorems of Debreu and others concerning the equilibrium or Pareto optimality of competitive systems can be assumed to apply.

EPILOGUE

Don't try to have a (conceptual) revolution and minimize it too.

Hilary Putnam

It seems to me that the explicit axiomatization of the *general* theory of choice, and the explicit recognition that theories such as those of consumption and production are particular *models* for the general theory of choice, are nontrivial changes.

This move throws light on the implicit value assumptions in special models for choice theory. To take just one example, conventional neoclassical thinking in consumption and production theory often took for granted that larger physical quantities of a given commodity will be preferred, and welfare claims were made in terms of this tacit assumption. Now we know that this requires the assumption of an Axiom of Dominance, also that no such axiom is required for general choice theory or even for consumption or production theory, and, above all, that if such an axiom *is* to be assumed[1] in a special model for choice theory *we will want to know the reason why.*

[1]As we did in the Edgeworthian theory of exchange, purely for simplicity.

If an economic system turns out ever-larger quantities of a set of commodities with which you are satiated, and possesses no mechanism for recognizing and implementing needs (yours and other people's) that are unsatisfied, you will not want to describe such a system as "growing" or "progressing."

Further, those who are concerned that economic science be "value-free" may be encouraged to show that the economic theories they endorse contain no assumptions not derivable from a value-free axiom set.

Likewise, those who feel that a welfare economics without value assumptions must amount to fiddling while America burns may be encouraged to build the values they feel necessary into explicit axioms, so that the manner of derivation of welfare theorems may be evident and open to criticism.

Finally, a point may be made concerning the relation between the *practice* of the techniques of optimization science and the problem of human values.

The physical scientists, whose work is in its nature apparently further removed from the sphere of values, have been brought face to face with this issue through the uses to which the hardware they produce has been put.

The *optimization* scientist is plunged into the thick of things. You will all be familiar, by now, with the sense in which choice theory is independent of values: one may use as a model for the theory a situation in which the objects of choice are never specified, except as some set of attainable elements. So far so good. Furthermore, a project may be described in highly general terms, as the search for optima given certain very abstract types of constraint.

But the moment such work is applied, the *content* to which it is applied is very unlikely to be morally neutral, even if the subject of investigation is not so momentous as the "optimal" use of nuclear striking power or some weapon system or an evaluation of the effects of techniques of chemical or biological warfare.

Anyone who applies optimization science to a concrete content makes an implicit moral commitment to that concrete content, and he should not be allowed to shelter behind the moral neutrality of pure science.

APPENDIX

Just before going to press I have found what I believe may prove to be a satisfactory axiom set for a general choice theory without the Axiom of Comparability or the usual Axiom of Transitivity. Development of these ideas properly belongs in my forthcoming advanced work, *Axiomatic Choice Theory*, but I cannot resist at least offering the axiom set, for any interested reader.[1]

As in the axiomatization in Chapter 9, we adopt "P," "A," and "C" as primitives. Indifference is defined as before, and we now define a new relation, x_0 Inc x_1 (read x_0 is incomparable with x_1) as follows:

$$x_0 \operatorname{Inc} x_1 \Leftrightarrow - (x_0 \operatorname{P} x_1 \vee x_1 \operatorname{P} x_0 \vee x_0 \operatorname{I} x_1)$$

Neither "I" nor "Inc," however, need appear in the statement of the axioms.

[1]In the development of this axiom set, without the Axiom of Comparability and with only a weakened Axiom of Transitivity, I have benefited greatly from discussions with Oswaldo Chateaubriand.

We then adopt as axioms of choice theory:

Axiom 1 $(x)(C_x \Rightarrow A_x)$

Axiom 2 $\exists x\, Cx$

Axiom 3 $(x_0)(x_1)(x_2)$
$\qquad [(x_0 \,P\, x_1 \,\&\, x_1 \,P\, x_2 \,\&\, Cx_0 \,\&\, Ax_2) \Rightarrow x_0 \,P\, x_2]$

Axiom 4 $(x_0)(x_1)(-x_0 \,P\, x_1 \,\vee\, -x_1 \,P\, x_0)$

Axiom 5 $(x_0)(x_1)[(x_0 \,P\, x_1 \,\&\, Ax_0) \Rightarrow -Cx_1]$

I think it will be found that any model for the axiom set of Chapter 9 is a model for this axiom set. On the other hand, this axiom set has as models structures that are not models for the axiom set of Chapter 9—or for any other usual axiomatic formulation of choice theory. [May, 1969]

NOTES
ON
FURTHER READING

The reader may be interested in the question: What is he now equipped to understand?

I shall not discuss the neoclassical literature, simply because it is readily available to every American undergraduate, and any good intermediate microtheory text will give references. It is important to point out, however, that the reader of this book knows quite enough economic theory to feel no strain from conventional undergraduate microeconomics. If anything, he should be critical of older standards of rigor. To be fair, and to see the neoclassical tradition at its best, however, it should be seen in its most formal dress; and to see it so requires a knowledge of classical mathematics, which has nowhere been presupposed in this book.

To turn to contemporary sources, one could go

straight to Kenneth Arrow's *Social Choice and Individual Values*.[1] There is a good deal to be said for this choice: a scientific education tends, of necessity, to be textbook-dominated. When the choice of reading a first-rate creative work of science is open, it should be eagerly seized. You should also read at this point Tjalling C. Koopmans' beautifully written *Three Essays on the State of Economic Science*.[2] And then Peter Newman's *The Theory of Exchange*[3] is all available at this stage (except for the last part of Chapter 6).

For a text at the next level of difficulty, which might be roughly described as the advanced undergraduate level, we are now excellently provided by James Quirk and Rubin Saposnik's *Introduction to General Equilibrium Theory and Welfare Economics*.[4] Some of the matters they treat will be immediately familiar, but they go into such concepts as the upper semicontinuity of a set-valued mapping and the use of the Kakutani fixed-point theorem to prove the existence of equilibrium for a general equilibrium system, at what is probably the most elementary level on which these matters can be meaningfully discussed. They take up precisely those issues that I felt were too complicated to be incorporated in an introductory treatment, and thus they offer a natural move to the next level of difficulty. At this point, I should mention an older book which was a pioneer in the dissemination of the new mathematical economics—William Baumol's *Economic Theory and Operations Analysis*.[5] Now in its second edition, it is a rich source, particularly of diverse concrete applications of optimization science.

At the next level of difficulty, an excellent, thoroughly contemporary, graduate text is Kelvin Lancaster's *Mathematical Economics*.[6] Indeed, parts of this book might be profitably used straight away by the reader of the present work. I am thinking of the excellent mathematical reviews,

[1] 2d ed., John Wiley & Sons, Inc., New York, 1963.

[2] McGraw-Hill Book Company, New York, 1957.

[3] Prentice-Hall, Inc., Englewood Cliffs, N.J., 1965.

[4] McGraw-Hill Book Company, New York, 1968.

[5] 2d ed., Prentice-Hall, Inc., Englewood Cliffs, N.J., 1965.

[6] The Macmillan Company, New York, 1968.

in particular R1 to R4 inclusive, and R8 and R9. To the best of my knowledge, R9, which is on point-to-set mappings, is (apart from Quirk and Saposnik) the only relatively informal discussion of any completeness. Lancaster should be acquired straight away and referred to as more and more becomes understandable in the light of other reading. Lancaster describes as more elementary than his the treatment of general equilibrium in Chapter 13 of *Linear Programming and Economic Analysis* by Robert Dorfman, Paul A. Samuelson, and Robert M. Solow.[7] But I think that in some ways the latter book, perhaps because much older, is heavier going. For one thing it lacks Lancaster's explicit, fully contemporary mathematical reviews. It certainly contains much important material.

At about the same level as Lancaster is David Gale's distinguished book, *The Theory of Linear Economic Models*.[8] Gale describes his book as a work on applied mathematics rather than economic theory, which brings up an important issue. I have not mentioned readings *specifically* in mathematics, simply because most of the books mentioned either develop the necessary mathematical notions themselves or refer the reader to relevant sources. I have thus not resolved the needs of anyone who wanted to pursue, in a strictly mathematical context, the specific mathematical notions hinted at lightly in the present book.

If you are interested in the axiomatization of choice theory (or any other science), you can, and should, immediately read Patrick Suppes' *Introduction to Logic*.[9] It should be mentioned that Suppes writes with the needs of the behavioral scientist specifically in mind. A new book, which is genuinely introductory to logic, yet strikingly contemporary and intellectually sophisticated, is Richard Jeffrey, *Formal Logic, Its Scope and Limits*.[10] Anyone interested in the logical and metamathematical background of axiomatization should find Jeffrey fascinating. He ends his book with a detailed guide to further study, including up-to-date references to the specialized advanced literature of logic and metamathematics.

[7]McGraw-Hill Book Company, New York, 1958.

[8]McGraw-Hill Book Company, New York, 1960.

[9]D. Van Nostrand Company, Inc., Princeton, N.J., 1957.

[10]McGraw-Hill Book Company, New York, 1967.

A treatment of naïve set theory forms Part 2 of Suppes' *Introduction to Logic*.[11] For axiomatic treatments, see Patrick Suppes' *Axiomatic Set Theory*[12] and the references in Jeffrey.

As for point-set topology, the elementary concepts are treated in many contemporary texts in pure mathematics. An introductory treatment will be found, for instance, in George F. Simmons, *Introduction to Topology and Modern Analysis*,[13] Part I. A standard advanced reference is J. L. Kelley, *General Topology*.[14] Certain topics of crucial interest to an economist (such as treatments of point-to-set mappings) are hard to find in introductory (and even some advanced) topology texts. The classic source, for the mathematical economist, is Claude Berge, *Topological Spaces*,[15] but it is not exactly light reading.

In conclusion, one might remark that quite an amount of reading now exists before Gerard Debreu's *Theory of Value*[16] must be met head on. Again the confrontation need not be all or nothing—The *Theory of Value* is a book to be acquired and referred to again and again.

[11]*Op. cit.*

[12]D. Van Nostrand Company, Inc., Princeton, N.J., 1960.

[13]McGraw-Hill Book Company, New York, 1963.

[14]D. Van Nostrand Company, Inc., Princeton, N.J., 1955.

[15]The Macmillan Company, New York, 1963.

[16]John Wiley & Sons, Inc., New York, 1959.

NOTATION

The following are the principal notations used in this book, in the order of their appearance in the text.

A the attainable set.

$-A$ the unattainable set.

X the set of all objects x.

$\{x_0, x_1, x_2\}$ the set composed of x_0, x_1 and x_2.

$\{x_0, x_1, \ldots, x_n\}$ the set of all objects x from x_0 to x_n, where n is some finite number.

$\{x_0, x_1 \ldots\}$ the transfinite set X.

$-p$ it is not the case that p, or, simply, not p.

$p \,\&\, q$	p and q.
$p \lor q$	p or q in the *inclusive* sense—p or q or both.
$p \Rightarrow q$	if p then q.
$p \Leftrightarrow q$	p if and only if q.
(x)	for all x; the universal quantifier.
$\exists\, x$	there is at least one x; the existential quantifier.
$x_0 \in A$	x_0 *is an element of* the set A; set-theoretic membership.
$\{x \mid A\}$	the set of all x such that x is attainable.
$\varnothing$	the set that has no members, the empty set.
$A \cup B$	the set composed of all the members of A and all the members of B; set-theoretic union.
$A \cap B$	the set of all elements belonging to *both A and B*; set-theoretic intersection.
$A = B$	the two sets A and B have the same members.
$A \subseteq B$	A is a subset of B; set-theoretic inclusion.
$A \subset B$	A is a *proper* subset of B.
$x_0 \,\mathrm{P}\, x_1$	x_0 is preferred to x_1; the primitive notion "is preferred to."
$x_0 \,\mathrm{I}\, x_1$	x_0 is indifferent to x_1; the defined notion of "indifference."
$x_0 \,\mathrm{R}\, x_1$	x_0 stands in some relation to x_1. R is used as a symbol for any two-place, or binary, relation. Specifically, R is an *equivalence* relation in a set $S \Leftrightarrow$ for all x_0, x_1, x_2 in S:
	$x_0 \,\mathrm{R}\, x_0$. R is reflexive.
	$x_0 \,\mathrm{R}\, x_1 \Rightarrow x_1 \,\mathrm{R}\, x_0$. R is symmetric.
	$x_0 \,\mathrm{R}\, x_1 \,\&\, x_1 \,\mathrm{R}\, x_2 \Rightarrow x_0 \,\mathrm{R}\, x_2$. R is transitive.
$\mathrm{A}x_0$	x_0 is attainable; the primitive notion of "attainability."
$\mathrm{C}x_0$	x_0 is chosen; the primitive notion "chosen."
X_i	the commodity set of the ith consumer.
(x, y)	the ordered couple, of which x is the first member and y the second.

$X \times Y$	the Cartesian product of X and Y, i.e., the set of all (x, y) such that $x \in X$ and $y \in Y$.
R_1	the real line.
$[0, 1]$	a "closed interval"—i.e., a segment of the real line from a point 0 to a point 1, including the limit points 0 and 1.
(a_1, a_2, a_3)	an ordered triple—specifically, a commodity bundle containing amounts of three commodities.
$(a_1, a_2, \ldots, a_n)$	an ordered n-tuple. A point in n-dimensional space, i.e., representing a commodity bundle of n commodities.
R_2	the real plane.
R_n	Euclidean n space.
X_L	the L-dimensional commodity space.
X_{2i}	the two-dimensional commodity space of the ith consumer, usually written simply as X to lighten notation.
A_c	the attainable consumption set.
$F_0, F_1, \ldots$	the frontier of an attainable region in different positions.
B_0	the better set associated with any point, x_0 or any trade t_0, in a commodity space, i.e. the set of points at least as good as (preferred or indifferent to) x_0 or t_0.
W_0	the worse set associated with x_0 or t_0.
I_0	the set of all boundary points of B_0 (which by Axiom 11 is the indifference set of which x_0 is a member).

WH	a wealth hyperplane.
U_0	the upper wedge associated with x_0.
L_0	the lower wedge associated with x_0.
$B_{D0} \cap B_{V0}$	the trading set (the intersection of Disraeli's better set associated with the point of zero trade, and Victoria's similar better set).
$f : X \longrightarrow Y$	a mapping, or function, f, from a set X (its domain) to a set Y (its counterdomain, or range).
$f(x)$	the image of x under the mapping f.
$N(b_0)$	any arbitrary neighborhood of b_0.
$f : p \longrightarrow [q_0, q_1]$	a point-to-set mapping, or correspondence, from a point p, to a closed interval, $[q_0, q_1]$.
$x \, T \, y$	x may be transformed into y; the primitive binary relation, T.
Y	the set of all productions.
Y_j	the production set of the jth producer.
λ	any nonnegative number.
$P_1, P_2 \ldots$	distinct technologically feasible processes.
$y_0, y_1 \ldots$	possible productions, i.e., points indicating possible outputs.

THE
AXIOMS

Choice Theory

1 $(x_0)(x_1)(x_0 \mathbin{P} x_1 \vee x_1 \mathbin{P} x_0 \vee x_0 \mathbin{I} x_1)$.

2 $(x_0)(x_1)(x_2)(x_1 \mathbin{P} x_0 \mathbin{\&} x_2 \mathbin{P} x_1 \Rightarrow x_2 \mathbin{P} x_0)$.

3 $(x_0)(x_1)(-x_0 \mathbin{P} x_1 \vee -x_1 \mathbin{P} x_0)$.

4 $(x)(Cx \Rightarrow Ax)$.

5 $(x_0)(x_1)[(x_0 \mathbin{P} x_1 \mathbin{\&} Ax_0) \Rightarrow -Cx_1]$.

6 $\exists x \, Ax \Rightarrow \exists x \, Cx$.

7 $\exists x_0 [Ax_0 \mathbin{\&} (x_1)(Ax_1 \Rightarrow x_0 \mathbin{P} x_1 \vee x_0 \mathbin{I} x_1)]$.

Consumption Theory

8 X_L is a subspace of R_n.

9 $(x_0) \exists x_1 (x_1 \mathbin{P} x_0)$.

10 B_0 is convex.

11 There are no interior points of $B_0 \cap W_0$.

12 $(x_0)\,(x_1)\,(x_0 > x_1 \Rightarrow x_0\,P\,x_1).$

Edgeworthian Exchange Theory

13   Where x_0, x_1, are points on I_0, and x_2 is on the line joining them, x_2 is an interior point of B_0.

14 $\exists\,x\,\exists\,y\,(Ax\,\&\,x\,T\,y).$

Production Theory

15   Any two transformations are indifferent $\Leftrightarrow$ their inputs are indifferent and their outputs are indifferent.

16 $x\,T\,y\,\&\,y\,T\,z \Rightarrow x\,T\,z.$

17 $x_0\,T\,y_0\,\&\,x_1\,T\,y_1 \Rightarrow (x_0 + x_1)\,T\,(y_0 + y_1).$

18 $x\,T\,0.$

19 $0\,T\,y \Rightarrow y = 0.$

20 Y_j is convex.

21 $x\,T\,y\,\&\,\lambda \geqq 0 \Rightarrow (\lambda x)\,T\,(\lambda y).$

22   The set of processes is finite.

23 $y_1\,P\,y_0 \Leftrightarrow y_1 > y_0.$

INDEX
OF
SCIENTIFIC
AUTHORS

INDEX
OF
SCIENTIFIC
AND
MATHEMATICAL CONCEPTS

This book was set in Linotype Falcon by Continental Graphics, printed by Peninsula Lithograph Company on permanent paper, and bound by Peninsula Lithograph Company. The designer was Janet D. Bollow. The illustrations were done by Judith McCarty. The editors were Robert D. Bovenschulte and Michael A. Ungersma.

about the author

photo by nancy hiltner, 1969

Vivian Walsh was an undergraduate at Trinity College, Dublin. He is also a Ph.D. of Dublin University. Before coming to America, he lectured for some years in Britain, chiefly at the London School of Economics and Political Science. He has held professorships in the United States and in Canada. Most recently he has been Visiting Professor of Economics at the University of Washington. His first book, *Scarcity & Evil,* was published by Prentice-Hall in 1961. For some years now his research has been particularly concerned with axiomatic choice theory; he has conducted graduate seminars and lectured in this area, and his scientific publications reflect this preoccupation.

McGraw-Hill Book Company
330 West 42nd Street
New York 10036

San Francisco · St. Louis · Toronto · London · Sydney · Mexico · Panama